# Praise for
## *WHAT DOESN'T KILL YOU MAKES YOU BLACKER*

"...t, like the work of bell hooks and Roxane Gay, should be required reading."
—**NPR**

"A fascinating exploration of how race, class and gender inform notions of black identity in American life [and] an astute critique of the contours along which black people survive the limitations of historic and systemic racism."
—*Pittsburgh Post-Gazette*

"One of the freshest, most important black voices on the internet."
—*Mother Jones*

"Made the page bend around my head and heart in a manner I honestly didn't think the essay or memoir forms were capable of bending."
—**KIESE LAYMON**, author of *Heavy*

"A painfully honest account of the toll that ennui takes on black social mobility. Young shines."
—*The New York Times Book Review*

"A humorous and deep dive into the culture and a life lived in that precarious state we call blackness."
—**MICHAEL ERIC DYSON**, author of *What Truth Sounds Like*

"A passionate, wryly bittersweet tribute to black life. . . . A must read."
—*Booklist* (starred review)

"By turns serious, political, self-reflective, and hella funny at the same damn time."
—**BRITTNEY COOPER**, author of *Eloquent Rage*

"Darkly hilarious."
—*Publishers Weekly* (starred review)

# PRAISE FOR *WHAT DOESN'T KILL YOU MAKES YOU BLACKER*

"Young pulls readers into his world, showing them his vulnerability, hitting them with unflinching honesty about the state of race relations in this country, and keeping them glued to the pages with his wit and humor. . . . An authentic, keen, and touching example of the black male experience. . . . The beauty of *What Doesn't Kill You Makes You Blacker* is that Young never tries to make it easy for readers."          —NPR

"A passionate, wryly bittersweet tribute to black life. . . . Young articulates the mingled bemusement, rage, and terror of living in a 'relatively safe and superficially black space . . . enveloped by whiteness.' . . . A must read."          —*Booklist* (starred review)

"A painfully honest account of the toll that ennui takes on black social mobility. Young shines."          —*New York Times*

"Language is itself a central character in *What Doesn't Kill You Makes You Blacker*. Mr. Young is fearless in reclaiming ownership of words and the diverse contemporary vernacular that represents strands of black culture in film, television, sports, literature and across social media."          —*Post-Gazette* (Pittsburgh)

"Young's book is, largely, a love letter to the parents who raised him, the wife who elevated him, and the friends who stood by him. You could also say it's a little like a love letter to Pittsburgh too, but one that doesn't let the city get away with any of its shit. It's a refreshing, honest look at a city that still has a long way to go, but one that has hope if people like Young are still creating inside of it."          —*Pittsburgh City Paper*

"Darkly hilarious. . . . Young uses pop culture references and personal stories to look at a life molded by structural racism, the joy of having a family that holds together in a crisis, and the thrill of succeeding against difficult odds. Young's charm and wit make these essays a pleasure to read; his candid approach makes them memorable." —*Publishers Weekly* (starred review)

"Examines the prevalence of overlapping forms of discrimination, classism, and otherness in the era of Trump and the microaggressions that black people routinely deal with but which fail to make their way into larger conversations." —*Christian Science Monitor*

"Documents the evolution of a city, a family, and a man using language that runs the gamut from irreverent to uproarious. . . . Explores the template upon which white supremacy is based and the recurring themes of oppression that permeate every aspect of black life in America. That Young does this vis-à-vis the tragicomedy of his own experiences makes each vignette that much more poignant. . . . Young sharply conveys important truths with powerful effect." —*Kirkus Reviews*

"His essays are pointed, ruminative, often barbed and funny reflections on how the fact of his skin color has posed particular lifelong challenges, questions, and anxieties." —*Weekend Edition*, NPR

"One of the internet's funniest social critics." —The Undefeated

"His writing is hilarious, as in laughing so hard that you end up in tears or, sometimes, laughing hard enough to stop the tears from flowing." —*Washington Post*

"Readers who know Young's work from the blog he co-founded, Very Smart Brothas, will recognize his voice, his fondness for lists, his precise, comprehensive and spectacular references to pop culture, his wit and his keen mind." —*Star Tribune* (Minneapolis)

"In *What Doesn't Kill You Makes You Blacker*, Damon is inviting us in, and tending so tenderly to what black folk in this country are afraid to admit we've seen. He does it by mediating the best of what folk call literary writing and the best of what folk call populous writing. Yet, the language, as Morrison says, never sweats; it laughs, it watches us laugh, it watches us hide, which means we are no longer hiding. If we look closely, I think we might see that Damon invented another literary form here. If we look ever closer, that literary form might actually save the parts of our lives that need saving. I am thankful to be alive during the artful and art-filled life of Damon Young." —Kiese Laymon, author of *Heavy*

"In this funny, illuminating, and occasionally gutting book, Damon Young wrestles with his own masculinity, fears, and lies, all while remaining unrelenting in his determination to learn and teach something valuable about blackness in America. He more than succeeds, in a volume that is a pleasure and an education."
—Rebecca Traister, author of *Good and Mad*

"*What Doesn't Kill You Makes You Blacker* is striking in its story-telling and imagery, in its honesty and humor, in its self-reflection and self-criticism, in its blackness and humanity. Damon Young produced an unobstructed and unsanitized memoir that few people have the courage to write and all people should be encouraged to read."
—Ibram X. Kendi, author of *Stamped from the Beginning*

"When I think about the cultural commentary that has consistently made me both ponder and praise-clap, I think of Damon Young's work via Very Smart Brothas. My gosh, his voice is so clear and so critical to this moment. I believe that future generations will look back on these days to reflect on the grace, gumption, and gusto of black film, music, fine art, photography, literature, and theater offered by our artists during this vibrant time. Our best thinkers will be in that reflection too: Coates, Blow, Ghansah, Cooper, Cobb, Smith, Gay—and Young." —Ava DuVernay

"Damon Young is one of the most fearless and important young writers today. A devastatingly funny critique of racism, *What Doesn't Kill You Makes You Blacker* is a humorous and deep dive into the culture and a life lived in that precarious state we call blackness."

—Michael Eric Dyson, author of *What Truth Sounds Like*

"I can't stand Damon sometimes because he goes and writes things that are so good that I wish I wrote them. So then I have to side-eye him for the pen envy. He is hands down one of my favorite wordsmiths and I wanna preorder any book he writes right now, just on principle." —Luvvie Ajayi, Awesomely Luvvie

"Whenever I read Damon Young's writing I get excited and angry in equal measure. I get excited because he has a way of comprehensively breaking down America's biggest societal ills while at the same time creating sentences that make me react like I was watching a slam-dunk contest with Michael Jordan, Dr. J, Vince Carter, Kobe Bryant, and the aliens from *Space Jam*. And that makes me angry, because I can't seem to write like that no matter how hard I try. His work hits you in the gut, the heart, and the brain at the same time." —W. Kamau Bell

"Damon Young is inarguably the stand-out satirist of our time. His ability to weave together incisive cultural and political commentary with humor is often the one thing that holds many of us together when we are confronted with the most horrific of experiences—the public killings of young black people by police, the aggressive racism of those who have the privilege of a national dais. That he does so without ever losing sight of our day-to-day ways and means of survival and activity takes him from the realm of the good to the rarified place of the brilliant." —Asha Bandele

"Damon Young is a fool. Not a fool in the traditional sense of the word, mind you. I'm talking the kind of fool of the Eddie

Murphy, Chris Rock, and Dave Chappelle variety—a satirist with a wealth of intelligence and raw wit, a finger on the socio-political pulse of pop culture and an incredible gift for making people fall out in side-splitting laughter." —Denene Millner

"In these highly serious times of social upheaval, Young always tells the truth, but you get to read that truth as you gulp for air, while reading his highly irreverent, comedic genius. His is the kind of writing you read as you laugh to keep from crying in the midst of this crazy world. And his words and insights never disappoint." —Brittney Cooper

"Equally profound, irreverent and profane, Damon Young is fresh air in a room with sealed windows. He's Prince's side eye. He's Obama's tightest line-up. He is Richard Pryor, David Sedaris, and Kendrick Lamar rolled up into one Pittsburgher's body. Young's wholly original, riotous reflections on class, race, sports, sex, and grilled meats will challenge and delight you. Get familiar." —Akiba Solomon, Editorial Director, *Colorlines*

# WHAT DOESN'T KILL YOU MAKES YOU BLACKER

## A MEMOIR IN ESSAYS

# DAMON YOUNG

An Imprint of HarperCollinsPublishers

HarperCollins books may be purchased for educational, business, or sales promotional use. For information, please email the Special Markets Department at SPsales@harpercollins.com.

A hardcover edition of this book was published in 2019 by Ecco, an imprint of HarperCollins Publishers.

FIRST ECCO PAPERBACK EDITION PUBLISHED 2020.

Designed by Suet Yee Chong

Library of Congress Cataloging-in-Publication Data has been applied for.

ISBN 978-0-06-268431-8

20 21 22 23 24  LSC  10 9 8 7 6 5 4

FOR THE BOOKEND VIVIENNES

# CONTENTS

# LIVING WHILE BLACK IS AN EXTREME SPORT

Every New Year's Day, hundreds of people gather together on the banks of the Monongahela, a 130-mile-long river that begins in Fairmont, West Virginia; runs along a stretch of factories, steel mills, and power plants through the Mon Valley; and flows to Pittsburgh, where it converges with the Allegheny River at Point State Park to form the Ohio River. Once there, these people strip and dive in. New Year's Day, as you probably know, occurs in January, and the average temperature in Pittsburgh then hovers somewhere between "hold my beer" and "fuck this shit." Which means that they're usually splashing butt-ass naked in an Appalachian Slush Puppie. They call themselves the Polar Bear Club (and their annual dive the Polar Bear Plunge).

Perhaps, while reading that paragraph, an image of a Polar Bear Plunger plopped into your head. Without knowing anything about you, I know—I am *certain*—that the bare-chested, shivering, and possibly inebriated person you envisioned happened to be white. And not just because whiteness is such the American default that it has even colonized our imaginations, but because willingly exposing yourself to frostbite, hypothermia, and the trillion-year-half-life Mon Valley isotopes floating downstream is about as "that's some white-people shit" as "that's some white-people shit" gets. Only someone so comfortably ensconced in privilege that they need to find ways to fabricate closeness to death to feel alive would leave their bed and blankets and house and clothes and city and the tens of thousands of years of civilization devoted to finding more efficient ways to protect us from the elements in the dead of winter to belly flop into a billion gallons of toxic ice. It's so white that if you happen to be a nonwhite member of the Polar Bear Club—and it doesn't matter if you're Barack Obama, Michelle Obama, Chaka Khan, or Shaka Zulu—you become, from the time you remove your clothes to the time you climb back out of the water, white by osmosis.

I've always been captivated by this peripheral effect of whiteness. Where the cushion of pervasive and metaphysical consequencelessness is so soft and thick that adversity must be conjured for neurons to fire and fight-or-flight to engage. This characteristic is so embedded in what we've come to know of what it means to be white that whiteness's unyielding affinity for artificial kamikaze is the standard for what falls beneath the "that's some white-people shit" umbrella. I'm especially enthralled by extreme sports, where white boys from Montana and Arizona and West Virginia perform athletic feats in competitions whose only purpose for existing is to bring participants close enough to death to give it an Eskimo kiss. The contests themselves don't excite me that much. I just love hearing these niggas talk when they're done, because they speak in quotes that sound like the names of embargoed Axe body sprays.

> Bro, that CLIFF DIVE was a FREAKIN BLAST. It was such a RUSH to GATOR PUNCH that NASTY CREVICE and that FURIOUS CREEK, even after I was SWARMED by a batch of CAVE CRICKETS and that MOUNTAIN LION. But I took a GENEROUS SWIG from my ENERGY PACK, felt the BRAIN FREEZE, rode THE WAVE of my ADRENALINE, and ignored my EYEBALL SWEAT and RUPTURED SPLEEN and pulled through.

Having to go to such extreme lengths to feel a rush is an alien concept for me, since living while black has provided me with enough thrills to make Wes Craven scream. Whenever I am followed by a police officer while driving, for instance, the theme song from *Mission: Impossible* plays on a loop in my head, and the mental checklist I run through reminds me of Ethan Hunt attempting to defuse a nuclear warhead.

"Okay, people. Relax. Stay calm, and do exactly what I tell you. Make a sharp right at this light to see if he's following us or just happens to be behind us."

*(Completes right turn. Cop follows.)*

"Okay, okay, okay, that's fine. Stay calm. We will be all right. Listen to me, people. *We will be all right.*"

*(A person named Kay gets hysterical.)*

"STAY WITH ME, KAY! STAY FOCUSED, KAY! WE WILL GET THROUGH THIS TOGETHER!"

*(Splashes some kombucha in Kay's face. Kay regains her composure.)*

"Okay. Now slowly and deliberately turn the music down.

The volume is at eighty-nine and the bass is on a hundred, and we're going to need those numbers to be thirteen and seven. We can do this. We've been trained to do this. Let's go!"

*(The volume knob is gently and steadily turned to the left. A single bead of sweat drips on the dashboard.)*

"What's the status, Frank?"

*(Someone named Frank replies.)* "The volume situation has been neutralized. The volume situation has been neutralized."

"Okay, great. We're not out of the woods yet, though. Kay, what's taking so long with the music? Why are we still listening to Rick Ross?"

"I . . . I just can't find . . . there are just too many . . . songs . . . on this Spotify playlist to choose from. These choices are overwhelming! I don't know what to do, Damon!!! I don't know what to do!!! Also, I'm pregnant."

*(Kay collapses in a ball of tears. I make a face communicating both abject shock and abject joy. It's a really ugly face. I put my arm around Kay.)*

"We're going to have a baby? Why didn't you tell me before?"

"There . . . there was just no time. I didn't know how to tell you. I remember how you treated that cat your ex asked you to sit for a month, and I thought you didn't want kids."

"I hate cats. But I love kids. And I love you."

*(We kiss.)*

"Now, Kay, we need you, babe. Can you do this?"

"Yes, Damon. Yes I can."

"Okay. Find us a new song."

*(Kay grabs the iPhone and furiously scrolls through it.)*

"I found one!"

"What is it?"

"Taylor Swift's 'Shake It Off.'"

"Perfect! I don't even remember adding that to my playlist—and can't think of a reason why I would have—but perfect!"

"You downloaded it for that spin class you attended in May, and just never deleted it because it's a really fun song with a solid chorus. Taylor is aggravating, but you can't deny her song-writing talent."

"Oh yeah, I remember now. Frank, does 'Shake It Off' work?"

*(Frank types on a really fancy iPad.)*

"It does! It does! The numbers add up!"

"Let's do it!"

*("Shake It Off" is selected on the playlist. And then I notice something.)*

"Team, is that what I think it is?"

*(I motion toward the rearview mirror. Both Kay and Frank look and can't conceal their excitement.)*

"Holy shit!"

*(The cop who has been following us has his turn signal on.)*

*(The cop turns at the next intersection.)*

"Crisis averted! Crisis averted! Crisis averted!"

*(Kay jumps into my arms, and we embrace. Frank smirks and pumps his fist, because an embrace from him too would make the driver's seat too crowded.)*

This hypercognizance of both my blackness and what the possession of blackness in America is supposed to mean has created a nigga neurosis—a state of being where *Did that happen because I'm black?* and *If this is happening because I'm black, how am I supposed to react as a Professional Black Person?* are never not pertinent questions. This neurosis can be amusing, as when I'm playing pickup basketball at a park I've never been to before and the guys there—who've never seen me play—still make me one of their top picks. *Did this happen because I'm black . . . and tall-ish . . .*

*and wearing appropriate athletic gear?* Probably. Mostly, however, it's unnerving and annoying. But it is also exciting as fuck. I never feel more alive and closer to death than when I am pondering ways for whiteness to ruin my life. If I'm walking down my street at night, I envision what would happen if I were coming from the gym and wearing a hoodie and one of my white neighbors didn't recognize me and this also happened to be the day that said neighbor decided to start carrying a handgun. When I go to the park with my daughter and sit on the bench while she's on the swing, I wonder whether the white moms there will reach into their fanny packs and pull out their pepper sprays if I happen to wave or smile at one of their kids. But then I also wonder if me *not* smiling and sitting there all constipated and Django-looking will alert their defenses too. Which is why I just split the difference now and wear a Zorro mask. If alone with a white woman for any reason—on an elevator perhaps, or in a coffee shop near closing when she's the lone barista and I'm the only customer still there—I have an internal clock telling me exactly how long I have until we've been alone together *too long*, and I start constructing feasible alibis in case something happens to her after I leave and I'm blamed for it. Sometimes I'll call a friend as I'm leaving.

**FRIEND**: What's good?
**ME**: Nothing much, just leaving this Commonplace Coffee on Buena Vista Street right now, at 5:56 P.M., and headed to the gym later.
**FRIEND**: That was a very detailed answer. You must have been alone with a white woman again, huh?
**ME**: Yup.

I know this probably seems foolish and sanity-consuming. But whiteness is in the life-ruining business, and nigger-life-ruining is its primary revenue stream. And all this attention to detail and context and inflection and body language and tone—and the multiple hypothetical reactions to the nigger-life-ruining business deciding to open an account on me—is a defense mechanism that keeps me breathing and never produces a dull moment. And then, once you take already thrill-producing blackness and add a generous helping of anxiety-inducing me-ness to it, you're left with a life full of GATOR PUNCHES on NASTY CREVICES and FURIOUS CREEKS.

What's the point of CLIFF DIVING if I feel a similar jolt while walking into a party where I don't know anyone and I feel everyone's eyes on me? And while walking into a party where I do know everyone and feel everyone's eyes on me? And while deciding exactly where to stand after I've walked into said party, because I never know where I'm supposed to stop and settle? And while preparing to take a picture with people, and deciding what to do with my face (usually frown) and my hands (I still have no fucking clue)? And while leaving a party, or a family reunion at a pavilion, or a room that people I know happen to be in, and I'm pondering how to make the quickest exit and say bye to the least amount of people? Not because I'm trying to be a dick—although I do realize that doing this is quite dickish—but because saying bye is really weird and hard and when I do it I also end up saying more words than necessary and then real-izing, midsentence, that I've said more words than necessary. And then I turn and walk away before the sentence is complete because I should have just ghosted in the first place.

Even masturbation, the most private and mundane of ac-tivities, is a CREVICE LEAP for me, because I have a deal with God where I only allow myself to masturbate on days that I've prayed. Which means there are days where I'm in the mood to rub one out, but I haven't prayed yet, so I get down on my

knees and have a pre-jerk-session conversation with God—
basically turning prayer into a masturbation delivery device.
Also, the guilt from doing this makes the prayer itself a batch
of EYEBALL SWEAT as I attempt to cram and shoehorn the
memories of everyone I know who has passed away and everyone I know who might possibly need a prayer into my prayer,
extending what I'm assuming is a two-to-four-minute process
for most people into a multilayered, sixteen-minute-long hom-
ily. And sometimes the pre-jerk prayer takes so long that by the
time I'm done, I'm not in the mood anymore, and I go make
some eggs. I eat a lot of eggs.

Maybe, instead of sending camera crews and commentators
to Alaska and Hawaii and wherever the fuck else these extreme
sports occur, ESPN should just have a crew follow me the next
time I'm trying to leave a party. We can even do the postparty
leaving interview in the parking lot, with much less exciting
sounding Axe body sprays:

> **ME**: OMG, bro. I knew at 11:37 that I'd been there
> LONG ENOUGH and needed to LEAVE SOON so I
> could GET HOME by midnight and watch *INSECURE*
> and then maybe *DESUS & MERO* afterwards if I was
> STILL AWAKE. So I TRIED REALLY HARD to
> ghost by just slowly MOVING TOWARD THE EXIT
> while everyone else was popping to "BACK THAT AZZ
> UP." But then THE SONG ENDED and this woman I
> was TRYING TO AVOID all night—not because I don't
> like her, but because conversations with her are always
> an UNNECESSARILY DENSE process involving flash
> cards and golf claps—saw me and attempted to MAKE
> EYE CONTACT. As she NEARED, I BEGAN TO
> PANIC. What was I going to do? I'd already STARTED

THE LEAVING PROCESS and I was fifteen feet from the door, FOCUSED ON THE EXIT, and it was too late to PRETEND I HADN'T SEEN HER. Trapped, I had to improvise. So I PRESSED MY HAND to my pocket like the phone in it was vibrating, made a CONCERNED FACE, pulled out the phone, and began a PHANTOM CONVERSATION with myself while waving at her and BACKING OUT THE DOOR. And, just in case there was anyone outside who ALSO WANTED TO TALK, I continued the FAKE PHONE CALL until I got to my car.

**ESPN GUY:** Wow. That was an amazing feat of athleticism and social anxiety. So tell me, Damon, will you be able to get home in time for *Insecure*?

**ME:** I should, but that PHANTOM CONVERSATION took so much out of me that I'm just going to go home, take a shower, and, um, pray.

---

To be black in America is to exist in a ceaseless state of absurdity; a perpetual surreality that twists and contorts and transmutes equilibrium and homeostasis the way an extended stay in space alters human DNA. Of course, there are other places that America takes us, and other places we jaunt to ourselves. It is perfectly sane, for instance, to be black and to allow outrage to conquer you. It is natural to be aware of our status and the extreme measures taken to expand and extend our subjugation and for this information to make you goddamn fucking furious. It is, all things considered, as predictable to be that if you're black as it is to bleed when decapitated. Because what else is there to do when your country decides to elect Donald

Trump president besides kick a hole through your living room drywall because your feet just ain't long or strong enough to kick craters through each of the motherfuckers who voted for him? How else are you supposed to react when first learning about redlining; when first reading about lynching; when first having gerrymandering and gentrification explained to you; when first studying the myriad and colossal racial disparities in everything from income to education; and when first encountering a white person intentionally oblivious to how being white in America is like being free to take an open-book exam on the same lesson materials that we weren't even allowed to study for?

Fortunately, our lives answer these questions. As natural and (occasionally) vindicating as that anger might be, allowing it to be the only response to the relentless absurdity of our condition would be suicide. Even worse, it would be *boring*, and existing while black in America is anything and everything but that. It is, sometimes, finding the farce and the humor embedded in the absurd, and allowing yourself to marinate in it long enough to lose your shit in laughter. It is, sometimes, stepping back and interrogating exactly when, why, and how white supremacy and patriarchy converged to construct the feelings you've internalized and the acts sprung from them, and then reckoning with what you need to do to rectify that. It is, sometimes, finding comfort and colony in a colloquial version of a centuries-old word created to destroy. It is, sometimes, just sitting on a futon with your homies at a game night, doing nothing but enjoying a shared moment where your personhoods need no explanation or alibi. It is, sometimes, a barbershop convo with a man who's been cutting your hair since before you were able to drive to the shop.

It is, sometimes, finding and jaunting to places yet to be discovered. Not a "new" blackness—never that—but a variation perhaps of how we choose to stand and where we mine our catharsis. It is, sometimes, just a familiar story you haven't yet heard. It is, sometimes, as simple as a song that moves you without your quite understanding the lyrics, or food made with love that you can already taste on your tongue before you actually eat it. It is, sometimes, a silent wonderment at all the beauty born in such ugly circumstances. And it is, sometimes, when necessary, a bone-vibrating celebration of all the blackness and all the life delivered from America's faithful and undeviating efforts to kill us.

I wrote this book because it's something that I have always wanted to read. I know my story isn't unique and that there are other similar works that explore many of the same themes. But I wrote this to examine and discover the *why*s of my life instead of continuing to allow the *what*s to dominate and fog my memories. I knew, for instance, that I didn't get a driver's license until I was twenty-six—which in a city like Pittsburgh is economic and social suicide. But why did I wait so long? How exactly did anxiety and the boundless scaffold of lies it produced converge to allow that to happen? I knew, also, that when I was twenty-four and teaching at a high school a rumor spread that I was gay. But why—if I knew it was untrue and if I believed there was nothing wrong or unnatural with being gay— did I allow that rumor to thoroughly unnerve me? What of the source of the disconnect between how progressive I said I was and how progressive I actually was? And what about the other disconnects between who I believed I was and how I actually conducted myself? And does this motley crew of disconnects and angst and anxieties and neuroses exist independent of race, or are they specifically and inextricably connected to it?

I wrote this book because in telling my story I'm also telling a piece of the stories of Vivienne Young (my mom) and

Wilbur Young (my dad). I want people to know them. Because to know them—even just the sliver of them that I was able to capture here—is to know how blackness doesn't just find space but conjures beauty in a country specifically constructed to crush them. And to know them is to know that they *knew* what was happening, and what would happen, but didn't allow that premonition to prevent them from fighting it, and also clawing and etching out a capacity to love.

I wrote this book because, well, I've never read about two niggas in suits about to fight at 3 A.M. over some buffet bacon while surrounded by black women with miniskirts and PhDs. Or about the distinct lexicon black porn stars use when speaking to each other on camera, something I discovered during the black porno bartering service I ran for two weeks out of my locker in eleventh grade. Or about the transparent and desperate and daffy measures some niggas took in the late nineties to model themselves after Darius Lovehall from *Love Jones*, because they (well, *we*) believed that writing bomb-ass poetry like he did would make girls want to give us some bomb-ass booty. Or about how true Kool-Aid connoisseurs can tell you which flavors go best with meat or fish. Or about what exactly makes someone an "Instant Oatmeal Crip." Combined, these tidbits and others assemble to remind me and inform whoever happens to read this that you can't tell my story the way I'd want my story told without comedy. It's been a security blanket providing catharsis when necessary—and company when the catharsis becomes too exhausting and corrosive. I've discovered how valuable humor and the laughter that sometimes drips and sometimes billows from it can be when resisting white supremacy. What I once thought of as elective is now understood as a necessity.

I also wrote this book because I was terrified to write it. I am terrified of refreshing long-dormant memories and challenging long-settled beliefs, which is exactly what this book did. I am terrified of the person this book says I am meeting the person I believed myself to be. I am terrified of what might happen when people I know and love read this. I am terrified of what might happen when people I barely fucking like might read this. I am terrified that people I hardly know and people I'll never know will read this and know things about me that I've never admitted to those closest to me. I'm terrified that this book sucks. That I'm maybe too glib. Or too awkward. Or too solipsistic. Or too insensitive. Or that maybe my story is either too esoteric or not esoteric enough. I'm terrified of the possibility of this book changing my life and terrified of the possibility that it *won't change anything*. I am nearing forty now, which unfortunately means that I don't have the same speed and stamina to run from these terrors as I did in my athletic prime. (Don't get it twisted—I'm still spry as fuck. A nigga just needs to stretch sometimes.) And so now I'm just going to turn and face them as best I can, and writing this book is me giving those terrors the finger.

I wrote this book because I believe, right now, that its existence means that instead of the events of my life occurring as random and haphazard incidents with no purpose, they're distinct pieces of a puzzle. Perhaps this is wishful thinking, a way to reverse-engineer deeper meanings to a mundane life. Kind of like how sports writers assign mystical and metaphysical properties to a thing achieved during a game—a clutch buzzer beater, perhaps—but if you ask the player about the act, he'll just say, "I was open, so I shot it, and it went in." I don't know. I just know that I haven't always believed that my life made any sort of sense. *What Doesn't Kill You Makes You Blacker* is, mostly, a series of attempts to find some solidity and lucidity in the relentless absurdity of existing while black in America. And right now, today, this book makes me believe my efforts matter.

1

# NIGGER FIGHT STORY

At seventeen, I wanted nothing more than for someone to call me a nigger.

Not a *nigga*. I was already that each time I talked to Brian Carroll, my best friend since we played against each other at Expos Basketball Camp at the Shadyside Boys & Girls Club when we were twelve and discovered that we lived a block away from each other. I lived on the 700 block of Mellon Street in East Lib, and he lived on the part of Negley Avenue where Black Street begins and starts to stretch up into Garfield. We shared an affinity for Wendy's junior bacon cheeseburgers and staying up until midnight to watch Pac-10 and West Coast Conference college basketball games on ESPN, and we'd argue in his parents' basement about who'd make a better pro—Oregon State's Gary Payton (Brian's choice) or Loyola Marymount's Bo Kimble. "Nigga, stop playin'. You know that gunning-ass beige nigga can't fuck with GP." And it still kills me that Brian was right because Bo Kimble never learned how to go left. The way we met reminds me of "You Got Me," that song from the Roots where Black Thought raps, *We use to live in the same building / on the same floor / And never met before / Until I'm overseas on tour.*" (Little hood niggas get meet-cutes too, apparently. How do you like dem apples, Nora Ephron?)

I don't remember when I first knew that a nigger was the worst thing you can call a black person. I suspect I was born with it embedded in my DNA, like how humans evolved to fear fire and black people evolved to fear potato salad made by white people. But I knew my parents used *nigga*. They wouldn't use it around me, but I'd hear them tossing it back and forth downstairs at night sometimes when I was in bed and they assumed I was asleep.

"Spike Lee gotta be the most bowlegged nigga in Brooklyn," Dad joked with Mom the night after they first watched *Do the Right Thing.* "Yeah," Mom agreed, "it's like that nigga's knees are horizontal." I'd love to hear those secret and comfortable *nigga*s escaping their lips because it meant they were getting along that day. And I'd just know that *nigga* was *different* from *nigger* because they'd say it with so much ease. There was no malice behind it. Just rhythm.

*Nigga* flew free and easy when I'd hang with my cousins and uncles in New Castle, the depressed steel town sixty miles northwest of Pittsburgh. It's where Dad was from, and my parents and I would drive an hour up I-79 several times a year for reunions, weddings, picnics, funerals, New Castle High School or Union Area High School basketball games, and sometimes just to bring back two boxes of Coney Island or Post Office Lunch chili dogs—both of which helped the city earn the distinction of the Hot Dog Capital of the World. I am forever grateful that I was indoctrinated with New Castle hot dog chili when I was a toddler and too naive to be skeptical. Because while it tastes amazing, it looks like refried regret and there's no fucking way I'd put that shit within a mile of my lips if I were first introduced to it now. On the midnight rides back home to Pittsburgh, I'd sleep underneath a blanket in the backseat of my parents' Thunderbird while they smoked Kools and listened to Steely Dan's *Gaucho* or one of the Charlie Parker mixes Dad would make on the living room stereo. Christmastime was my favorite time to make those trips, because then we'd listen to "Soulful Christmas"—the dad-curated compilation of Christmas standards performed by artists like Take 6, the Boys Choir of Harlem, and Louis Armstrong. And while I abhor cigarettes now—I've never smoked, and my annoyance with them congealed into abject hate after lung cancer killed Mom in 2013—the warmth and the haze from the smoke inching back from the front seats always made me feel protected. Like my parents had been compressed into a fog and were wrapping around me.

And at Peabody and Pennley and Mellon and Reizenstein—the East Liberty basketball courts where I'd practice and play, for hours at a time, every day the weather permitted—I could chart my progression as a ball player by the type of nigga I was to the oldheads. At nine I started off as "that eggheaded little nigga." By eleven, they dropped the *egghead*, and I'd just be "that little nigga." By the time I was thirteen and able to smack boards, I was "that nigga Damon." (They knew my name!) Soon after, I was "that nigga D." And then, when I was approaching sixteen and I'd finally surpassed most of them and they wanted to be on *my* team, I graduated to "my nigga."

But as essential and lubricative and anointing as *nigga* was, it didn't fulfill me. I wanted someone white to call me a nigger, and I needed that *nigger* to have ill intent and be meant to beat the black out of my feelings. And I craved that experience because being called a nigger by a white person was a necessary requirement for what I really wished to possess: the *nigger* fight story.

My parents had one. A *great* one. You will never find a *nigger* fight story better than the one they possessed. It was 1985. I was six. Mom and Nana (my mom's mom) were post-Sunday-brunch browsing and shopping in Squirrel Hill, a thriving, dense, and traditionally Jewish neighborhood on the East End. They stopped at Isaly's, a then-popular Pittsburgh-area cafe chain, to buy some ice cream.

Nana, after her quart of French vanilla was rung up by the white boy behind the register: "Four fifty? I thought this was on sale."

"No. It's four fifty."

Mom chimed in: "But the sign on the window said it's on sale."

"The ice cream is four fifty."

"You should do something about that sign."

"And you black nigger bitches need to go somewhere else."

"What the fuck did you say?"

"You heard me."

Furious, my mom snatched the ice cream out of Nana's hands, threw it on the marble floor, and warned, "We'll be back." My mom was the Terminator. They left, went up the street to the Giant Eagle on Murray Avenue to find Dad, and returned to Isaly's.

Dad walks up to the white boy—who, according to the story, looked to be eighteen or nineteen—and calmly asks him to apologize to Mom and Nana. He refuses. Dad repeats himself. "I'm going to say this again. And if you don't apologize, I'm going to jump back there and kick your fucking ass with this baseball bat." Oh yeah, I forgot to mention that Dad had a baseball bat with him. It had been sitting in the trunk of our car. My dad is black beatnik John Wick. The kid, who is clearly showing signs that he just might be the dumbest motherfucker on earth, still doesn't apologize.

This makes Dad, a man who takes his fight cues from *Shane* and the rest of the thousands of westerns he watched as a kid, threaten, "I'm going to count to ten. And when I reach ten, I'm coming back there." Then he actually counted to ten.

(In hindsight, the kid behind the counter really had no way of knowing that if a black parent starts counting, once that black parent *stops* counting, you need to brace yourself because furniture will start moving.)

At ten, he tried to pull the kid over the counter by his collar and hit him with the bat. The kid slipped out of his grasp, and somehow managed to grab a butcher knife that was randomly lying around and swing it at Dad. Because why wouldn't a butcher knife be readily available in an ice cream shop? Because this Squirrel Hill Isaly's was also apparently the House of Blue Leaves from *Kill Bill*.

During all of this, my bank-teller mom and my award-winning-organist nana are smashing random bottles and display cases in the store, leaving destruction and M&M's everywhere. Mom is also encouraging Dad: "Whoop his ass! Whoop that white boy's ass!" I come from amazing black women.

My John Shaft–with-an-NPR-membership dad smartly realizes that a butcher knife beats a baseball bat in literally every conceivable way and backs off. But not before Mom grabs a jar of olives—again, this apparently was the randomest deli of all time; I wouldn't have been surprised if it were a jar of live frogs—and chucks it through the window and into the street, sending shards of racist glass and chunks of bigoted salad olives onto the sidewalk.

By this point, the police had shown up and Nana and my

parents were promptly questioned, detained without incident, and taken to the station. While there waiting for whatever black people who start race riots at neighborhood delis wait for at police stations, they were approached by a black woman with some sort of authority. A sergeant or a lieutenant, perhaps.

"You decent-looking, brunch-attending, and Bonneville-driving black people aren't supposed to be here. What happened?"

They explained, and she left. Moments later she came back.

"You're free to go."

"What happened?"

"You were racially intimidated."

"So, no charges?"

"No."

"What about the store damage?"

"If y'all negroes don't get up and sprint out of here before these white folks figure out I'm letting you go . . ."

Even my sister, Jamie, who's nine years older than me, had a cool story about the time she beat this girl up in high school choir practice for calling her a nigger. The aftermath is even better. She got suspended from school and was terrified she'd get in trouble when my parents heard what happened. But once Mom and Dad found out *why* she got suspended, she didn't get grounded. She got butter pecan ice cream. I wanted my own post-*nigger*-fight-story ice cream party, with cake and candles and cards and Polaroids documenting everything, just so I wouldn't be the only *nigger*-fight-story-less nigga in our house.

Being called a nigger would seem to be an easy task for a kid growing up in Pittsburgh, a city so historically, hilariously, and hopelessly white that Rick James once tried to snort it. But although surrounded by whiteness, I existed in a *nigger*-free zone. A *nigger* vacuum. A *nigger*-deficient silo. A *nigger* event horizon.

From the time my parents moved there when I was nine until the summer before my seventeenth birthday, I lived in East Liberty. Which used to be predominantly black before gentrifiers and colonizers transformed and rebranded it into the *"Portlandia* but with Pierogies" it is today. So it's not like I was going to hear it there. The only white people on my block were either cops or cameramen actually filming the TV show *Cops*. (Seriously. *Cops* was in my neighborhood so often that I once spent an entire summer following cop cars on my bike, hoping to catch some screen time if they happened to be filming. It didn't work.)

And while I attended predominantly white schools, I wasn't going to hear it there either. At St. Bartholomew, where I went from sixth to eighth grade, most of the white boys—and *all* of the cool and popular and tough ones—were my football and basketball teammates. And I was good at both. And if you're good at sports in middle school, all your teammates are your friends by default. And all the girls either like you (which is good) or don't actively dislike you (which, when dealing with thirteen-year-old girls, is fucking great). That's just how it works. And basketball friends don't call basketball friends niggers. Especially if the black kid is the point guard and you want to continue receiving perfect pocket passes off of high ball screens and staggered double-flex cuts. Call me a nigger and, well, you probably weren't getting the ball until midway through the third quarter. And I'd make sure the pass was out of rhythm.

And, although I had no idea what the nuns at St. Barts did when they weren't teaching us about quadratic equations and the spiritual benefits of natural family planning—complete with surprisingly graphic diagrams and pie charts about the rhythm method—I strongly doubt they were slipping *nigger*s into casual conversations at the rectory pool tables. I had myriad fantasies about what the nuns did in their spare time. Gambling on hockey games, spelunking at Laurel Highlands, spades tournaments in Homewood; you name it, I daydreamed it. Still, I just couldn't picture Sister Mary Margaret throwing back a Miller High Life while sprawled on a musty futon—her veil swinging from a ceiling fan, her black utility shoes splayed on a mostly empty bag of Purina Cat Chow—and opining on how niggers made her teeth itch.

This *nigger*-less existence continued through high school. The suburban Penn Hills Senior High was much larger and blacker than St. Barts. I had multiple black classmates and basketball teammates and there was even a rumor that there was a black teacher actually teaching there somewhere. And this wasn't a school with much apparent racial tension. The black kids and the white kids generally got along, united in a collective love of $1.04 Whoppers from the Burger King on Frankstown Road and a collective hate of Woodland Hills High School and Silkk the Shocker. This just was not an optimal setting for *nigger* use and usage. It was definitely subprime *nigger*. By the end of my junior year, I realized that if I wanted to be called a nigger before I graduated, I'd probably have to transfer.

Still, despite these very obvious conditions that cultivated this increasingly surreal *nigger* void—and despite the fact that, traditionally, actually being called a nigger tends to suck—I felt ambivalent and insecure about it. Did I want to be called a nigger? No! Well . . . *not really*. I just, I don't know. I didn't want to be called one. But I didn't want to *not* be called one either.

Most of my friends had their own "this is what happened when that white boy called me a nigger" stories too. And these were *amazing* stories. Some involved the type of witty and pithy off-the-cuff comebacks it would have taken me months

to think of. ("Maybe I'm a nigger today, but you'll be ugly forever, bitch.") Some involved teachable moments right out of an
eighties-sitcom Very Special Episode. ("After she called me a
nigger, I grabbed her hand, peered into her soul, and said a
prayer for her. And then she prayed with me.") But most involved fights. Glorious and violent fights.

Brian had one, which he shared with me while playing *Tecmo
Super Bowl* in my bedroom. "Yo, Dame, I had to beat this little
white nigga's ass at the busway yesterday for calling me a nigger."

My homeboy Frankie had one. "This crew of white boys
called me a nigger at the mall, and I chased them out the food
court with an empty Clarks Wallabees box and a stale funnel
cake."

Even this mousy little light-skinned girl Tiffany who was
in my physics class in eleventh grade had one. "That cashier at
Wendy's on Rodi Road tried calling me a nigger 'cause I asked
for extra ketchup, but I mushed the taste out her mouth before
she could finish the 'er.'"

While all of these *nigger* fight stories are harrowing, I felt
left out. Like I was missing a crucial and fundamental rite of
passage; a stolen step on my ascent to fully realized blackness.
And would maybe receive a demerit on the mythical and om-
nipresent Black Card I kept in my sock drawer. I wanted to be
able to share my own *nigger* fight story and not just listen when
it was *nigger*-fight-story sharing time. I desired the opportunity
to reflect on the time *"that power forward from Franklin Regional
called me a nigger, and I threw the ball in his face and got a tech."*
Or perhaps how I single-handedly warded off a group of *nigger*-
spewing street urchins on my way home from the busway. Or
maybe how I heard a classmate mouth *nigger* under his breath
to me during homeroom, spent the following six hours stew-
ing and plotting about what I'd do to him, found his locker,

waited for him there after school, and said something slick and cool like *"Your nigger's here now, bitch"* before quick-jabbing his spleen.

But mostly I just wanted to see how I'd react. Would I go Super Saiyan and throat-punch the offender? Would I punk out and pretend I didn't hear it? Would I think he said it but not really be sure, ask him to repeat himself, have him say, *"Oh, I was just saying that you're a trigger"* and leave confused? How could I test and assess my own level of blackness if it was never tested?

I spent so much time pondering what I'd do if it ever happened that it not happening left a void. Like I'd studied the scouting report for a team I never played against.

This *no one has called me a nigger yet and I feel a certain way about it* unsettledness eventually congealed into a pervasive doubting of both my perception of my environment and my relationship with it. Perhaps this *nigger* vacuum I existed in wasn't a *nigger* vacuum at all. Maybe me never being called a nigger wasn't a product of circumstance or chance but was an intentionality. Maybe the white people around me just didn't believe I was threatening enough or *black* enough to waste one of their precious *nigger*s on. Maybe they were primed to say *nigger*, saw me, thought about it, and said, "Nah," saving it for a more deserving black guy. A *blacker* black guy. Maybe they believed wasting a *nigger* on me was like wasting a bullet on one of the zombies from *The Walking Dead*. Perhaps *nigger*s, like bullets, are scarce and only to be used with unambiguously black blacks. *"Damon's nice and cool and quiet and has a great crossover so he's totally not enough of a threat to my whiteness to use a 'nigger' here. In fact, let's invite him to a sleepover."* Maybe I was the guy white people referred to when they said things like "I'm colorblind" and "I don't even see race." Maybe I was the magical race-neutral negro; the seventeen-year-old manifestation of every character Rashida Jones has ever played.

Yet, whether I was acceptably black to other black people wasn't much of a worry to me. I drank too much grape Kool-Aid and owned too many African American College Alliance short sets for that to ever be a serious thought. I also never suspected that other black people possessed that suspicion of me. The popular and dangerous American cultural trope of the smart black kid getting teased by other black kids for "acting white" just didn't apply to me. If I had a dollar for every time I received protection and free passes from the neighborhood gang members and dope boys, I'd have enough to bail them all out of prison.

Instead, the primary source of my blackness angst, then, was whether white people believed I was black enough to find a place within their arbitrary, constrictive, and patently false definitions of what it meant to be black. Being just black wasn't enough. I wanted—needed—to be black enough to not be the guy white people asked for directions or sat with if the seat next to him on the bus was free. I wanted them to see me as worthy of their overt racism. So I could finally prove to myself that I had what it took to overcome it. To persevere past it. To smack the fire out of a white motherfucker.

Even then I recognized the ridiculousness of this mind-set. But it was my reality. And *nigger* became my barometer.

And then, three months into my senior year at Penn Hills, it happened.

I was on Frankstown Road waiting for a 77B bus that would take me from Penn Hills to East Liberty, where I would connect to a 71A to the University of Pittsburgh's campus in Oakland. Once there, I'd pretend I was a Pitt student and sneak into Trees Hall, where I planned on spending the rest of the evening hooping.

A red pickup truck approached. And in the passenger seat of that truck, a guy who looked exactly like post–*Silver Spoons* Ricky Schroder draped his head out of the window, looked at me, and screamed "NIGGER!" as the truck sped away. There was no one else there, so there was no doubt I was his target. I even turned my head to confirm. *Nope. No one else is here. He was talking to me.*

Initially, I was overcome by the surreality of being called a nigger in 1996. It didn't sting as much as it felt like I was watching a tape of myself watching *Mississippi Burning.* And then the questions came. What was his motive? Was he trying to intimidate me? Upset me? Anger me? Did he not realize he just wasted a *nigger* on me? That I wasn't the nigga you scream *nigger* at? And why did he look exactly like Ricky Schroder? *Shit, was it actually Ricky Schroder?* Did the star of *The Champ* and a three-season stretch on *NYPD Blue* get his jollies trolling bus stops in the east suburbs of Pittsburgh for lone teenagers to scream racial slurs at?

And then out of nowhere I started laughing. A wild and hysterical and decidedly ugly laugh—the ugliest of laughs; the Steve Bannon of laughs—with tears dripping from my eyes and saliva tickling my windpipe. I coughed and hiccupped and even almost choked. I was tickled. Shit, I was beyond tickled. I was fucking verklempt. Not because I'd finally received the vindication I'd believed I needed, but because hearing that word had zero effect on me. He screamed *nigger* but he might as well have screamed "Bingo!" or "Yahtzee!" or "Planters Honey Roasted Peanuts!"

I was only called a nigger that day because I happened to be the one standing at that bus stop. It wasn't about *me.* Or how black I happened to be or assumed I wasn't. I just existed as a convenient proxy for all black people. Which, I surmised, was likely the case for most uses of *nigger*. Even the ones that resulted in the best *nigger* fight stories. It didn't matter if it was me or my dad or Master P standing there; Yinzer Ricky Schroder was primed and ready to release one of his *nigger*s and I just happened to be the one to catch it.

And it's not that *nigger* is meaningless. It's just that I'd attached so much meaning to finally hearing that word and finally possessing the ability to share how I reacted when hearing it that I hadn't considered the possibility of the absurd. Of having it screamed by an eighties child star's doppelganger from the passenger seat of an F-150 that didn't even bother slowing down. Of realizing that my *nigger* fight story, the one I'd been itching to tell since I became aware of *nigger*-induced fights and that *nigger* fight stories were a thing, would be anticlimactic. And how foolish I'd been to assign any measure of my own level of blackness to a word that was both the greatest and most impersonal slur in America's lexicon.

# 2

# STREET CRED

Dad refused to tell Mom when I was expelled from Linton Middle School midway through my freshman year. In an effort to keep this secret from her, he encouraged me to partake in an elaborate daily ruse where I'd pretend to leave for school when she was leaving for work, and then I'd return home when the coast was clear. Each day she'd prepare to trek downtown to her job verifying people's insurance for University of Pittsburgh Medical Center, I'd walk to Stanton Avenue from our row house in East Liberty to catch the 94A to the Penn Avenue business district. Before I got kicked out of school, this was where I'd catch another bus that would take me out to Linton in Penn Hills, a suburb ten miles east of downtown Pittsburgh. But now I'd just catch a different bus back home after an appropriate amount of time had passed.

For Dad, the nineties were a stretch of ferocious joblessness occasionally interrupted by microbursts of underemployment. The last consistent job I remember him having before he was unemployed then was with Prudential, a gig hyperdependent on reliable transportation. When our car was stolen in 1990, it began a recurring spiral where he'd be out of work for a couple of years. My parents would scrounge together enough coins to buy a "beater"—the type of hooptie sold in strip club–adjoined used auto lots to niggas with dyspeptic credit. And then he'd find work for a few months. And then the car would die— maybe an engine would explode or a catalytic converter would find Jesus—and he'd be back home again. He'd been jobless for two years when I was expelled from school, and we'd spend the mornings and early afternoons together eating Cream of Wheat, reading *USA Today*, and watching *The Bold and the Beautiful*, which I preferred to *The Young and the Restless* because of the font on the credits.

Since it was illegal to attend a suburban public school if you lived in the city, my parents—well, Dad with Mom's permission—had forged a Penn Hills address for me to be able to go to Linton. I'd been at St. Barts (also in Penn Hills) from sixth to eighth grade, which wasn't a problem then because St. Barts was a private school. I could live in Memphis or on fucking Mars and still attend as long as my parents paid tuition. When it came time for high school, though, the plan was for me to attend Linton, which schooled kids from sixth to ninth grade, for a year and then matriculate to Penn Hills Senior High School with the rest of the rising sophomores. Penn Hills regularly had outstanding basketball teams, and my parents' elaborate machinations were mostly fueled by a desire to put me in the best position to earn a basketball scholarship. "It will all be worth it when he doesn't have to pay for school," Dad would say to Mom, leaning on insurance-salesman-elevator-pitch templates to convince her.

In 1994, during my freshman year, Penn Hills won the

Western Pennsylvania Interscholastic Athletic League championship and probably would have won states if star shooting guard E. Robe didn't tear his ACL in the state semis. I was the starting point guard on the junior varsity team—which I and three other Linton students had been chosen to play on—and was a virtual shoo-in to start on varsity the following year. But someone's parents were annoyed that this egg-headed little nigga from East Lib was stealing their son's shine and snitched on me living in the city. We never quite figured out who it was. But we knew it was a parent because that's the type of thing that parents do when they believe potential scholarships are on the line. I was kicked out of school in February.

After two months of Dad trying and failing to find a way to get me back into Linton, he enrolled me in Peabody High School, which was three blocks up the street from our home and tried very hard to mirror the first fifteen minutes of *Lean on Me*. My first day there, I saw two fights and somehow neither involved actual students. I also didn't hesitate to tell other students and my teachers that I was only going to be at Peabody until the end of the year because my parents were moving to Penn Hills and I was going back to school there. My existence at Peabody was a small glitch in the Matrix, I thought, and I'd soon be back where I belonged. Only, my parents didn't move that summer. By the time fall came back around, I was still at Peabody. Mom still didn't know that I had been expelled and was attending an entirely different school.

It seems, even as I write this, impossible to extend a deceit for that long right underneath her nose. But she had no reason to doubt the truth of such a mundane certainty, no reason not to believe that her honor-roll and budding-basketball-star son was still enrolled in the school she believed he was in. Also, Dad's house-husband status meant that he was the one available for parent-teacher conferences, that he'd be the one home if the school called for any reason, and that he'd be the first person to see any mail. We had all the bases covered. I knew Dad was terrified of disappointing her again. He couldn't be unemployed *and* the type of nigga who'd allow his son to get kicked out of school. Making certain I stayed centered on the master scholarship plan was his only job, and he couldn't face failing at that too. That type of fear and shame can make men do strange things. Including making their sons their accomplices, allowing a disappointing but understandable setback to stretch into a months-long conspiracy.

The jig finally ended in November when basketball season began. Of course, Mom was interested in attending my games, and she might've killed Dad if she caught the 77B from downtown after work all the way out to Penn Hills just to learn that I hadn't been in that entire fucking municipality for nine months. I don't know exactly how Dad broke the news to her. He asked me to go to my room, and as I did, I could hear Mom shrieking and screaming downstairs. After fifteen minutes, she stopped. It sounded like she'd just run out of energy, like a hot air balloon struck with a harpoon gun. A half hour later, she came upstairs to my bedroom—her entire face damp and shiny and drained and faded. She looked *tired.* "I'm so sorry, Damon, that you were put in a position where you were forced to lie to me. I'm so sorry." She started crying again and went to my parents' bedroom. I didn't see her again until the next morning.

I'd spent that night bracing myself to hear, when I woke up, that they were getting a divorce. Dad's habitual joblessness had already strained their relationship. "Why don't you just get a shit job at Giant Eagle or something? Do you know how hard this is for me?" I remember Mom pleading with him one night. And this ordeal would be the final straw. I'd probably live with

Mom, I thought, since Dad didn't have a job. And where would he live? Would he be homeless? Would he move back to New Castle and live with Grandma and Uncle Terry? Or perhaps would the divorce be the impetus for him to get his shit together, like Robin Williams in *Mrs. Doubtfire*? And maybe, after a year or so, Mom would notice his efforts to be self-sufficient, and they'd slowly and cautiously start dating again. And then they'd get married again. But a proper bougie wedding in a Marriott ballroom or one of them big-ass churches in Oakland, instead of in my Nana and Papa's backyard like the first time they got hitched.

But when I got up that morning, Dad made me a drippy egg, two slices of bacon, and an English muffin, like every other morning. Mom showered, sang to herself, and applied cocoa butter to her skin and Maybelline to her face while sitting at her vanity, like every other morning, and we both left for the day. That night before would be the last time either of my parents spoke to me about that lie.

The next April, my parents found a nice little house for rent on a nice little street on Clinton Drive in Penn Hills. It sat on a hill, one hundred feet from the Frankstown Road bus line and a fifteen-minute walk from Giant Eagle and the BP gas station on the corner of Frankstown and Robinson. You couldn't have asked for a better spot for a family of carless niggas from the city in the suburbs. We moved in May, and by that fall, I was enrolled at Penn Hills High, ready to start my junior year, finally settled after attending school in four separate buildings in a three-year span.

Penn Hills Senior High School sat three miles up Frankstown from where we lived. Although the district was steadily losing population—in 1987, my sister graduated from Penn Hills with nine hundred classmates; in 1997, I graduated with five hundred—it still was one of the largest schools in Western Pennsylvania. It was famous in the Pittsburgh area for two things: the football team (which was ranked number one in the country by *USA Today* in 1996) and its preponderance of pretty black girls. It was so known for the latter that while each Allegheny County school district had its own Kennywood Picnic—the day in May or June when the entire district spent the day at Kennywood Park—the Penn Hills picnic was the only one city niggas plotted to crash just to potentially meet and bag or just fucking *see* a Penn Hills dime.

(Also, if you happen to be in the greater Pittsburgh area, you might hear someone make an offhand reference to a "Kennywood outfit." Usually as a snarky dig at the conspicuous effort someone puts into being fashionable. This term stems from the fact that Kennywood Picnic Day is such a big deal for school-aged kids and teenagers that you put as much thought into what you wear on Kennywood Picnic Day as you do with your prom. There are shoe stores in the Burgh that have "no Kennywood refunds" policies in place specifically for teens who bought a too-expensive pair of Jordans just to stunt at the picnic and return the next day—a fact I discovered in 1996 after attempting to return a too-expensive pair of Jordans to David's Shoes in East Liberty the day after wearing them to Kennywood.)

The high school was perhaps 60 percent white. It had the type of Irish and Italian white kids whose parents owned construction companies and Laundromats and who totally, definitely, absolutely were not scared of black people at all despite the fact that they all seemed to stop growing in eighth grade. Imagine a school full of seventeen-year-old Joe Pescis and Marisa Tomeis rocking gold crosses and Levi's and giving niggas five-step pounds and hugs in the hallways. Still, the school *felt* blacker than its actual demographics reflected, perhaps because Pittsburgh itself is so segregated that any place within a ten-mile radius of the city with more than seven black people there at one time feels like the Essence Festival.

Despite our new house, our new address, my new school, and my new middle-class classmates, I was still a nigga from the hood. And not necessarily in a rough-around-the-edges, fish-out-of-water way, but just that I knew I'd seen and been through some shit that these Penn Hills niggas only read about in *The Source*.

The beginning of my junior year at Penn Hills is when I first met James Adams, the only person I've ever hated. It's been more than twenty years since we were teammates on the basketball team and at least fifteen years since I've last seen him, but I still root for bad things to happen to him—not death or disease or anything, just a perpetual parade of shitty mundanities, random misfortunes, and miscellaneous pratfalls. I hope that every time he runs for a bus he misses it by seconds and is close enough to see both the bus pass by and the perfunctory shrug of feigned pity bus drivers tend to make when that happens. I hope that at least once a week he attempts to make spaghetti, and while transitioning the Giant Eagle–brand angel hair pasta from the box to the pan, it slips from his hand and falls to the floor—and the five-second rule doesn't work because the floor is covered with cat hair. Because he's a grown-ass man with four cats, one of which wakes him every morning by blowing humid cat breath into his eardrum. I hope that while driving to dinner with a woman he really likes, he nears the restaurant and finds a parking spot. But it's a parallel parking spot and he's so flustered by her presence that he keeps taking the wrong angle and can't fit into the space. And then he keeps starting over and trying to correct it. And keeps failing. And then gets so frustrated by the cars beeping behind him—at this point he's causing a mini traffic jam—that he gives up and goes to a pay lot. And the woman never looks at him the same way again. I hope he doesn't get as many "happy birthday" wishes on his Facebook wall this year as he assumed he would, and I hope he gets upset that he cares enough about a Facebook birthday wish to get upset. I hope that every time he goes to the Popeye's drive-through at 9:53 P.M.—rushing to get there before it closes at 10:00—they tell him they just ran out of chicken two minutes ago. I want his relationship with fast food fried chicken to be star-crossed and overwrought. I want him to think of an extra-crispy two piece and a biscuit and get hives.

Mind you, this is not an active rooting. I do not possess any voodoo dolls or decapitated effigies with his likeness. But if his name happens to come up in conversation, or his face happens to appear in a memory, I'm reminded of my passive and petty antipathy, and I become possessed with and entertained by the thought of his life sucking ever so slightly for as long as he's alive.

This irrational, decades-long hate stems from a bus ride. We were on our way back from Shaler Area High School. We'd beaten them pretty handily, and I'd scored somewhere between fifteen and twenty points, so I should have been happy. But I dreaded this ride home—as I did many others that year— because I feared it would inevitably turn into a ripping contest, which it did. And, at that time, I was cursed with the dual misfortunes of not being particularly good at ripping and being an occasional source of others' rips.

*Ripping*, by the way, is a Pittsburgh-area colloquialism for playing the dozens (also commonly known as *roasting*), which is often depicted in media and in conversation as an innocent and fun and funny and nostalgia-worthy aspect of black culture. A favorable rite of passage we all happily and willingly go through. I've lost count of how many television shows and movies I've seen featuring witty and quick and dimpled preteen and teenage black kids that have also featured a scene where the kids trade barbs about each other's looks, parents, girlfriends (or lack thereof), and whatever else could be mined for jokes. And while some creative and cruel comments are made, all the kids seem to be having fun. And all seem to be *really fucking good* at it.

The reality, however, is that the primary function of the dozens is to either reinforce established social hierarchies or create new ones. The cool and popular kids generally don't get ripped on, and if they do, it's most often good-natured teasing from other cool and popular kids. The type of rips intended to make everyone—including the target of the rip—laugh. Rips that aren't even really rips. Rips like "*Yo, did you see the face Dwayne made after he scored his fifth touchdown? He looked crazy, yo! Ha! Wayne, man! The next time you score five touchdowns, don't look like you're eating a Happy Meal!*"

The coldest and cruelest (and best) insults, however, are reserved for when you're either anticipating or instigating a fight or genuinely attempting to shame and embarrass a lower-status person. If you're often at the receiving end of those kinds of rips, the mere thought of being somewhere where that might happen—particularly if you're a guy and there are girls around (like a school bus filled with your teammates and the cheerleading squad)—is enough to induce panic attacks.

Navigating the world of postgame bus ride rips my junior year was particularly tricky because of the paradoxical nature of my existence and status at Penn Hills. On paper, I was an alpha. The leading scorer on one of the best teams in Western Pennsylvania. My name was frequently in the *Pittsburgh Post-Gazette* and the *Pittsburgh Tribune-Review*. I was beginning to get attention from colleges, some of which would mail letters that were sent to Penn Hills' athletic office and delivered to me while I was in class. Which would get nods of appreciation from the guys and even occasionally a girl or two stopping her daydreams about Method Man to ask me where the letter was from. I was in all the honors and AP classes. Getting B-minuses in them, but still in them. I was one of the few kids who looked forward to being called to the principal's office, because for me it was always good news.

This on-paper status, however, didn't extend to our team's internal ecosystem. There, I wasn't Damon Young, the leading scorer and best player for the 13-3 Penn Hills Indians. I was "Yolk"—a moniker a senior gave me during my freshman year when I was playing on the junior varsity team and hadn't been expelled from school yet. It was an allusion to my unusually large and egg-shaped head, a head that made me so self-conscious that I wasn't comfortable leaving the house without a hat until my senior year of *college*. A head that would cause me to get annoyed with Mom when she'd insist that my head was perfectly fine. Of course, I wasn't Yolk to everyone. To my friends on the team, I was Dame or D.Young. But while James Adams was my teammate, he was not my friend.

This intrateam dynamic was an extension of my general status within the school. I was too popular to be objectively uncool, but I was definitely the most uncool popular kid. The honeydew melon in the popular-kid fruit salad. This dynamic was largely self-determined, a manifestation of a form of self-consciousness that resulted in me always giving myself whatever the opposite of the benefit of the doubt would be. I assumed everyone else was as hyperconscious of my flaws and insecurities as I was. If I dared walk outside without one of my dozens of fitted baseball hats and camouflage fisherman's caps, I'd conjure a roomful of eyes, all glued to the crown of my head. If I smiled or spoke in front of the class, I'd *know* the people who saw me were more focused on and transfixed by the eighth-of-an-inch gap between my two front teeth than what I actually said. I would hide within myself, shrinking and shriveling within my own skin like I'd been left in the dryer. I didn't want to be seen, unless it was exactly how I wanted to be seen by exactly who I wanted to see me. Through these efforts, I became the world's most anonymous star basketball player. The intermittently invisible man. Unfortunately, this ceaseless need to self-constrict also sometimes served as an advertisement for those desiring targets to rip on, which is what I was to James that night in the back of that bus.

James had a minor role on our team that year. An imposing six foot five and roughly 220 pounds, he had the body and the athleticism to be a much better player than he actually was, but he spent his first three years of high school doing literally nothing besides vacillating between being "cool" and being "kinda sorta a member of the Crips." Although he made the team as a senior—the first year he was actually academically eligible to play—his basketball IQ was so underdeveloped that besides giving the starters someone big and strong to play against in practice, he wasn't much help.

Yet, his status at Penn Hills was the inverse of mine. A bit of a loser on paper who, through familiarity and force of personality, managed to be one of the most popular people in the school. Despite being our eighth man—the third person off the bench—he owned prime back-of-the-bus real estate on our trips to and from games, a status usually reserved for people who actually scored points during them.

On most trips, James would hold court back there, talking shit about the hos he was fucking, the whips he planned to cop in the summer, or maybe even the niggas in Homewood who were snitching. Because, remember, James was an Instant Oatmeal Crip. I'd be near the middle of the bus, either engaged in spirited debates about who was the weakest member of the Wu-Tang Clan (U-God) or laid up against a window with my Walkman blasting one of my recorded mixes from WAMO 106.7. On that ride back from Shaler, however, I'd left my Walkman at home, so I couldn't pretend to not hear James when he shifted his mindless humble-brag bukkake to "Who has the least amount of hos on the team?" and then promptly nominated me.

"Yo, how you gonna drop twenty a game and not have no hos?" James asked, rhetorically, to a bevy of muffled snickers emerging from the 10 P.M. back-of-the-bus darkness. He followed with one of the seven dumbest analogies I've ever heard: "It's like being a millionaire and no one cares."

The entire bus—including the cheerleaders, all seated near the front—became invested in how I'd respond. "Come on, D!" the chorus collectively urged. "You ain't gonna let him get you like that, are you?" I eventually obliged and said something about how James must be a magician because I couldn't see him, but I could hear his voice. (Which was a "joke" because James is very dark-skinned. And it was nighttime. And I told you that I wasn't good at this.)

Luckily, being overtly color-struck was still in vogue in 1996 and that induced some laughs, which naturally made James double down on my abject holessness. For the next ten minutes, he continued on my (lack of) popularity with the girls at school. Not even that they didn't like me, but that I was so irrelevant they didn't think enough of me to even bother *not* liking me. I sat there and took it, humiliated (because there was nothing I could do) and near tears (because I believed it was true). I stared out the window, counting the Route 28 exits and then, once we got on Allegheny River Boulevard, the signs and road markers to calculate how soon I'd be able to jump the fuck off of that bus. It was my own personal episode of *Fear Factor*, trapped in a dark, damp, screeching metal box while each of my most pressing anxieties—a fear of my fear of girls being addressed and made fun of *and* a fear of my fear of girls being addressed and made fun of *in front of actual girls*—suffocated me. If I could have engulfed myself somehow—unhinging my entire jaw to swallow and disappear myself whole—I would have.

When we'd passed the McDonald's on Frankstown Road, which meant we were five minutes from the school parking lot, James said something I do not remember. Probably something about bitches or the Monroeville Mall or something. Whatever it was, it conjured something in me that made me get up, walk to the back of the bus, and confront him. If we were in an eighties teen movie starring John Cusack or Ralph Macchio, this would be the moment when I punched James Adams's Billy Zabka in the mouth, and then he'd cry like a little pussy-ass bitch, and then the finest and flyest cheerleader would jump into my arms and plant a prolonged closed-mouth kiss on my lips. (This being a PG-13 movie, obviously.)

But since this was real life, I decided to tell James about *his* life.

"You have hos now, and that's great. But your life is never going to get better after this point, and mine will. High school will be the highlight of your life. So, keep talking back here, telling jokes about me and having fun, and I'm going to go back to my seat to sit down."

The bus fell silent—a silence that was the result of the prolonged and exaggerated shock of someone successfully subverting the ripping dynamic by completely eschewing rips and morphing into a high school guidance counselor from hell. I'd ruptured something in the space-time continuum, effectively creating my own ripping wormhole. He went at my status with girls; I went at his *soul*.

I returned to my seat, and James never ripped on me again.

At this point, I can imagine you, person reading this right now, being somewhat confused by the way this story ended— not that it was anticlimactic (it kind of was, but that's annoying, not confusing), but that the climax didn't correspond with the exposition. I've hated this man for twenty years, so much so that I wish for his perpetual comeuppance in the form of random chicken-related calamity—which is a terribly cruel thing to wish on a black man—but the story actually ended quite well for me. At least not the way you'd anticipate a story about a guy the author has hated since high school to end. In fact, if his life did indeed peak in twelfth grade and is currently best characterized as a series of unfortunate events, he would be perfectly justified to carry a decades-long animus toward *me*. If his life does suck, it's good I haven't seen him in so long, because he'd probably shank me on sight.

So, why do I hate this person whom I have no justifiable reason to hate two decades later? I hate him because I let him off easy on the back of that bus. I actually possessed the perfect trump card, and the memory of his fucking face reminds me of a time I was too self-conscious to realize I could play it. He's a proxy for the mélange of self-doubt and ceaseless self-deprecation that infested my psyche, and I hate him because he reminds me of when I didn't love myself enough to be hateful toward him then.

Remember, James was a member of the Crips street gang, but he was a "member" in name only. He lived in the fucking suburbs and had enough money to have a car in high school and lived in a house with a front and back lawn and a porch. (A gotdamn porch!) He lived on a street with trees with leaves and shit and cheerful white toddlers with Big Wheels and complete sets of Power Ranger accessories. Although he talked a great game and looked the part, James was actually about as *hood* as Gwyneth Paltrow.

I was uniquely qualified to call him out on this—to doubt his hood bona fides and dis his faux gang affiliations, ultimately revealing him to be a fraud—because *I was actually from the hood.* In the nineties, East Liberty served as a nexus point for three extremely violent gangs terrorizing the city: the Bloods, the Crips, and the LAW (Larimer Avenue and Wilkinsburg). I lived on the hottest block, the 700 block of Mellon Street.

Before I continue, there are a few things you should know about my experience living in a gang- and drug-infested neighborhood as a teenager.

1. If you were to peek in my closet and in my bedroom
   dresser right now, you'd probably notice a gaggle of gray
   clothing. Shirts, undershirts, shoes, jeans, suits, ties,
   boxer briefs—if it can be worn on an adult human male's
   body and it comes in gray, I own that bitch. *Gaggle* doesn't
   even really do my disturbing level of grayophilia justice.
   You'd think I owned *all* the gray clothes or that I shopped
   exclusively at stores that only sold gray merchandise. Or
   perhaps even that there was an unrealistically attractive
   woman working one day at the Gray Clothes Depot—
   Nicole Beharie or Yaya Dacosta somehow stuck hawking
   gray sweat socks to writers—who convinced me to buy
   everything in aisles four through seven by flirting with
   me long enough for me to think I'd have a shot at getting
   her number if I spent $2,500 that day.
   
   You'd then probably assume that I must just really,

really, really like gray shit. That assumption would
be correct, but this affinity for gray is not arbitrary.
It developed over time as a natural and eventual by-
product of a very intentional survival mechanism. For
a teenager in East Liberty in the early and midnineties,
your clothing options were limited by circumstance and
environment. You couldn't wear a ton of blue because the
Crips (in neighboring Lincoln and Homewood) owned
blue. Red was out because of the Bloods in neighboring
Garfield. And the LAW in neighboring Larimer draped
themselves in black. This was also a decade or so before
Cam'ron and the rest of the Dipset made it cool for black
men to wear pink and purple again, so the only colors left
were white (which gets dirty too quickly), green (which
doesn't match with enough colors), brown (which the
Cleveland Browns wore and fuck the Cleveland Browns),
yellow (which is too bright and jolly and you couldn't
be looking too bright and jolly in the hood), and orange
(which is the Kia Optima of colors). Gray, however, was
neutral and versatile. And in 1995, neutral and versatile
meant life-saving. Now, it just makes people assume I
must really like Drake.

2. I've witnessed and/or experienced each of the following
   things:

   a. A drive-by shooting fifty feet away from my front door,
      which killed a close friend of my cousin's and caused
      Dad to break down in tears—the first time I ever saw
      that happen.

   b. An M-80 exploding in our front window, shattering
      it completely and ruining both the plants on the
      windowsill and the couch sitting underneath it. It was
      placed in our window by a man who wanted the people

inside our house to be so shocked by the explosion that we ran outside, where he planned to shoot and kill us. No one went outside, however, so he fired shots up into the second-story window facing the street. This happened to be my parents' bedroom, and Mom—who was still asleep—was awoken by a burning sensation on her forearm, a bullet that ricocheted off the wall and landed there.

We later learned that the shooter mistook our house for a house belonging to a drug dealer who lived three doors down. (I had a crush on that drug dealer's niece, who also lived on that block. And it was surprisingly requited. But nothing ever developed between us because the whole "your uncle almost got my entire family murdered" thing made the situation awkward).

c. We lived in a collection of row houses. Each house came equipped with a twenty-by-ten-foot fenced-in yard in the back as well as a carport. My bedroom window faced the back. One night, sprung awake by some commotion, I got up, looked out my window, and noticed that a car in a carport four houses down was ablaze. I could also hear a man screaming and crying hysterically, which struck me as even odder than the car being on fire at 3:30 A.M., because who gets that damn upset about a car? (Even as a twelve-year-old, I was a pragmatist about insurance). I later learned after eavesdropping on my parents that his car was burned because of a drug debt and the next thing to burn would be his house if he didn't pay. But, without a car now, he wouldn't be able to get to work. So he was fucked.

Also, this drug debt had no connection to the drug

dealer neighbor mentioned a couple of paragraphs ago. The 700 block of Mellon Street was apparently a prime focus group for creative and entrepreneurial ways to settle crack-related disputes.

d. For two years, our next-door neighbors were a family of somewhere between 6 and 149 people. So many people went in and out of that house at all times of the day that we stopped trying to determine exactly who lived there. Mom called them "gypsy negroes" in a way that totally actually said *fucking gypsy hoodrat niggas*. We were very sure about one of the residents, though, a fifteen-year-old named Jerome who moonlighted as a prostitute.

We were always suspicious about what Jerome did with his time. Once, Dad asked him where he went to school, and Jerome pointed toward the horizon and said, "Over there, somewhere," as if he attended class on the moon. Dad didn't press him.

Months later, while we were walking home from Giant Eagle one night, we noticed a slight young woman sitting on the stoop of an apartment complex a few blocks away from our house. She was wearing a slip and house shoes and sitting the way certain types of women sit to make plain that certain types of things are for sale. She was a pro, or, at least, an amateur mimicking and wanting to appear to be a pro. As we got closer to her, it became clear that this slight young woman was Jerome.

Dad called out to him. "Jerome, is that you?"

Jerome lied, "No."

Dad didn't press, and just replied "Well, Jerome, if that is you, be safe out here."

(Decades later, I've come to realize that Jerome likely wasn't just working. Considering his age and that neighborhood, he was probably working *for someone*. And, when also considering that Jerome's age made him legally unable to have consensual sex with an adult, this just adds another level of tragedy to Jerome's situation.)

A couple of months after that, their house burned down—not because of a drug debt, but because when you have 149 gypsy negroes living in a house, it catching fire is an inevitability. Fortunately, no one was hurt, and the firemen were able to contain the blaze so it didn't spread to our house. One thing that did spread, however, was a family of roaches that had been living with the 149 and were now refugees. We learned quite quickly that Lysol kitchen spray is actually much more effective than Raid at killing them.

e. My parents were evicted twice. Not a full eviction where you come home and all your shit is on the street like in the movies, but an eviction where the eviction guy posts a big-ass red notice on your door—announcing, "These triflin' niggas ain't pay they bills" to the neighborhood—and your locks are changed until you've caught up on your rent. Fortunately, both times happened when I was still small enough to be propped up on Dad's shoulders so I could crawl in the house through the kitchen window and unlock the back door.

f. My favorite recurring activities on the block were the touch-tab and stop-grab football games the other kids and I would play in the middle of the street. Light poles seventy feet apart demarcated our end zones, the sidewalks were deemed out of bounds, and parked cars were extra and painfully effective defenders. If a car happened to turn on our block, we'd stop playing until it passed. One evening, however, we took a bit too long to get out of the street for the driver's liking, so he beeped a few times. Annoyed now, we stood, defiant, and started taunting him. ("Nigga, what you beeping for? You ain't gonna do shit.")

And then he put his car in park, opened the door, and got out—*with a shotgun.* We scattered like Skittles dropped in a sink; some ran into people's backyards, some hid behind cars, and me and a few others ran through a dirt pathway between a couple of houses.

And we all—each one of us—had smiles on our faces and laughs escaping our mouths, like we were in an especially intense round of Release the Den and not "hide from the nigga with the gun."

3. I witnessed and experienced some legitimately scary-ass fucking shit. My neighborhood wasn't quite *The Wire.* And my parents, despite their limited resources, scratched and clawed and cheated their way for me to attend St. Barts. So, while I lived on Mellon, I was able to escape it for eight hours a day every day. Still, my reality was far closer to the Barksdales than the Cosbys. But I never felt scared. I never felt in fear for my life. I never felt poor. I never doubted that whatever happened, I'd be all right. I was far from oblivious; I knew the mortal dangers surrounding me on each side. I knew how one wrong walk through the wrong block, or even one right walk through the right block at the wrong time, could end my future. My life. And if there was any inkling of a chance of me not knowing any of this, my parents never hesitated to remind me. But I was more scared for and protective of *them* than I was myself.

I knew I was from the hood, but I didn't actually *feel like* I was from the hood until we left it and moved to Penn Hills. It was there that my parents not owning a car and my dependence on the PAT bus became another thing that I needed to be self-conscious about. The faux-bougie black kids in Penn Hills with dads who owned barbershops and moms who worked at Highmark had access to their parents' cars. And when you're waiting for the 77B and a Nissan Altima driven by cute and nice and curvy Carmen from your third-period AP history class speeds by your stop, you dead any thought you have about asking her to go to the Showcase Cinemas with you next weekend because no cute girl with a car is gonna date a nigga on the bus.

I didn't realize, though, that a more confident and self-assured me could have easily leveraged the from-the-hood thing into my favor. How? Street cred! I had street credibility and realness seeping out of my pores! I had so much real actual street cred in me that I could have shit it out! Parts of my pre–Penn Hills life could've been a skit from a Mobb Deep album! I saw niggas die with my own actual eyes on my own actual street! I knew crackheads and crack dealers! Shit, I knew what crack *smelled* like! I had guns pulled on me! I knew like four dudes named Man Man and three dudes named Day Day and like three Nieceys and at least five niggas from Homewood and Garfield with inexplicably Spanish names like José Washington and Alejandro Jenkins! The only breeds of dog I'd ever seen were pit bulls and rottweilers! I regularly played basketball on milk crates attached to telephone poles and indoors in the hinges of metal doors propped open! I didn't (and still don't) know how to swim! I got expelled from school! And then played hooky with my own dad (my *dad!*) for months afterward! I knew how to kill roaches better than most exterminators! I played tackle football on concrete pavement! I didn't just know niggas in prison, I knew entire families—brothers, uncles, sisters, grandmothers—of niggas in prison! My fucking mom was shot! Shot—*in her own fucking bed*!

It would have been so easy too. I could have regaled the cafeteria and study hall tables with my daily tales from the hood. I could have done the whole "thug with a smart and sensitive side" like Tupac did. I could have been vulnerable—well, "vulnerable"—and watched the girls line up to soothe my troubled and damaged psyche. I could have made the PAT bus *cool* by lying and saying that's where it's really poppin' and that only lame niggas drove cars. I hadn't been in an actual fight since seventh grade, but I could have given myself a tough city-nigga-sounding nickname, like Knuckles or Bumpy or Wing-Ding. And if James Adams dared to make me the focus of his rips, I could have told him, in front of everyone, that real niggas don't have porches.

Of course, I didn't do any of this, because of that self-doubt and self-deprecation. But also, to be fair, because I was pressed against an even greater force, one that I likely wouldn't have recognized and overcome even if I *were* an unusually confident and self-assured sixteen-year-old. For many black American families, the dogged and grim pursuit of upward mobility—of the American dream being actualized instead of aspirational—cultivates a dynamic where performative mobility replaces actual mobility. This, of course, is a by-product of the historical constrictions and conditions placed on our financial ascension. Moving up the ladder from working poor to lower middle class, from lower middle class to middle class, and from middle class to upper middle class is possible. And it happens often enough that actively pursuing it can't be dismissed as silly.

It just tends to happen so much fucking *slower*. And, if it does happen, it has a way of feeling fraudulent. Counterfeit.

Like someone is going to show up at your door one day to tell you they made a mistake. (Or call you to the principal's office during third-period biology to tell you that you have to clean out your locker, be escorted out of school and back to wherever the fuck in the city your black ass came from.) That all of your success—regardless of how minor and mundane this success happens to be—is the result of a clerical error. An intern in accounting forgot to cross a *t* and dot an *i* somewhere, and now it's back to the hood for you.

The tenuousness of this mobility connects to why, despite my parents' obvious lack of great financial means, I had every pair of Jordans from the time I was eight until I graduated from high school. It has roots in why, after not having a car for at least five years, my parents bought a freakin' Cadillac. I couldn't embrace my humble and hood background because it wasn't something to be embraced. It wasn't considered something to be proud of; and it was definitely not considered something to promote as some sort of standard of desirable legitimacy. The appearance of doing better than we actually were doing was so ingrained, so vital to our collective spirit and self-esteem, that I couldn't commemorate my East Liberty roots—mining each morsel of street credibility out of them—but instead wanted nothing more than to escape them. I ran as far away from 740 Mellon Street as I possibly could.

By doing that, I ran smack-dab into James, who was also running in his own way. He was battling the same neurosis I was, but from the opposite end of the spectrum. Instead of escaping his realness—his *blackness*—he was performing it. The performative thuggishness, the hyper-heterosexuality, the apathy toward school and basketball practice and anything that would force him to break his delicate and intricate "hood nigga" facade—this was an effort to be what he believed it meant for

him to be black. It was a perpetual appeasing of expected blackness from a man-child as insecure about his background as I
was, only his act was more popular and, in Penn Hills, more
prevalent. There were dozens of James Adamses swaggering
the halls at this suburban and solidly middle-class high school,
all desperately wanting to be exactly what America would see
when it saw them. All searching for a fabricated authenticity that
didn't exist. All allowing their zip codes to convince them that
they weren't convincingly black enough. Perhaps he singled me
out specifically because I was legitimately from the hood. Maybe
it bothered him that while I was from the place he wanted to
mimic and possessed the cred he wanted to capture, I didn't actually want any part of it. I just wanted to hoop and fit in with
the rest of the Penn Hills niggas. I wanted the porch James
pretended he didn't have and the car he feigned like his mom
couldn't afford. I just wanted my life to be "normal." And he just
wanted to be "black."

I'm two decades removed now from that night on the back
of the bus, and I understand, better, the impulses and impetuses
that forced James to be who he was back then. This, apparently,
is called perspective, and I have enough of it now to grant him a
sympathy that I wouldn't have dared to twenty or even ten years
ago. Unfortunately, I am also petty as fuck, and I'm choosing
not to employ all of this perspective and sympathy and magnanimity and whatever else I've gained in the last two decades
of living, book learning, and churchgoing. I am enjoying this
decidedly one-sided grudge, and I intend to squeeze the shit out
of it until there's nothing left but pulp. Perhaps it's that East Lib
in me. Who knows?

Instead, I'll settle for hoping that James accidentally butt-
dials someone he really, really, really, really, really doesn't want
to talk to today and ends up in a forty-five-minute-long conver-

sation with them. Or perhaps that he goes to the theater tonight to watch a movie in 3-D, only to be told all the 3-D glasses have been given out, but he already paid and this is the only time he has free, so he has to sit there and watch a blurry movie for 120 minutes. And this gives him a headache that makes his sleep that night quite uncomfortable.

# 3

# BOMB-ASS POETRY

Darius Lovehall was trash.

He was also the main character in *Love Jones*—Theodore Witcher's 1997 romantic drama about the love lives of a group of black Chicagoans who, while not millennials, lived and acted and dated quite millennially. And the black cinema counterpart to the emotive, immature, romantically volatile, and hopelessly lovelorn male characters popularized in eighties teen comedies by John Cusack, who perfected that archetype in *Say Anything*... and *Better Off Dead*, and then gave us the grown-up version of it with *High Fidelity*. And played so well by Larenz Tate that it was near impossible to fathom that, only four years earlier, the same actor portrayed the nihilistic, psychopathic, and plaited-up O-Dog in *Menace II Society*. And, for smarty-arty black people who were in high school or college when *Love Jones* was released, either the most common prototype for the type of relationships you hoped to have with women or the template for the type of man you wished to be wooed by.

That said, just know and do not allow yourself to forget that Darius Lovehall was a fraud, a creep, and a criminal, and that all of this was revealed within the first fifteen minutes of the movie.

*Love Jones* begins in a smoky and hip lounge called the Sanctuary with Darius onstage reciting a spoken word poem detailing exactly how he would seduce and have sex with a woman he desperately wanted to seduce and have sex with. Which is par for the course at most open mics, as the majority of poems performed at them are usually either about orgasms, racism, or granola. Unfortunately, the woman at the center of Darius's poem (Nia Long's Nina Mosley) was in the audience. And we know the poem was about her because the name of the poem was "Brother to the Night (A Blues for Nina)." And we also know that Darius and Nina met for *the very first time ever* at the bar five minutes before Darius's performance, because that was the scene directly before Darius strode to the stage. Which means that Darius wrote a poem explicitly articulating the sex he wants to have with a woman he just met *and* performed said poem in front of dozens of people while said mortified woman—WHO HE JUST FUCKING MET—was sitting in the audience. We also know that there's no way in hell he could have written and memorized an elaborate three-minute-long poem in five minutes. Which means he already had that poem written and prepared for another woman, and he just made a couple of quick edits to it when he met Nina.

A week or so later, Darius tracks Nina down by convincing a friend who works at a record shop Nina happened to be browsing in to give him Nina's home address. Which I'm sure is some sort of crime and, since the friend is complicit, a conspiracy to commit some sort of crime too. He then drops by her home, unannounced, just to tell her he can't get over how desperately he really, really, really wants to fuck her. He's had countless sleepless nights because of that ass. He needs some Ambien 'cause of dat ass. But since this is a movie, instead of kicking him in the shins, emptying a can of pepper spray in his grill, and hurdling over his crumpled body to dash into the street and yelp, "THIS BLACK-LEATHER-JACKET-IN-THE-DEAD-OF-THE-CHICAGO-SUMMER-ROCKING-ASS POETRY-ASS NIGGA IS STALKING ME!" she lets him in, agrees to go on a date with him, sleeps with him, and eventually falls in love with him. They also, occasionally, wear black leather jackets together.

To be fair, this synopsis of *Love Jones* is much harsher than my actual feelings about it. It's a movie that makes me warm and fuzzy each time I see it. I find myself actively rooting for Darius and Nina, and I'm so in love with how in love Ted Witcher is with his characters and their city and the easy and smooth and vibrant and limitless blackness they're ensconced in that I even excuse the fact that none of said characters seem to be very employed but all of them live in houses with wide porches or tastefully furnished lofts with mezzanines and floating staircases and shit.

*Love Jones* is also known and lauded for accurately capturing the general zeitgeist then among the upwardly mobile and educated niggas who appreciated Biggie and blunts like everyone else but were also enamored with the abstract concept of "deepness" and even more enamored with reminding everyone how enamored they were with the concept of deepness. This was the era of kufis and anklets and head wraps and ponchos. When words like *aura* and *essence* and *chakra* and phrases like *keep your third eye open* were regularly cited in conversation, unironically. And conspiracy theories about everything from AIDS (*created by the government to stop African birthrates*) and Magic Johnson (*rid of HIV after he purchased the cure from the government*) to Timberlands (*the tree logo etched on every pair represented the lynching of black people*) and Tommy Hilfiger (*went on Oprah to explain why he didn't want black people wearing his clothes*) were considered verifiable facts. And everyone seemed to be into passion fruit. And I strongly suspect we were into passion fruit because we just enjoyed saying *passion fruit*, as if fruit salad and smoothies with emotional pepo somehow made us blacker. Niggas were just too good for grapes.

And if the day party and the bottomless brunch are the nexus points and fulcrums for contemporary bougie blacks, the bluesy and electric neighborhood lounge with regular poetry readings and interpretative dance performances and random niggas going table-to-table selling incense, shea butter, and Pre-Paid Legal served that purpose at the turn of the century. *Love Jones* was just one of several popular forms of media to reflect that spirit, a canon that includes 1998's *Slam*, *Russell Simmons Presents Def Poetry* (which ran on HBO from 2002 to 2007), and Jill Scott's 2000 debut *Who Is Jill Scott? Words and Sounds Vol. 1*.

But this encapsulation is false. *Love Jones* didn't capture the zeitgeist. It created it.

Now, open mic night culture did exist before *Love Jones*. Saul Williams was already quite popular, Jessica Care Moore had already won the *Showtime at the Apollo* talent show five consecutive times, *Aloud: Voices from the Nuyorican Poets Cafe* had already been released, Maya Angelou's "On the Pulse of Morning" could already be found scrolled out in italicized block letters on every self-consciously conscious black chick's Black-Planet profile page, and every pan-African recording artist—from the Roots and Erykah Badu to Common Sense and the Wu—already regularly incorporated the confusing, contradictory, and conveniently alliterative lexicon of the Five-Percent

Nation (the official religious sponsor of open mic night culture) in their music. It was still somewhat fringe, though, something that only super-duper extra-Vantablack black people and niggas into turkey bacon and patchouli were a part of. But *Love Jones* was such a force within the bougie black American subculture and made open mic night culture seem so damn *cool* that it pulled it up out of the fringe and mainstreamed it. Now *everyone* started snapping their fingers during readings the way the patrons at the Sanctuary would honor standout poems instead of clapping. And at jazz concerts. And solos at church. And basketball games. And really impassioned spontaneous 2 A.M. speeches at parties about the virtues of garlic parm chicken wings. And there was a rash of niggas with names like Edward and Frank and Joseph who all of a sudden wanted you to call them "Knowledge" and "Wisdom" and "Thermostat." And poetry writing and performing—which before stayed pretty much confined to actual poets, theater arts majors, and inmates at maximum-security prisons—became ubiquitous. Everyone wanted to be a fucking poet. Which led to a decadelong boom period for pretentious, verbose, faux-feminist, and spectacularly shitty poetry. Unfortunately, I made frequent contributions to this archive.

I started writing poetry my sophomore year at Canisius College, the Jesuit school in Buffalo, New York, that was kind enough to give me a full scholarship to play basketball for them, for the same reason every nineteen-year-old heterosexual male decides to start writing poetry midway through college: to impress women enough that they perhaps begin to actively consider the idea of giving him some ass. In my case, my muse was a girl named Tracey, who was also a sophomore. We first met two weeks into our freshman year. We both missed a campus bus to a Sigma party at nearby Buffalo State University, and were left stranded on a balcony outside our main cafeteria when she approached me, cigarette in hand.

"Do you have a light?"

"I don't smoke."

"Why not?"

"Because cigarettes will kill you."

"Everything will kill you eventually."

"Even you?"

"Maybe."

She had long brown hair with barely detectable auburn streaks, a raspy voice marinated by Newport smoke and draped over a still-to-this-day unplaceable and inconceivable accent— she was from Binghamton, New York, but sounded like a black chick from Toronto impersonating Holly Hunter—and a bemused slyness that frequently vacillated between *Is she flirting with me?* and *Is she making fun of me?* Naturally, I immediately fell in deep like with her. And twenty-four hours later, when we went to another party together, left that party together, walked a mile back to our dorm, and both ended up in my twin bed—her in the leggings and gray T-shirt she retrieved from her room a floor above mine, and me still wearing the jeans and boots I wore to the party because it all happened so quickly that it didn't dawn on me that I should probably have taken them off before she came back downstairs—I assumed that night would be the first in a promising romantic relationship. Instead, it was the first of perhaps sixty nights that year of us lying in bed (and always her bed); her in PJs, me in sweatpants and a harder-than-a-concrete-park-bench dick awkwardly repositioned in my boxer briefs and pressed up against my belly so it wouldn't poke her in the ass, and us both surrounded by at least a dozen of the Tickle Me Elmo dolls and figurines she had in her room, all witnessing us having conversations about search engines and

La Nova chicken wings and not having anything even closely resembling sex.

We grew to be homies. A month into freshman year she was already my closest friend on campus. But I wanted more than a friendship, figuring that attaching occasional sex to our easy compatibility and already frequent cuddle-buddying would be the optimal romantic relationship. She didn't see the logic, however, and pretended to be oblivious to the feelings I never quite articulated but knew she knew about. (Which, to be fair, was probably her best option.)

So I did what I thought I needed to do to convince her, which was hang out with her, hang out around her, hang out next to her, hang out beside her, and, if necessary, hang out underneath her, like the bottom mattress on the world's saddest bunk bed; hoping that being with and available to her literally all of the fucking time would somehow dull her defenses enough to convince her to reconsider the stance she never officially took.

By sophomore year, I'd devised a new strategy. I would woo (or guilt) her into submission with some bomb-ass poetry. The type of poetry that would make her say things like "*I didn't know you wrote bomb-ass poetry, Damon*" and "*Did you get taller over the summer?*" and "*Take my panties off because that bomb-ass poetry got this bomb-ass pussy all wet.*" Some Darius Lovehall–ass bomb-ass poetry.

I pounded away for weeks. But aside from discovering myriad new ways to incorporate "after parties we bone" with "Bacardi Limón" into the verses I'd memorize for rap cyphers in the cafeteria with my teammates, I kept coming up blank. I didn't anticipate that the whole I'd-never-actually-written-a-poem-before thing would be a problem. Running out of patience, I enlisted the help of a talented and prolific friend, and eventually we came up with something workable together, which I typed up and emailed to Tracey.

> No doubt, you got the best trout there can be
> Not an everyday, average, Chicken of the Sea, candidate
>     for H.I.V.
> You'd rather deal with monogamy Queen to be held,
>     Black Mahogany
> You're bout to bust damnit, sugar walls comin down
>     Now you can't stand it, you've been touched That's
>     when I felt the blood rush
> Gettin closer and closer with every thrust, take me there
> Volcano's about to erupt, I love you much

If you're familiar at all with late-nineties East Coast hip-hop, this poem might sound familiar. It might even sound exactly like an edited version of Method Man's verse on "Sweet Love"—track three off of his *Tical 2000: Judgement Day*. Which is exactly what it was. My "help" was just me hopping on the Original Hip-Hop Lyrics Archive, cutting and pasting Meth's verse into Microsoft Word, and slicing it in half. I even sent it to Tracey with *To You, From Me* in the subject line—which also became the poem's title—as if she wouldn't have somehow deduced that a message sent from my email account to her email account would be from me and to her. I was volunteering an alibi for a crime no one suspected me of committing.

I knew Tracey wasn't a hip-hop head, so there was minimal chance she'd recognize my plagiarism. Not only had I committed the perfect crime, I was convinced my thievery might result in some ass. I'd even allowed myself to fantasize about more slightly amoral acts I'd commit to keep the stream of booty flowing, because of course she wouldn't be able to re-

sist a bomb-ass-poetry-writing-ass nigga with some safe college student thuggishness in him. Perhaps the next time we
were partners while playing Spades and our opponents wanted
to bet on the game, I'd use the flex cash on my meal plan as
collateral *even though I'd already spent all my first-semester flex
cash in September.*

She replied to my email the next day with sincere gratitude
and appreciation. But not the type of gratitude and appreciation
that suggests immediate bomb-ass pussy moisture. More the
type of gratitude and appreciation that occurs when a seven-
year-old nephew draws you a really sweet picture of Rosa Parks
slam dunking a football.

Undeterred and armed with my newfound friend, I sent her
another poem, this one an even more obscure verse from an
even more obscure Wu-Tang-related track—Inspectah Deck's
"Femme Fatale."

I was so intoxicated by this easy thievery that I didn't even
bother editing it down *and* I gave it the exact same title of the
song I stole it from. To my dismay, her response didn't change.
"This is very sweet. You're so talented Damon!" read her reply
this time. Stilted compliments were her only option now, since
my feelings by this point were too obvious for her to continue
to feign obliviousness. I took her polite appreciation to heart
and sincerely attempted again to write my own poems, which
would range in quality from "That's actually not the worst
thing I've ever read before" to "Yeah, that's the worst thing I've
ever read."

There was "Strawberry Klondike," a disturbingly illustra-
tive ode to eating pussy—something I hadn't actually done
before—which was given that title as a cheeky way to refer to a
black woman's vagina.

"Twice Born" came as a result of listening to Ursula Rucker's harrowing "Return to Innocence Lost"—the concluding track on the Roots' *Things Fall Apart*. After nailing cunnilingus, I wanted to try my hand at something harrowing too, because why should Ursula Rucker have all of the harrowing fun? So I attempted to duplicate her cadence, her command of language, and her talent, and ended up creating a ColecoVision version of Rucker's work.

"Twice Born" was the first of my practice of barely concealed mimicry that stretched for a year. I'd hear or read something, and then I'd write something similar, beat for beat, eventually sharing and passing off that haphazard facsimile as authentic. "Miss You"—wherein I saw an attractive woman while on the subway and fantasized about the future we'd have together if I ever gathered the gumption to approach her—was a carbon copy of the first verse from Inspectah Deck's "Lovin' You" (where he saw an attractive woman while on the subway, and fantasized about the future they'd have together if he ever gathered the gumption to approach her).

Also, at this point in my life, I'd never been on a subway, or any type of train. But subways were such effective narrative devices—in my head they were steel and sleek buckets of shy glances, sneaky winks, and subtle flirtations and not the dank and dirty portable roach motels they actually tend to be—that I couldn't allow the limitations of my own reality to influence my bomb-ass poetry.

"Who Am I" straight-up jacked the concept, the flow, and even some of the words from Company Flow's "Patriotism"—a track from the *Soundbombing II* compilation album. And it was actually a double lie because I was nowhere near as cynical about America as I pretended to be in it.

Although exaggerated, this then-performative disgust with our country was essential to my newfound identity as a bomb-

ass-poetry-writing-ass nigga. I wasn't Muslim or a Five Per-
center. I liked bacon too much to give up pork. Soy-infused and
soy-dependent food products gave me bubble guts. I preferred
Avirex leather jackets and Nike Air Maxes to loincloths and
Dr. Martens. I still spelled America with a *c* instead of three
*k*'s. My jewelry of choice was a gold chain, not an Africa me-
dallion. And I was from beige-ass Pittsburgh—not Brooklyn
or Harlem or Chicago or D.C. or Philly. I didn't meet any of
the usual benchmarks of extra-super-blackness necessary to
be a convincing black bohemian or backpacker, so I pretended
to be angry, allowing manufactured racial fury to be the co-
signer for this change. But only on paper. In person I was still
the same Damon. On paper, though, I was the horniest Black
Panther ever. And my poems vacillated from strained militancy
and artificially extraneous pro-blackness to ballads of barely
concealed desperation either enunciating the extravagant and
ethereal sex I wasn't actually having or convincing women to
drink almond milk.

The worst of the latter was probably "I Got Your Letter"—a
typo and malapropism-riddled response to a nonexistent black
woman's nonexistent letter lamenting a shortage of eligible black
men. It begins with a well-intentioned but clumsy laud of sistas
that suggests they're specifically equipped with unusually large
vaginas to handle my unusually large penis, and concludes with
the threat of me growing so tired of waiting for these unusually
large-vaginaed sistas to recognize and appreciate *my* awesome
that I give up and start dating white chicks.

> I hear you sis'.
> your kiss?
> shiiiit, I'll NEVER dismiss
> them lipsthick-asshipsthighseyesvoice . . .

GODDAMN, GIRL, you got me moist
other choices? PLEASE
give a brother some credit
you think Ally McBeal could deal
with my long, strong Mandingo steel?
chills in the summertime
spine tingles at the thought
perfection embodied in a black sundress, hour-glass
    frame, caramel
complexion, hips swaying my direction
let me permeate your pores
calm your mentals
your heartbeat's my instramental
in the night
brown eyes bright like candlelights
exciting me,
inviting me to stay in your landscape
thoughts NEVER sway
you're too beautiful
fruitful,
smart
huggable
doable like art
of my life, I want you part
forever
made my blues MO' BETTER
positive like neutrons their's no better
I love you like the fourth letter
and the twenty-fifth
but . . .
BLACK WOMAN
there's no shortage,

I'm HERE
right within ear-
shot
we aint all locked up
we aint all slangin' rocks,
hanging on blocks,
smoking pot
this talk of "there's no good men"
has got to stop
cause it hurts
hurts me that the ones you desire
are them same stray cats that try their DAMNEST
to quench your fire
but BLACK WOMAN . . .
I'M still here
while your chickens cluck in your ear
saying "there's no men left out there"
I'm still here
patiently awaiting your return to the throne
I'm still here
cause aint no way I'm bringing snow white in my home
I'm still here
cause your presense and effervescence cant be covered in
    no Essence
or Ebony magazine
want to conversate and innovate
my dream's protagionist
Cleopatra, queen of the nile, I'll cross the battleline . . .
BLACK WOMAN
I'm here for you
PLEASE make up your fuckin' mind
(Ally McBeal's starting to look fine)

Fortunately, the bar for what passed as good poetry then was so low I could've banged my shin on it. I'd email these to multiple friends, and they began to anticipate my new poems like they were advance singles from a secret album recorded specifically for them. And for the first time since landing on campus, I had a thing I was specifically known for and thought to be better than (most) everyone at, a status I'd been searching for since realizing basketball wouldn't be it for me anymore.

I did not enter college with any pretense of anticipating a career in the NBA. Did I dream of one? Of course. But the same way an eighteen-year-old me might have dreamed of taking Aaliyah or Tatyana Ali to the prom. I was self-aware enough then to know that a person my size (six foot one and a half and 190 pounds then) had to be an athletic freak of nature to play at that level, which I wasn't. And I was savvy and neurotic enough then to also realize that professing a desire to play professional sports aloud fit the racially codified narrative of what black boys were supposed to want to do. Telling people you wanted to be a ballplayer or a rapper was essentially broadcasting that your parents failed at raising you and the only possible remedy was being duct-taped to a couch and forced to watch seasons two through five of *A Different World*. So if asked if I wanted to play in the NBA, I'd lie and say I'd rather be in sports management. Or maybe a network TV weatherman.

I did, however, anticipate having a successful college basketball career. I even alluded to this in a *Pittsburgh Tribune-Review* profile of me published the July after my senior year of high school, where I assumed that because Canisius's starting point guard had graduated the year before I arrived, I'd be able to step right in and perhaps even be a starter immediately.

I did not anticipate finally getting to school that fall and struggling so badly with the preseason conditioning on the track that I'd have to suffer the indignity of running extra laps when everyone else was done; sometimes even kicking over random garbage cans in disgust after running another seventy-five-second sprint in eighty-one seconds. And then being ordered to stop running, pick up all the trash my furious kicks scattered on the gravel, and, of course, resume running. Or not making the five-minute-and-thirty-second mile time required of all guards to culminate the month of conditioning, which meant I couldn't practice with the team until I was able to. Or finally making the time two weeks after everyone else did, and falling so far out of the team's rotation that I was essentially a walk-on. Or not getting on the court at all in any of our first three games of the season in a tournament at the University of New Mexico. Or finally getting some burn in our first home game—which happened to be against the University of Kentucky—and doing surprisingly well against them. And not realizing that those four points and two assists against the eventual national champion Wildcats would be the apex of my entire college career.

There were games I played more minutes, scored more points, grabbed more rebounds, dished more assists, and snatched more steals. Particularly during my sophomore year of playing, which actually occurred two years after my freshman year, because I tore the anterior cruciate ligament in my left knee the June after my freshman year, rendering me unable to play during the weeklong trip to Italy we took that August and forcing me to take a redshirt year because the rehab and recovery period at the time for a torn ACL was approximately twelve months. But that Kentucky game was the last time I harbored any reasonable hope that my college basketball career would be a successful one. By the end of that season I'd fallen out of the rotation. I scored six points *total* all year.

Each consecutive season would begin and end similarly.

Me struggling with the preseason conditioning tests—which I'd later realize weren't so much tests of physical endurance as mental fortitude and mettle. Me falling out of the rotation before the regular season even began. Me dealing with some random injury and/or illness:

- a bone bruise in my right knee the fall before my sophomore year,
- a torn hamstring the day before our conference tournament began that same year,
- a bout of mono the spring after my junior year so intense that I lost forty pounds and somehow gained a terrible case of acid reflux that left me unable to play at all during my senior year because the coaches and team trainers thought I had the bubonic plague.

And me searching for space within this new and cruel reality, where this game I'd allowed and wanted to define me— existing as my sole source of favorable identity, the only way I could look in the mirror and smile at what I'd see—became my shame. Everything about me up to that point was predicated on the status associated with being able to walk into any space within my sphere of influence and know that I was the best person in my age range in that space at this one particular awesome thing. But my career distorted this dynamic. I was still better at basketball than 99 percent of my peers. I was still a Division I basketball player. I still belonged to the basketball team, which at Canisius was the most exclusive and powerful group on campus, and I still received and cashed in on the free admittances to frat parties and the luxury of choosing class times and housing assignments before everyone else and the rest of the perks of that position. I could still walk through the yard between Bosch Hall and Frisch Hall, or down Main Street to the Koessler Athletic Center, or past the off-campus upperclassmen housing on Delavan Avenue, or even out to the food court in the Galleria Mall in Cheektowaga with my team sweats on and my swaying nuts firmly ensconced in my right hand. But every minute on campus was spent with the knowledge that I couldn't assert the same status I did in Pittsburgh—a status I'd spent a decade molding, maintaining, perfecting, and allowing to exist in place of me—because I was, objectively, the worst scholarship player on the team. I was still better than everyone, except the only people who actually mattered. The same people who happened to be my teammates. And roommates. And classmates. And friends.

This dynamic is why, since then, I've always carried a soft spot for people like Michelle Williams of Destiny's Child and others who've been the least heralded member of a supremely popular group. Imagine, for a second, existing your entire life as the most talented, best singing, prettiest, and overall baddest chick wherever you happened to be. School, church, summer camp, back corner booth at a Memphis-area Chipotle—it didn't fucking matter. If you happened to be there, you were the motherfucking temperature. The template. The benchmark every other aspiring bad chick measured herself by. People would bring your name up when you weren't around, would be disappointed to go places and not see you there, and would think of you when thinking about MAC counters at Nordstrom and turtleneck sweaters and bubble gum and wind machines and the rest of the shit I assume people think about when mindlessly pondering bad bitches. Guys would craft entire schedules and lunch breaks and contrived bike paths to work around the mere possibility of you maybe, hopefully crossing their path, and women would befriend you solely in the hope that they'd be able to exist in and off of your residue, retaining coolness by osmosis and perhaps even scooping up your discarded men like a plover snatching what's stuck between a gator's teeth. (Of course, I don't know what life is like for women who look like this, since I've never been one of them. Which is why this hypothetical is mostly based off of characters Stacey Dash played in the nineties.)

Now, imagine taking that status and that position and joining a group with motherfucking Beyoncé. And Beyoncé's cousin and best friend Kelly Rowland. A three-person group with Beyoncé and Beyoncé's cousin and best friend Kelly— that's managed by Beyoncé's dad and outfitted by Beyoncé's mom. Imagine how surreal your world would be then. Imagine the psychedelic and soul-snatching fusion of hypervisibility and invisibility; where everyone is looking at you—or, at the very least, in your direction—but people aren't paying much attention to you. (Unless, of course, you fuck up.) But because you're more privileged than everyone except your two most immediate peers, any type of lament of your own circumstance would be considered ungrateful. Obscene, even.

Perhaps I'm projecting. Maybe Michelle Williams didn't wrestle with the same sort of status-dependent angst that I did. Maybe she only joined Destiny's Child for the paycheck, the music, and the free postconcert vegan chorizo burritos that Solange would order for them, which I'm certain is what happened after their concerts because Solange looks like she knows where to get the best vegan chorizo burritos in every city. Maybe she wasn't so annoyed by the years of always having to pause mid-song to adjust to another one of Momma Tina Knowles's arbitrarily malfunctioning Lycra bodysuits that she didn't have to do what I did, which was to latch onto another possible source of elevated status when realizing I needed something to fill the void left by basketball leaving me.

By my junior year, the transformation from "that dude who's on the hoop team but doesn't actually play" to "that dude on the hoop team who writes that bomb-ass poetry" was complete, and I embraced this metamorphosis with open arms. It didn't matter to me then that my start was fueled by plagiarism and desperation. Like that *Seinfeld* episode when George pretends to be a marine biologist and then, when encountering a beached whale, becomes possessed with the spirit of a marine biologist, I *became* that bomb-ass-poetry-writing-ass nigga. Fitted caps and race car jackets were replaced with kufis and peacoats; the gold and faux-platinum chains draped around my neck replaced by a necklace composed of beads, acorns, and bronzed pumpkin seeds copped from a table at an African Arts Festival in Erie, Pennsylvania, the summer before and empty dog tags from an army/navy surplus store in downtown Pittsburgh. I had all the rubber bands—wrapping them tightly around my wrists like Ace bandages nursing a sprain—and I started wearing the glasses I had been prescribed my freshman year but refused to wear in public and to parties until realizing that they added an easy, desired layer of character. I wanted all the easy layers of character.

I even created my own signature bomb-ass-poetry-writing-ass-nigga distressed jeans. I'd put a quart of bleach in a mop bucket, lightly dip an old pair of Timberlands in them, lay a pair of blue jeans on the floor, skim the jeans with the bleached boot soles—turning the blue a greenish beige in the spots my hand was the heaviest—and then cut a half inch off the bottoms so the tattered threads left hanging would make the jeans appear even more seasoned.

I also no longer needed the Original Hip-Hop Lyrics Archive's assistance. All of my poems now were original, and they even began to get less terrible. And by "get less terrible" I mean "get the attention of white people." I submitted "Nomad" to

*Quadrangle*—a student-run biannual literary arts magazine at Canisius—and was invited to read it at the spring issue's launch party.

I eventually used the poetry genesis and my burgeoning confidence in my voice as a springboard for more experimental and less dramatic essays, regular columns in *Nia News* (Canisius's black newspaper) and an eventual head editor position there. But my complicated relationship with Tracey remained my fundamental inspiration; the connective tissue threading each year in college together. I wanted her to be the Nina Mosley to my Darius Lovehall. I dreamed of us punctuating deep midnight conversations about gentrification and chunky peanut butter with sublime and celestial and embarrassingly sloppy sex. I'd fantasize about rocking matching black leather jackets with tastefully militant pins adorning the sleeves and lapels to Wegmans and women's volleyball games. I pictured us smoking weed and climbing rooftops to study stars and squirrels and other shit I assume people study while blazed on rooftops. I'd imagine us doing really witty and silly and slutty things with chocolate syrup. I'd allowed *Love Jones* to completely subsume my reality, wishing to etch and live out a real-life dramatization with her, and I grew increasingly frustrated that Tracey possessed, well, agency. And was able to decide, for whatever reason, that while she adored me, those feelings would remain platonic. She wanted no part of my fantasy.

And then, after two years of this, this want for her began to compete with and was eventually completely swallowed by a want for her to want me. I didn't want her to be my Nina as much as I just wanted her to somehow validate the time, the effort, and the energy I expended cultivating that mirage, feeding it oxygen and imagination and histrionic allegory like some sort of insatiable poetic jabberwocky.

I knew, even as I continued to lug the flaccid torch of our romantic potential from year to year, that I didn't want her as badly as I pretended to. That I needed, instead, for her to legitimize me in the eyes of my friends and roommates and teammates. And her friends and roommates and lovers. And any potential lovers I'd be interested in after Tracey and I had run our course. And the professors and academic advisers and resident assistants and cafeteria workers and bouncers and bartenders and sales clerks at T.J.Maxx who'd see us together and assume we were a couple. And I needed that validation—that I had the game and the raw sexual magnetism necessary to pull *her*—to believe myself to be legitimate. I knew that I needed to win her. Not because I wanted whatever prize winning would grant me, but because I couldn't accept losing so demonstratively and publicly. Especially after I'd lost so much with basketball.

I also knew that she was my alibi. That as long as I possessed some sort of romantic connection to her, I could lean on that and her if ever pressed by those same friends and roommates and teammates—whom I allowed to assume that we did, in fact, have a complicated romance—about why I didn't just find someone else. I knew that, as maddening as our relationship was, it was safe. That allowing people to believe that the fantasy was my reality gave me a convenient excuse; a justification for never making a serious effort to pursue anyone else. The fear of professing a sincere interest in someone else and having those feelings ignored or unreturned *again* was so paralyzing that I chose comfortable romantic indifference instead of possibly adding another piece to the Jenga tower of rejection renting space in my head. And I knew how tenuous this dynamic was; that it wouldn't take much of anything for this subterfuge to be exposed. And mostly I knew that my status as Canisius College's Darius Lovehall would be incomplete and, ultimately, revealed as counterfeit without a Nina. I have no doubt that Tracey realized all of this, and if a slender possibility of romance ever existed, it was likely preempted by her sensing that I wanted to be with a proxy—a landfill to dump all of these anxieties and insecurities into—and not a real actual person.

I was so captivated with the melodrama of *Love Jones* and the ethos of open mic night culture that it didn't dawn on me until two thousand and fucking eleven, after watching the film in full for the first time in twelve years, that I'd based my fantasy on a fraud. This was the movie I'd allowed to set the temperature for my entire romantic experience in college? This was my template? This was what led to the paradox of owning three black leather biker jackets but no bike? This was why I shaved my chest hair with a disposable Bic razor that one time in 1999—leaving me with so many welts and razor bumps that my skin looked like the back of a man-sized Nestlé Crunch bar—because Darius Lovehall didn't have chest hair and if Darius Lovehall didn't have chest hair neither would I? This was the movie I took my courting cues from, (wrongly) assuming that bomb-ass poetry would be enough to convince anyone to do anything other than say "That was a bomb-ass poem"? And it wasn't that *Love Jones* was anachronistic, it had just done such a great job convincing me that it *should* be real that I forgot it wasn't.

Because if it was, if Darius Lovehall would have been an actual real-life black man in Chicago, the movie wouldn't have ended with him and Nina driving away on a Harley but with him sitting on a curb somewhere, his eyes swollen and watery from Nina's pepper spray, his hairless chest scratched and bloodied from her furious fingernails clawing into it, and his feelings crushed as he tearfully recited "A Blues for Nina" to himself while waiting for the L.

# 4

# YOUR TURN

I forget sometimes that my parents and I were homeless for three months in 2001. Our landlord lived in Tampa, but decided to move back to Pittsburgh and back into his house, and he shared this information with Dad six months before he planned to return. Which fucking sucked. Our home on Clinton Drive was a simple two-story brick house with three modest bedrooms, two baths, and a tattered green awning stretched over a forty-square-foot front porch, but after escaping Mellon Street, it felt like the Taj Mahal. *Cozy* sometimes has a connotation of slight condescension, a smirking and backhanded commentary on an item's size. But for us *cozy* meant safe, stable, and settled, and this was the safest, stablest, and most settled my family had been in a decade. Dad's habitual joblessness ended, and he'd been employed at the same telemarketing firm for three years. My parents even finally had a car—a wolf-gray and whistle-clean 1995 Cadillac DeVille. Still, six months was more than enough time for my parents to find a new place and move. Dad,

however, kept this information from Mom until a *month* before
they had to leave. They weren't able to find a new place in time,
and they were forced to cram their belongings in a storage facility while crashing at Nana's. This all happened my senior year
at Canisius. I didn't learn they'd lost the house until I was home
for spring break.

In 2012, eleven years after that spring, a series of late
paychecks from *Ebony* magazine (where I was employed as a
full-time freelancer) began a string of financial setbacks that
eventually led to the repossession of my car. After borrowing
several hundred dollars each from Brian, my homegirl Liz, and
a church's credit union—and telling each of them my car was
impounded by the police for unpaid speeding tickets because
that was less embarrassing than the truth—I was able to get it
back. But that experience left me with a fierce bout of PTBD—
post-traumatic brokeness disorder. From then on, whenever I'm
home and I hear the distinct *beep . . . beep . . . beep* of large trucks
backing up in the street, my adrenaline and my anxiety spike as
I fear it's a tow truck coming for my car again.

Perhaps Dad was also suffering from PTBD in 2001.
Maybe he'd been so used to being broke, and to having tenuous
employment, and to navigating the world of overdraft fees and
debt-collector-phone-call ducking that those habits and those
fears stuck with him. And instead of just telling his wife about
their unfortunate but less than dire predicament, he hid it from
her for as long as he could, so possessed by the haunts of East
Liberty that he couldn't see anything but shame. Maybe he was
paralyzed by the thought of that impending doom. Maybe he
did what I did in the weeks before my car was repossessed, when
I'd ignore the relentless calls and letters from Ally Auto as if
they'd just forget about me if I refused to acknowledge them.
Maybe Dad thought that if he didn't tell Mom about their prob-

lem it would just wither away. Like the owner of their house was Candyman, and he'd only appear if you looked in a mirror and said his name five times. Or maybe Dad kept this information from Mom with the hope that he'd be able to fix it, somehow. Maybe he believed he'd be able to pull through in the clutch and just didn't want her to worry about something he'd eventually handle.

I don't know. I do remember how I felt after catching the bus home from Buffalo that spring, being picked up at the Greyhound station by my parents, and being told during the drive that home was now Nana's and they'd been living with her for a month. It felt like we were stuck in a morass of peanut butter. It felt like we were trapped underneath the tarp used to cover in-ground pools. It felt like we kept walking through invisible and unbreakable cobwebs. It felt like our lives would forever be drenched in static. It felt stupid and fake. It felt like *"What the fuck, guys?"* It felt like I was missing something. It felt like we were missing something.

Mom and Dad met on a blind date in 1975, and they came to each other heavy. Mom's sister (my aunt Toni) was dating one of Dad's niggas from college, and Aunt Toni—who also knew Dad from school (they all went to Knoxville College in Tennessee)—thought her baby sis would be a good match for him. Dad, who was named after my granddad's brother Wilbur but is known as "Weeb" by everyone (except my grandma, who always called him Wilbur Allen as if she were calling his name from a porch after the streetlights came on) had already been married to and divorced from his college sweetheart. Mom, who was named after Vivien Leigh (Nana's favorite actress) but spelled her name Vivienne, had a child—my sister, Jamie. She got pregnant while in high school and was subsequently sent, by Nana and Papa, to some sort of home in

Cleveland for fast teenage girls who shamed their respectable negro parents. Mom gave birth to Jamie, came back home, somehow managed to earn a scholarship to Carnegie Mellon University, and attended for three semesters but never finished. I'm not quite sure how my parents were able to find each other and then fall in love through all of that noise. Dad used to joke that he hooked Mom with roses and a batch of New Castle hot dog chili, but I think they both just needed a reliable Spades partner.

Dad and Mom were two of the brightest, funniest, wittiest, worldliest, sharpest, and blackest people I knew. Dad taught me how to write. He'd revise and rewrite the take-home essays assigned to me in seventh and eighth grade. I'd—well, *he'd*—get A's, and then I'd eventually attempt to mimic the stylistic choices he'd made and the flourish he'd peppered his sentences with. He taught me words like *permeate*, *conniption*, *obtuse*, and *behoove*, and I'd incorporate them at recess with moderate success ("I BEHOOVE YOU TO PASS ME THE BALL"). Mom taught me, while watching *Goodfellas*, how breaking the fourth wall was a Scorsese trademark. And also what the fourth wall was. And also that Scorsese could break the fourth wall because he'd mastered the fundamentals of filmmaking. And that after you've mastered the basics, you can break rules. Mom taught me how to be a badass, if I wanted to be one. (I didn't.) I also learned from them that it was bad luck to place a hat on a bed or a couch. And where to position a motorized fan on a cracked windowsill in the summer so that it best replicated an air-conditioning unit. And that if a black man was the first person to enter your home on New Year's Day, it was promised to be a good year. And that respectability politics were a fucking fraud. "Don't break yourself trying to appease white people," Dad told me while we were sitting at the dining room table a day after they took me to see *Malcolm X* on my thirteenth birthday, and an hour after I lamented to them that Tommy Weismen's parents wouldn't let him come to my birthday slumber party because East Liberty was "the ghetto." "Martin Luther King was killed in a suit."

I just didn't understand how these beautiful and talented people kept finding themselves in hardship. And it felt like whatever it was that was infecting them—whichever invisible and arbitrarily cruel entity was committed to keeping them an inch away from exhalation—was contagious, and I wanted no part of that. Or them. I still loved them. I was just tired of seeing them like this. And tired of them seeing me see them like this. When they picked me up from that Greyhound station and told me about the house, I wanted them to drive me back downtown so I could hop on the bus and get back to Buffalo.

The source of that invisible force and that unstoppable inertia that kept teasing them, that kept allowing them to break through for a stretch before tripping them up and pulling them back again, that would lay latent until it saw fit to remind them it was there, is obvious to me now. White supremacy is so gargantuan and mundane that sometimes its existence and its proficiency can't be measured, addressed, or even seen without a stark change in perspective. It isn't like gravity. It *is* gravity. It *is* a ceaseless pressure intended to keep blackness ground-bound and sick.

And it wasn't that my parents' blackness itself was pathological. It wasn't. It never has been and never will be, for anyone. It's just that blackness in America meant that setbacks, like my parents getting their car stolen in 1990, were tsunamis. It meant that there were and would always be environmental factors they needed to overcome. It meant a permanent cushionlessness where tripping and falling left broken bones instead of bumps and bruises. It meant supporting and relying on an entire economy dependent on that perpetual vulnerability. It meant emergency room visits and Rent-A-Center living room sets. It meant payday loans and phone bills in toddlers' names. It meant standing in line at Money Mart and "ridin' dirty" for so long you forgot what it meant to be clean. It meant participation in that self-mutilating symbiosis was necessary if you wished to survive. It meant that, in order to combat and withstand this force, they needed to be perfect. Or lucky. Or perfect and lucky. It meant that any victory, regardless of how definitive it seemed, was tenuous. It meant that the black people who seemed to be able to escape it—the families like Brian's whom I envied because they just didn't seem to be awash with the same burdens—were exceptions. It meant that even those few special and lucky and perfect niggas weren't exceptions. It meant that the tsunami could hit those special perfect lucky niggas too. It meant that special perfect nigga luck just placed those special perfect lucky niggas a little farther inland. For my parents, it meant an aggregation of tiny little defeats culminating in twelve weeks on the couch in Nana's frigid and mildewy game room, sleeping next to stacks of ten-year-old *Jet* magazines and boxes of artificial Christmas trees and broken ornaments.

I slept in that game room with them, in a tree-bark-brown Barcalounger that had belonged to Papa and hadn't been sat on that much since he died in 1985, and I'd rock and seethe myself to sleep. I was too selfish and too *twenty-one* then to be as empathetic as I needed to be; as they needed me to be. Too hoggish to realize that I was able to return to my off-campus town house with my bomb-ass-poetry-writing-ass-nigga starter kit in Buffalo if I pleased *specifically because of them* and the sacrifices they made. Too myopic to be proud of them for fighting that behemoth long and hard and fierce enough to eke out some safe space for me in East Liberty and at St. Barts, Penn Hills, and Canisius.

And then, one day, it all changed.

---

The biggest takeaway from season four of HBO's *The Wire*, which is the year centered on the lives of four adolescent boys (Namond Brice, Michael Lee, Randy Wagstaff, and Duquan Weems), was that the only way for a young person from West Baltimore to not succumb to the streets was for someone to come and *literally* lift him out of them. It didn't matter how talented or resourceful or dynamic you were. (At least it didn't matter as much as it should've.) Your destiny was largely dependent on magnanimity and luck. Which, in the right context, can be a fancy way of saying charity. By season's end, the only member of that crew to escape those corners is Namond, who was first introduced to the audience as a spoiled and nasty scion of an infamous mass murderer. So spoiled and nasty that he was removed from his eighth grade classroom (he called it "gen pop") and selected to be part of an experiment where the school's worst and most disruptive students—the "corner boys"—were all placed in the same classroom and taught a street-based curriculum. It was here that he met retired and disgraced policeman Howard "Bunny" Colvin, who helped teach and mediate that classroom, took a liking to Namond, and eventually adopted him. The last scene of the season shows Namond doing homework on Bunny's porch in a still and presumably middle-class neighborhood. He looks like a regular kid. Which is exactly what he is when he's able to be one.

On the third day back from spring break, while we were sitting in the car outside of Guardian Storage in Shadyside, waiting for Dad to retrieve a coat he'd accidentally packed away there, Mom shared something with me. "Hey, Dae, your dad and I are trying to buy a house. There's one on Graham Boulevard we really like, and we're going to view it tomorrow. You should come."

The concept of homeownership was unfathomable to me then. My parents had never owned a house. And while I didn't know much about credit and bank loans and mortgages and down payments then, I knew enough to know that my parents had shitty credit and didn't have much (if any) savings. She might as well have told me they were building one of those transporters from *Star Trek*. It was just something that people other than people like us did. But we were apparently going to see that house tomorrow.

Mom, you should know, was a bit of a trickster. It wasn't uncommon for me to walk into a bedroom or a bathroom and then be startled out of my skin by her jumping out of a closet or from behind a shower curtain. "Your turn!" she'd scream. I'd spend the next week plotting for ways to get her back, but she'd usually outsmart me and sniff out my hiding places before I even had a chance to return the scare. When I was young, she had me convinced she was magic. It wasn't until I was a teen that I realized she'd always find me because I was breathing too loudly and couldn't keep a straight face.

We did view that house the next day. And it was on Graham Boulevard. But they were not *trying* to buy that house. They'd already bought it. Mom broke the news while showing me the bedroom that would eventually be mine. "I know you know your dad and I have gone through some things" she told me as we stood in that empty room. "We didn't want to tell you anything. You worry so much and we wanted you to be focused on school and not your little old parents."

I couldn't believe what I was hearing. Not simply that they'd bought a house, but that they were able to. It just didn't compute. Mom saw the look on my face and continued. "We . . . we went to three separate banks. This house was on the market, and your dad and I had been saving. The first two denied us. But that third bank . . . Damon, I begged that woman. I begged that woman's boss. I begged her boss's boss. I prayed while we were sitting there. Your dad and I stayed in that bank for five hours. We whipped out so many forms and papers . . . I think I even showed them your SAT score. And somehow, through the grace of God and the skin of our teeth, we got approved. We got approved, Damon. Your dad and I got approved."

I went back to school a week later. When I returned home in May, I slept in my new bedroom for the first time. The same room Mom and I cried in after she told me it was my room. I woke up the next morning to the familiar scent of vanilla extract, maple syrup, and nutmeg, which meant Mom just made some French toast and bacon. I got out of bed, stretched, put on some sweats and a T-shirt, and walked down the hallway. As I neared the living room, two mysterious ghost hands reached out behind me and tickled my underarms. I yelped and flinched so quickly I almost stubbed a toe on a loveseat. I turned around. It was Mom. Of course it was Mom.

She laughed. "Your turn!"

# 5

# NO HOMO

The first time someone asked me if I was gay, I was playing *Tecmo Super NBA Basketball* in Brian's basement, and beating the shit out of him with the Jordan-era Chicago Bulls.

"So my mom," Brian mumbled between chomps of Cool Ranch Doritos, "the other day was like, 'Does Damon have . . . like . . . girlfriends?'"

"Woooooow" I replied, in the incredulous and flabbergasted and faux-haughty way that niggas say "wow" when they don't yet have an answer to the question they were just asked.

"What did you tell her?" I followed.

"Nigga, I said, 'I don't know.'"

Brian was the least helpful nigga on earth.

We played a few more times and then walked five blocks to the courts behind the Pennley Park Apartments, where we shot around for a half hour, then walked back across Penn Avenue to watch the Connie Hawkins Summer Basketball League games that night. After those games ended and the audience cleared out, we stayed at that court and played five-on-five with the rest of the niggas too young to play in the Summer League but old enough to be out past 10 P.M. Since the lights above the court were timed to go off at 11, we only had an hour. But with Brian and I on the same team, we didn't just beat them, we beat them quick enough to get six games in.

We were thirteen then and Brian was already six foot two (and would grow to be six foot eight). Lean and lefty, he was hyperactive and physical on defense, a gifted but arrogant passer—sometimes he'd be so impressed with and excited about his vision that he'd whip no-look and uncatchable fireballs at teammates—and a streaky shooter. He also talked shit. So much fucking shit. His favorite player was Gary Payton, known then as the NBA's premier trash-talker, and Brian modeled his steez after him. He even started calling himself "GP."

"You weak, nigga!" Brian would say after the guy he was guarding had the audacity to miss a jump shot. "Get up, bitch!" or "Get the fuck off me!" if Brian happened to snatch a re-bound. "AAANNNNND OOONE!" he'd scream if he was fouled while making a shot. We were a perfect match out there. The lanky and bombastic lefty and his deceptively quick and aggressively quiet boy with the killer crossover would run nig-gas our age off the court and annoy oldheads with Brian's re-lentless shit-talking and our talent.

Brian never asked for an answer to his mom's question. Not about girlfriends—he knew I didn't have one—but about what she was actually asking. I told myself that his lack of following up was because he knew the truth. But I suspected he wasn't quite sure either, and only shared his mom's ask to get some sort of clarity. I needed some too.

I knew I was attracted to girls. Girls were the only ones who made me sweat and stammer at the mere thought of talking to

them. Girls were the ones I'd daydream about in social studies class and on the twenty-seven-minute-long bus rides on the
77B from Penn Hills to East Lib. Girls were the reason I'd just
recently started waking up in the middle of the night with my
dick glued to my Hanes. I also didn't quite know what it meant
to be gay. I knew what it meant to be soft. Or, at least, what it
meant to be the type of boy who other kids called soft. I didn't
walk like them or talk like them. I hooped and I played video
games and I rocked Blacktop Reeboks and I ate nachos and I
had farting contests with my niggas and my dad. But being soft
and being gay weren't the same thing. According to my parents
and that one episode of *Roc* where Richard Roundtree played
Roc's gay uncle, being gay wasn't bad. You were just born like
that. Like my cousin Michael, who was gay but wasn't soft because he had the fastest hands in the family and he'd whoop a
nigga's ass for looking at him wrong.

But if there was nothing wrong with being gay, why was
there something wrong with being "soft"? And how were these
two things connected? And what the fuck did *soft* even mean?
It was used to describe the boys who seemed to be more interested in the things girls were supposed to be interested in than
the things boys were supposed to be into. Like clothes, music
that wasn't rap, dancing, and cooking. But some of those soft
boys had the baddest girlfriends, which would seem to negate
that distinction, because I thought that not having one is what
made you soft. (Also, who the fuck *didn't* like Guess jeans, who
the fuck *didn't* try to do the Butterfly after watching TLC's
"Creep" video, and who the fuck *didn't* want to learn how to
make bomb-ass Steak-umms? Why were these amazing things
*soft*? Had these niggas ever had a Steak-umm with onions,
ketchup, scrambled eggs, and Food Club American cheese?)

It was also sometimes used to describe the boys who didn't

play sports. But then sometimes it'd be used to chide the kids who *were* playing sports, but weren't playing the sport as arbitrarily aggressively as they were supposed to be playing it. In basketball, preferring to shoot jump shots instead of barreling into the paint each time you touched the rock was considered soft. Because it was assumed you were scared of contact. But if you're good at shooting jump shots, and if successful jump shots count as two points (and deep jump shots count as three) how the fuck is partaking in an effective strategy to win basketball games soft? And if calling a boy soft was a way of doubting his masculinity, and if masculinity doubting was actually heterosexuality doubting, wouldn't engaging in unnecessary physical contact with other boys be the soft thing to do? None of this made any sense.

Perhaps, I thought, having a girlfriend would have provided some lucidity; a solution for these unanswerable questions. But I hadn't kissed or even danced with a girl yet. I spent all of the time that I assumed niggas with girlfriends spent with girls with Brian. Playing *Contra* in his basement and playing one-on-one for hours at Pennley and Peabody. Riding the 71B together to Oakland to hoop and the 94B to Waterworks Mall in Fox Chapel to watch *Above the Rim* and *Hoop Dreams* and *A League of Their Own*. Eating Taco Bell with his parents, and him eating Vento's Pizza with mine. Sleeping over at his house some Saturday nights, and attending service at East Liberty Presbyterian Church with his family the next morning. He was an honors student at Frick International Studies Academy, and it would crack me the fuck up that this kid who'd tell niggas to suck his dick after he pinned a layup to the glass was also always on the high honor roll. My parents even had a nickname for us: "Gloom and Doom"—a nod to our preternatural curmudgeonliness. We acted and bantered like seventy-two-year-old men trapped inside thirteen-year-old bodies. About the only thing we didn't do together was the shit that boys and girls did with each other when they liked each other. But if I wasn't doing those things with *anyone*—no dancing or hand holding or hugging or kissing—and the only things that distinguished straightness from gayness were those things, how could I be sure if I was either? I believed I was straight. But maybe that immobilizing anxiety I felt around girls was the gay bursting out. Or maybe all boys felt a measure of anxiousness, but what made those other boys with girlfriends straight—or, better yet, *straighter*—was their willingness to overcome those fears. They were so straight that their straightness overpowered their doubts and jitters, while my flaccid straightness succumbed to them. Perhaps I wasn't gay, but maybe I sucked so much at being straight that it didn't matter.

At Schenley (his high school), Brian became an even bigger star than I was at Penn Hills. He made first team All-City twice and earned a full ride to Loyola College in Maryland, which was in the same conference as Canisius. We weren't able to spend as much time together once we got to college, but we'd still talk on the phone regularly. Our convos would consist of what we'd heard about niggas back home, who in the NBA was doing what, Wu-Tang and Killarmy album release dates, and Brian's threats to transfer schools because he was fed up with his teammates and coaches. "Yo . . . I gotta get out of here," he'd say between bites of what sounded like Cool Ranch Doritos (Brian had consistent tastes). "You wouldn't believe it. This Baltimore shit so fucking wack."

We'd also, for the first time, talk extensively about the girls we were seeing. He had a girlfriend on campus, and I had Tracey, who I'd speak about as if she was my girlfriend on campus. We talked about girls the way that barbers on TV and lazy comedians do. How girls were "crazy," how we were the clear-minded pragmatists, and what we'd do as a reaction to their insanity, reflexively incorporating that language and those tropes because it was the way we thought we were supposed to talk about them. It felt good, though, to not have to worry anymore about whether my best friend had any suspicions about my straightness, even if my evidence was based on a lie.

During these conversations about girls, and also when we'd talk about what we talked about when we weren't talking about girls, we'd often begin or end our sentences with "no homo."

"Yo, no homo, but I took Jackie to see *The Players Club* last night."

"You see Marcus Camby had seven blocks last night? That nigga's arms long as shit. No homo."

We weren't alone. At some point in the late nineties, *no homo*—a masculinity-asserting phrase attached to any sentence or statement that could possibly have gay undertones—had become so ubiquitous among high school and college-aged black males that it essentially served as a punctuation. At Canisius, it had become so ingrained that we shortened it to *no mo*. By then, you'd *intentionally* say things that were "gay-sounding" just so you could attach *no mo* and induce what I guess were supposed to be ironic laughs.

"No mo but that psychology test was hard. Like a rock, yo. But no mo, though."

"I'm tired as shit, man. Can't wait to go home and fuck my pillow. No mo."

The farce and the tragedy of how obsessed we—the black men and boys who considered ourselves to be straight and wanted said straightness to be conspicuous and foolproof—were with what it's supposed to mean to be a straight man enabled a creeping and indiscriminate dehumanization of ourselves that swaddled and permeated us. It lived in the words we said (and currently say), the music we listened to (and currently listen to), and the way we thought about ourselves and women and our relationships with ourselves and women. We were, and still are, soaked in it. We marinate in it and are pickled by it. It brutalizes us. And that brutalization brittles and breaks us. We spent, and still spend, so much effort, so much time, so many resources, trying to match or maybe just perform the hyper-rigid heterosexuality we were socialized to aspire to, for fear of being seen as soft. And we used, and still use, gay men as proxies instead of people; as adaptable poltergeists for our egos and personal political narratives. How masculine, how straight, how authentically *black* and authentically *male* we wished to be considered existed in concert with how we regarded homosexuality. If you maybe wanted to be seen as so straight, so manly, so masculine that you gave no shits about gay men, you'd perform tolerance and enlightenment with ironic homophobia. If you maybe wanted to be seen as so straight, so manly, and so masculine that your heterosexuality was too pure to risk a homosexual contagion, you performed hatred, adopting a rigid and unceasing animus toward gay men that you didn't quite understand or maybe didn't even really *believe*. But you did it because other people did it and told you that you were supposed to do it and that company was safer than what you feared might have happened if you maybe just admitted that you didn't know why you were supposed to care about how men who didn't appear to be straight walked and talked. And that you didn't know why you were supposed to care about appearing to be straight. And that you didn't know what it even *meant* to appear to be straight. (Or gay.) And that the only reason you gave a shit was because what we'd come to define as manly and masculine was measured by its distance from softness. And that you didn't understand why or how these things were intertwined. Or what softness meant. Or why some things were even considered soft, and why the distinctions between softness and masculinity were necessary.

Being a convincingly straight black dude was *hard as fuck* if you weren't bedding enough women to exhaust any arbitrary quotas of sufficiently vigorous heterosexuality. Which was (and is) both the only acceptable form of heterosexuality and a sham determination. So hard that it even started to affect the clothes I wore.

On a journey through Pittsburgh's Shadyside neighborhood the summer after I graduated from Canisius, I discovered its Walnut Street shopping district: a block of upscale retail shops, art galleries, restaurants, and boutiques hidden between Fifth Avenue and Centre Avenue. This block sat only a mile and a half from the block I grew up on, yet my universe then was such a stark contrast from the universe Walnut existed on that it might as well have been on fucking Neptune.

Clothing had always been a way for me to both hide from the world and carve out some sort of prominence and status in it. I'd use clothes to shield me from whatever anxieties I possessed. Better you notice this rare and expensive-ass fucking shirt on my chest and these shoes on my feet than my face or my head or my teeth. Also I hoped that clothes would do such a great job concealing these imperfections that they'd effectively replace me—that people would be so enamored with and impressed by my clothes and my fashion sense and the money I must possess to be able to afford them that it would eventually allow them to forget that the person wearing them was, in fact, the person wearing them. And that they'd be so impressed by them that they'd eventually be impressed with me by association. I wanted my clothes to make me. And so while working in a University of Pittsburgh Medical Center (UPMC) mail room that summer—a ten-dollar-an-hour, three-month-long assignment Mom hooked me up with a month after I finished school—I'd spend the bulk of my paychecks at Moda and Quasi Moda, the Walnut Street shops with $125 Dolce & Gabbana belts and $275 Versace crew necks adorning their racks. Purchases made far easier by the zero dollars in rent I was paying while living with my parents.

I'd burrow inside these designer clothes, hoping they'd pull some sort of Jedi mind trick on the people who'd see me. In 2002, baggy jeans and loose-fitting jerseys were still what was considered fashionable and *acceptable* for straight black men in the Burgh. The form-fitting D&G T-shirts and Armani Exchange jeans were not that. They were intentionally tailored for men built like mannequins and Olympic swimmers, not six-foot-one, 200-pound niggas with thick thighs and ass. But maybe those extra smedium shirts and slacks would communicate that I was secure enough in my manhood and my straightness to wear the type of clothes that niggas would consider soft or gay. I gave all of the fucks in an effort to convince these still nonexistent niggas doubting my sexuality that I didn't give any. To me, fucklessness was the pinnacle of manliness. My dream was for women to see me sauntering down Walnut Street—my skin-tight Versace button-down draped across my shoulders; my obnoxious-as-fuck D&G belt buckle sitting three inches above my dick and reflecting sunlight—and think, *Damn. That nigga doesn't give any fucks. That nigga is a MAN. I want his number in my phone and his babies in my mouth.* (In this dramatization, of course, they definitely wouldn't notice that the only reason my posture seemed so correct was because that dumbass buckle poked my stomach each time I relaxed, reached into my pockets, or just fucking exhaled. I think that belt lacerated my spleen.)

My next job after working at the mail room was at Wilkins-burg Junior/Senior High School. I began in January as a sub-stitute teacher. And after a series of serendipitous (for me) and unfortunate (for him) events involving a teacher who caught some sort of toe gout and might have actually died or some-thing, I ended up with my own classroom after my first week there: ninth grade English.

I had switched majors the last semester of my senior year, from secondary education with an English concentration to straight English, specifically to avoid student teaching and be-ing a teacher when I graduated. I made this change because I didn't want to teach. I didn't know what the fuck I wanted to do, but I definitely knew what I didn't want to do. It wasn't very long, however, before teaching began to feel like an inevitabil-ity. What the hell else was a twenty-two-year-old English grad going to do besides teach? My grades were too low for me to get into grad school without acing the GRE, which I had no interest in studying for. My writing was still too embryonic to have any-one pay me for it. And my summer at the mail room transport-ing boxes, fighting dollies, and dodging typhoons of dust in the building's basement taught me I was structurally and spiritually unfit for manual labor. I'd come home each day that summer and immediately strip, shower, and sprawl naked on my bed like I'd just completed a sixteen-hour shift in a Hancock County coal mine. The countless paper cuts acquired from opening and stuffing envelopes were my black lung disease. I'd convinced myself that another month of letter cutting and box breaking down would leave my hands too cracked and callused to do any-thing useful with them other than open tightly screwed bottles of Mountain Dew.

I was notified of an open position at Wilkinsburg by a friend who worked there. I applied, was invited to meet with the superintendent (who happened to be friends with Brian's dad), and began, with no classroom experience, teaching at one of the poorest and lowest-performing districts in the state. And as with other inner-city schools in similar neighborhoods performing at similar levels, Wilkinsburg's reputation cultivated unfavorable presumptions about the type of kids who went there. It was assumed that they were a bit rougher and a bit less inhibited and a bit more adult than the average kid. Which is a presumption that exists for black kids, and black people, in general. And the poorer the person, the stronger the presumption. If you're just black, America adds a decade of age, a vat of sass, and a coating of Kevlar to your skin because of course niggers don't feel any pain. If you're poor and black, America acts like you emerge from the womb twenty-seven years old, with four kids, five predicate felonies, and a lit Newport already between your lips. White people get to be babies. And they get to still be babies when they're adults. Poor black people are born Avon Barksdale.

Despite growing up broke and black in East Lib, I fell victim to those presumptions, allowing America's dehumanizations to be contagious. My first few weeks there, I'd walk into that building bracing myself for violence and being just as violent toward my students as I waited for them to be with me. I wasn't physically abrasive, but I was less interested in teaching them than I was in guarding myself from them—erecting a facade of performative masculinity manifesting as unnecessary gruffness toward them—and expecting the worst out of these kids was an act of violence. For many of the kids there, the school was a respite from the rest of the world. It's where they knew they'd be warm. It's where they knew they'd get two hot meals. It's where they knew they'd have structure and routine, even if some of them fought against it. It's where they knew they'd be (relatively) safe for eight hours a day. It's the only place some of them would encounter adults equipped with the energy and resources to help them. And me knowing this and still seeing them how America saw them and wanted me to see them was an act of violence. Guarding myself from them with the same shields they'd see whenever they left the school was an act of violence.

But they were susceptible to the same angsts and anxieties and insecurities associated with kids who didn't happen to be so demonstratively at risk. The main difference between the Wilkinsburg kids and kids from Fox Chapel or Mount Lebanon or any other district steeped in affluence was that the Wilkinsburg kids didn't possess the privilege of mistakes. They were expected to fuck up and forced to exist in a universe where fucking up had disproportionately dire consequences. Because of the harshness of their environments, they had to etch and chisel and bite out space to still be young.

Eventually I became the living and breathing embodiment of the stereotypical young teacher in every movie about schools in the hood. You know, the one who's shunned and teased at first and thinks about quitting, but then gets a pep talk from his doting and eternally supportive girlfriend (who's always in the kitchen chopping eggplant and making some sort of pasta). And eventually reaches his hard-edged but actually really sweet students with tough love and Hemingway quotes over DJ Premier beats.* And then takes them on impromptu field

---

* This is not hyperbole. For an entire week, my figurative language lesson was just me printing out rap lyrics from the Original Hip-Hop Lyrics Archive, making copies, distributing them in class, and instructing the students to outline the analogies and circle the ono-matopoeia in songs such as Nas's "Second Childhood" and Inspectah Deck's verse in "For Heavens Sake." Which was either an ingenious and relatable way to cultivate, capture, and engage the students'

trips to zoos and museums and morgues and offers occasional speeches where he says things like "I'M TRYING TO SAVE YOUR LIFE, TANISHA!" and "THESE WHITE PEOPLE DON'T GIVE A DAMN ABOUT YOUR LIFE, KHALID!" and "I JUST WANT YOU TO LIVE AND HAVE THE BEST LIFE, LATONYA!" and "DON'T YOU DIE ON ME, DEMARCUS! LIVE, DAMMIT, LIVE YOUR LIFE!"

I also learned, in September of the following school year, that there was a rumor going around that I was gay.

Although I had my own classroom, I didn't have Pennsylvania state teaching certification, which meant I was still technically a sub and required to do substitute teacher shit. Like walk up the stairs to the junior high school during one of my off periods to cover seventh grade science because Mr. Livingston, the science teacher, was somehow allowed to take a field trip to the Carnegie Science Center with seven fucking students, leaving the rest of his class in school and science-teacher-less. I entered that classroom annoyed I had to be there, a feeling surpassed only by how annoyed the students were at being stuck all day in those mousetrap chair desks while their seven classmates and their bitch-ass teacher were out frolicking in sexy robotics labs and interactive dinosaur exhibits. Those motherfuckers probably even went to Quiznos.

It was here that a kid who looked like a twelve-year-old Scottie Pippen mumbled, "But that's why you a faggot, yo," under his breath in response to me writing him a referral to send him to the dean of students. I ejected him from the classroom as a response to him refusing to do the worksheet I distributed to

---

interest in the utility of words or some lazy shit from a shiftless fuck who only created lessons out of printed rap lyrics because he couldn't think of shit else to do.

the class. Instead of completing it, he chose to ball it up and hit it like a Wiffle ball with a foot-long, fluorescent green plastic wrench he was carrying in his pocket. I was tempted to allow him to stay because I desperately needed to know why the fuck he was carrying a foot-long fluorescent green plastic wrench, but classroom management trumped my curiosity.

Now, being called a name didn't bother me too much. While a teacher, I'd been a "bitch-ass nigga," a "smarty-arty nigga," a "straight bitch yo," a "bitch-ass bitch," a "meanie," a "booger-face," a "motherfucker," an "ugly motherfucker," a "fuck boy," and a "republican." High school classrooms are basically Internet comment threads with acne. So having an occasional insult hurled my way when a student was upset was expected. Also, middle school kids are notoriously subhuman, so I anticipated pushback when attempting to deliver that lesson.

(Seriously, if you happen to know a parent of a thirteen-year-old or a person who teaches or coaches or even lives in a neighborhood with them, the next time you see this person, buy them a drink, a doughnut, and a lap dance, recite the Lord's Prayer with them, and slide them a hundred-dollar bill. From twelve to approximately fifteen years old, children are prickly, insecure, sadistic, and smelly little dicks. For good reason, of course. Puberty hijacks their bodies and souls like the xeno-morph in *Alien* latched onto a human host. So it's not their fault that they turn into a humanistic subspecies because of it. Still, avoid those shady and shitty motherfuckers at all costs.)

This was different, though. His "faggot" wasn't snide or nonchalant. It wasn't a perfunctory insult quickly snatched out of the bag of bad words twelve-year-olds knew after listening to Lil Wayne. It was *intentional*. And he said it under his breath while exiting the classroom. For most kids that age, an insult like that is performative. They say it so the other kids will snicker or say, *"OOOOH. He called Mr. Young a* faggot*!"* But this *faggot* was for my ears only.

I heard it again two weeks later while on cafeteria duty, but this time from a couple of high school kids. I was walking past a table, talking to another teacher, when I overheard a girl ask another girl if I was a faggot. She replied, "'Faggot' is a bad word and you're not supposed to say that." Which, considering the place and context, was the awesomest thing I'd ever heard. I wanted to stop in my tracks and give that miniature Melissa Harris-Perry a high five and a free raspberry iced tea. But the fact that this wasn't even meant to be an insult—just an innocent query from one seventeen-year-old girl to her progressive friend—reinforced the idea that my sexuality was now a thing people in the school openly wondered about. A week or so later, Brian (who also worked there as a sub) told me that one of the security guards asked him if I was "sweet." From then on, the *boogerface*s and *motherfucker*s and *smarty-arty nigga*s dissipated. Now, when a student was upset enough with me to whisper or toss an epithet, I'd hear "fag" or "faggot" or "gay." And it would only come from students I'd see in the cafeteria and hallways or when subbing in for their regular teachers. The ones in my classrooms and the ones I already had relationships with would still occasionally get loose-lipped when in trouble. But they'd never take it *there*.

This rumor was likely a result of those same Dolce & Gabbana belts and Chanel eyeglasses and fitted jean shirts and slim-cut corduroys that I'd hoped would distinguish me enough from the typical Pittsburgh nigga to attract women. At Wilkinsburg Junior/Senior High School, however, this distinction from the norm meant I dressed and acted just a little differently from what they were used to. My shirts and slacks were a little snugger, my gait and diction and demeanor were a little less hood.

And there, *dressed and acted just a little differently than what they were used to* meant *gay*.

Perhaps it was some sort of karmic justice that I'd eventually be saddled with a gay rumor, a thing I actively attempted to avoid despite pretending I was too evolved to give a damn about it. The rumor also happened to be impervious to pushback. I couldn't exactly begin stopping random kids and security guards in the school hallways to shake some heterosexual sense into them. I had a job to keep, and angrily informing them of my true sexual orientation would imply that there was something wrong with being gay.

By then I was ten years removed from that day in Brian's basement, but what a few eighth graders and security guards thought about me bothered me the same way that learning that Brian's mom asked him if I had a girlfriend had. It didn't even matter that I finally *had* a girlfriend. The summer before that school year, I'd met a girl named Teresa while at the Carnegie Library in Oakland. I was there using up the forty-five minutes of Internet time they allotted you on busy Saturday afternoons, and she was studying at a table. Not wanting to interrupt her—and not realizing (or caring, really) that what I did was *still* an interruption—I found a notecard, wrote the world's shittiest haiku on it (Girl in Library/Studies Intensely While Guy/Thinks About Approach), scribbled my number and my name and a note saying *I didn't want to interrupt you* on the back of it, approached her, asked her if she could read it for me, and walked out. She called a day later, we went out a day after that, had sex the day after that, and then we were official. (If there was any doubt that we were official, the conversation we had right after sex—where she lay next to me and joked, "I guess we're official now?" and I replied "I . . . think so"—solidified it.)

Teresa was twenty-one years old and a senior at Duquesne

University. She lived with her mom, handled the accounting for her church—and had broken up eleven months earlier with the pastor's son—and loved *The Golden Girls* almost as much as she loved her five-year-old nephew Duece, who she doted on like he was her son. She also looked and was built so much like Tyra Banks that if we were out somewhere together, we'd be able to predict when a person was about to ask, "Excuse me, but has anyone ever said you look exactly like Tyra Banks?" just by the way they'd double take at her.

Her physical attributes mattered because it's why I was so quick to lock her down. She was that solution I was searching for. Something to prove, to everyone, that I possessed sufficiently vigorous heterosexuality. And she was *something* to prove that and not *someone*. I was infatuated enough with her to believe that I loved her, and I think I treated her as well as you can treat a girlfriend when you're still struggling with how you believe your personhood is perceived and your relationship is your solution and the girlfriend isn't quite a person but a two-dimensional projection where the dual dimensions are *How good does she look?* and *How good does her good-looking make me look?* I treated her like she was a diamond. Which probably means I treated her like shit. We split two years later, after finally realizing we didn't have much in common besides my desire to possess a trophy and her evaporating willingness to appease me.

She should've been enough to satisfy any residual need for proof of my heterosexuality. But that was impossible. That I still somehow needed proof *was* proof there was no way to placate my anxiety, and each mumbled slur at Wilkinsburg took me back to the time when I wasn't quite sure if I was doing the straight thing *correctly*. So in order to combat those rumors, I leaned on the same thing I leaned on at fourteen.

Although a few of the kids and the teachers knew I hooped,

my basketball background wasn't yet common knowledge throughout the school. I was just the ambiguously gay new black teacher with the glasses and the tapered slacks. So as a way to assert my masculinity, I'd shamelessly name-drop basketball at every opportunity. Conversations with students would start with them asking about hall passes or homework assignments and would end with ". . . you need to dot your *i*'s and cross your *t*'s, Jerome. Just like how I once crossed Baron Davis at the Adidas Big Time AAU Tournament in Columbus, Ohio, in the summer of '96." I'd walk through the hallways and pretend to hoop, doing shake moves with an invisible basketball on the students walking past me and windmill dunking on the top of the door whenever I'd enter the classroom. I'd place the garbage can ten feet away from my desk instead of underneath it, so an impromptu one-man three-point contest would ensue each time I'd have to throw something away. And whenever there was an opportunity to hoop with the students—at lunchtime, after school, or even when subbing for the art teacher and taking the entire classroom next door to the gym because the gym teacher (also a sub) didn't mind—I would. I wanted everyone to know that the best ballplayer in the school was the effete ninth grade English teacher.

I'd also have Teresa visit me at school whenever she could. I'd ask her to bring my lunch to work, a process that would require her to pass through a metal detector at the entrance, sign in at the vice principal's office on the first floor, and walk down two forty-foot-long hallways to my classroom. This would allow her to be seen by at least twenty-five and sometimes up to seventy-five different people in a five-minute span. I also brought her to Wilkinsburg's football and basketball games, and even once convinced the principal to allow her to man a table during a bake sale. (She made sugar cookies.)

Between the basketball pantomiming and Teresa's public service, the Wilkinsburg Junior/Senior High School narrative eventually shifted from "*Mr. Young might be gay*" to "*Mr. Young got bitches, yo.*" Which was still inaccurate. I hadn't reached or even particularly desired plural-bitches status yet. One girlfriend was enough. Plural bitches just seemed too time-consuming and inefficient, and I didn't have enough experience with sufficiently vigorous heterosexuality for that type of ambition.

I even heard from Brian one day while we were watching a Pitt basketball game that one of the security guards admired my clothes.

"Drew from the second floor asked if I knew where you got those brown boots you wear sometimes. He walked up to me all nervous at lunchtime and then said, 'Yo, B . . . um . . . but do you know where your boy Mr. Young be shopping? Them boots he had on yesterday were fire. No homo.'"

"He really said 'no homo' after 'fire'? That's just so . . . out of context."

"Everyone moves at their own pace."

# 6

# DRIVER'S ED

The Caesar salad with extra shrimp at the bustling Union Grill on Craig Street in Oakland wasn't the best shrimp-infused Caesar salad I'd ever eaten. That honor was reserved for Simmie's Restaurant on Frankstown Avenue in Homewood, which maybe had oxycodone in its dressing. But it was close. It was so good that I began to fantasize, midmeal, about how many more lunch dates and meetings I'd have there in the upcoming months and years. *Meet me at the Grill at noon*, I imagined typing in emails on my yet-to-be-purchased MacBook and text messages on my yet-to-be-assigned BlackBerry while I sat in my yet-to-be-commissioned office. After meeting my companion for lunch, I'd attempt to encourage him to also try the Caesar salad, but would quickly follow with "but everything here is good" with the easy and intentional and obnoxious familiarity of someone who eats somewhere so often that servers approach the table with "I thought I was done with you this week!" instead of "What can I start you out with?"

It actually wasn't a far-fetched fantasy. I was at the Union Grill because it was within walking distance of Carnegie Mellon University, where I'd spent the three hours before lunch interviewing for an open admissions counselor position, and where I'd spend the four hours after lunch completing the day-long vet. My lunch companions that day were two counselors already employed by the university. I'd met them a week before during my initial interview on campus, and they believed, as I did, that lunch would be a perfect time to pick their brains about a position I was an obvious shoo-in to fill. It had been revealed earlier that day that out of the 150 candidates for the gig, I was the only one to make it to interview three. "How does it feel to be the final survivor on the island?" one of them asked. "Good, I guess," I answered. (I never watched that show.)

By the end of the exhausting day—which also included an extensive campus tour and an hour-long round-robin session where each of the five counselors currently on campus surrounded me in a room and peppered me with questions (at that point, I wasn't quite sure if they were going to interview me or jump me into the Craig Street Crips)—I found myself in the office of the head of admissions, Mr. Rooney, who was prepared to offer me the position. The salary was $41,000 a year, double what I was making as a substitute teacher, and a small fortune for a twenty-five-year-old nigga in Pittsburgh with a bachelor's degree. It also came with full medical benefits (which I'd never had), a 401(k) (which I'd only heard of in commercials featuring Sam Waterston), life insurance (which I'd always dismissed as some "white-people shit" as if white people were the only ones who needed coffins), fifteen days allotted for vacations (which I'd never been on) and a generous tuition reimbursement package that would allow me to attend CMU for free and would cover 80 percent of the bill if I chose to go to Pitt. It was also the first time I'd actually get the type of unabashed hookup white people lean on for gigs, interdepartmental promotions, bank loans, college placements, investments, rental applications, health inspections, mortgage approvals, doctor referrals, venture capitalist funding, peak-hour restaurant reservations, generous grades, reduced speeding tickets, Kickstarter campaigns, criminal record expungements, book deals, and Republican presidencies. Mom had attended CMU after high school and knew a man named Robert Fisher who had also gone to CMU, currently worked in the school of business, and was apparently dating Miss Tammi, one of Mom's best friends. Miss Tammi let Mr. Fisher know I applied for the position, and he made the call to the head of admissions, asking him to "look out for his boy." The ease with which I was passed up the chain was fascinating and terrifying. I had been trying for two years to leave Wilkinsburg and find something better. Something that would allow me to move out of the east bedroom of my parents' split-level ranch in Penn Hills and carry a savings account with more than a pack of bite-size Snickers in it. And my efforts were futile until a fifty-five-year-old black guy with a key to a super-duper-secret wormhole of whiteness looked my way and was able to make it happen, granting me some golden ticket like a nigga Willy Wonka. This hookup was, without a doubt, the most Caucasian thing that ever happened to me. I felt whiter than a Patagonia fleece.

The chairs in front of the cavernous desk in Rooney's office were plush and sexy. *This must be where he meets with parents*, I thought as I rubbed my palms against the bark-brown leather and leaned slightly back to test the chair's lumbar support. (It was spectacular.) I felt like I was in Crate and Barrel or West Elm, browsing living room collections and nodding my head while pretending not to be horrified by the prices. I would have eaten a meal off of this chair. Shit, with a dollop of Dijon mustard and a quart of raspberry Simply Lemonade, I would have eaten the chair.

I concealed a grin when he repeated the starting salary. I'd known it since first finding the position posted two months earlier on CMU's website, which I'd checked for job openings three times a week for the previous eighteen months. I also checked Pitt's website, and Duquesne's and Chatham's and Carlow's and Point Park's and Robert Morris's and CCAC's with a similar frequency, figuring—well, hoping—that there had to be something on one of these campuses that I was qualified to do. More than just a considerable bump in income, the pay would finally cement my status as a fucking grown-up, which I believed eluded my grasp as long as my meager paycheck was solely determined by how many days I managed to show up for work. The kids at Wilkinsburg would joke and complain that I was there every day. I even overheard one telling his homie "that nigga don't ever get sick," obviously oblivious to the fact that eighty-five dollars a day bought a conditional immunity to sniffles, headaches, fevers, coughing spells, and Lyme disease.

My facade of coolness finally cracked when Rooney officially welcomed me to the team, and I beamed as I stood up and shook his hand. It was large and soft and pale yet surprisingly firm, like a sheet of Marriott Rewards continental breakfast biscuits before the complimentary sausage gravy. I gripped it and thought of all the similarly biscuited hands of parents and guidance counselors and school principals I'd shake on recruiting trips to San Diego and Seattle and Austin and Aliquippa, and all the conversations over coffee and stale cookies we'd have where I'd expound on the benefits of attending a "top-tier, private, global research university that challenges the curious and passionate to deliver work that matters" and that exists at the "intersection of technology and the human condition" making it "uniquely positioned to address global challenges" and other passages I'd memorized from the school's mission statement. I couldn't wait to be a faceless CMU shill.

For a moment, I even allowed myself to consider that I might possibly meet someone on one of these trips. Perhaps we'd catch each other's eyes while at the same college fair and share a smile at the act of finding another brown face. And I'd learn, after catching her eyes again at the happy hour for out-of-town admissions counselors at the Hilton that evening, that she was from the University of Chicago. And we'd trade a dozen easy and familiar laughs about how *She Hate Me* is the most "quintessentially Spike" Spike Lee movie and maybe about the unnecessary insurance Enterprise tacks onto car rentals and perhaps even about "these white motherfuckers" (always a reliable source of bonding and mirth for black professionals) while I tried very, very hard to make eye contact without staring. Which would eventually lead to a "nightcap" in her room and a very adult and tasteful and occasionally guilt-ridden dalliance that would occur whenever we happened to be in the same city. Or maybe—rather, hopefully—I'd decline the nightcap offer because I'd remember I had a girlfriend. And she'd say, *"It's just drinks."* And I'd say, *"I know what drinks lead to."* And she'd say, *"Me too. More drinks!"* And I'd laugh while my ego underwent a deep-tissue massage at the fact that someone so witty and fun and flirty (and also so familiar with *No Country for Old Men*) was actually interested in sleeping with *me*.

Back on earth, Rooney handed me an offer sheet to peruse and a contract to sign and asked for my driver's license to send a photocopy of it to human resources.

It's been, now, more than a decade since he asked that question, and my response to it still perplexes me. I knew that the position would require me to travel to cities. And that while in those cities, I'd be required to rent cars to get from place to place. And even if I wasn't yet aware of those duties, the job posting stated that both a bachelor's degree (which I possessed) and a driver's license (which I did not) were required.

I knew my lack of a license would be something I needed to deal with at some point, but I hoped that Rooney—like everyone else—would have just assumed that a twenty-five-year-old man, born, bred, and currently residing in Pittsburgh, knew how to drive, and that he would hire me without asking for verification. And that enough time would pass between being hired and my start date for me to get a license. And if that still wasn't enough time, I assumed that my first several weeks at work would be in the office, and not on trips. Because of course I'd have to go through all types of orientations and post-hire vetting before they trusted me to travel. Perhaps I'd even need to get fitted for a nifty burgundy CMU polo shirt. I had, in my head, at least two months before I'd actually *need* to drive.

Still, I should have prepared for the question. Which I'd already been asked on a job interview before. And I should have thought of one of the lies I'd regularly volunteer when I was single and dates would ask why I caught taxis—which *no one* in Pittsburgh ever did then; you were either on the bus, catching a jitney, driving a car, or riding in a hearse—or why I always requested to meet at restaurants and movie theaters that sat near convenient bus lines. "My license was suspended" was my favorite one, because it (A) suggested that the inconvenience was temporary and (B) assigned to me a level of law-indifferent badassness. "*Oooh,*" I'd imagine my date processing between bites of herb-crusted salmon at the Cheesecake Factory (which sat a block away from a 51C bus stop), "*this bespectacled teacher nigga has a bit of thug in him.*" To make the appearance of subtle academic thuggishness more convincing, I'd occasionally order a Hennessy and Coke with dinner instead of my usual Malibu rum. (If she had tattoos I'd order a double.)

Simply telling Rooney that I left my wallet at home after running out of the house that morning would have granted me a temporary reprieve; enough time to go home, regroup, and concoct a more elaborate lie for when the weekend had come and gone and I still hadn't returned to campus with my license. I should have had that ready. Lying about what I didn't do and hadn't yet done had become such a reliable crutch that I'd genuinely surprise myself when I told the truth about a fact I assumed would be uncomfortable or unflattering. But Rooney's question somehow caught me off guard. Perhaps because I knew that no lie would allow me to escape the question. If I didn't produce the license today, I'd need to do it *soon*—within a week or even a day—before he'd naturally assume something was up and would just refresh the interview process with one of the 150 other applicants.

So I told him the truth. And watched his smile drop, his eyes blank, his forehead flinch and contract, his biscuits dive into his pockets, his neck tilt, and that super-duper-secret wormhole of whiteness—which was close enough for me to reach through and steady the ladder of Caucasity I'd finally be able to climb—shutter.

---

The worst lie I ever told came ten years before that day I shared that inconvenient truth in Rooney's office. It was also a few months after discovering that the white guy working behind the counter at PA Video in East Liberty either didn't know how to distinguish a sixteen-year-old black teen from a twenty-one-year-old black man or just didn't give a damn about attempting to, an act that eventually led to me using the family video card Dad received as part of his membership package to rent pornography. It was a no-brainer, really. For a mere $2.50, I'd be able to possess 120 minutes of the finest ethnic and ebony adult titles Western Pennsylvania had to offer for three whole, entire days. More than enough time to conduct my anthropological analyses about positions and placements and the peculiar porn-specific grammar actors and actresses would use to describe sexual acts that were either currently happening or they wished to happen very soon. (Instead of "suck my dick" or "fuck my pussy" they'd say "suck *this* dick" or "fuck *that* pussy" as if the dicks and pussies in question belonged to a disembodied torso they had dominion over. Black porn is basically *Avatar* with baby oil and fluffers.)

Unfortunately, a major obstacle sat between me and this porno nirvana. Although I apparently looked old enough to walk into the adult films section without question, I still wasn't mature enough to alleviate the rush of self-consciousness I'd feel about actually doing it. Each time I'd take a step in the direction of that section—which was located in a back corner of the store and partitioned off—I'd feel like I was being judged and silently admonished by the poor-man's Paul Giamatti behind the counter. And by the rest of the customers in the store. And by my late grandpa, my recently deceased aunt Toni, the first Aunt Viv from *The Fresh Prince of Bel-Air*, Maya Angelou, and the ghost of that guy Morgan Freeman played in *Glory*. I just *knew* my ancestors shed a tear each time I held a copy of *All Dat Azz* or *Ghetto Booty* in my hands, and hoped I'd do something more meaningful with my displaced semen than shooting it into a Kleenex after watching *My Baby Got Back 18*.

To circumvent this shame, I repeated a process where I'd

go into the store and pretend to browse the foreign films and romance sections until the guy at the register left the front counter to answer a phone or retrieve a video for a customer, which would then be my cue to sprint into the back. Sometimes I'd even go as far as renting two or three other videos I had no intention of ever watching just so I'd be able to slip the porno rental in as an afterthought. Like *"Yeah, lemme have* High Anxiety, Blade Runner, Aliens, Friday . . . *oh, and* Cream-Filled Phatties 12, *if you have that too."* If too many people, or a black person who looked to be over fifty, or a black woman who looked to be under thirty, happened to be in the store, however, I'd abort the porno mission. But would still rent a video I had no plans of watching, just to throw anyone potentially tracking my rental tendencies off the scent. And I'd leave with a copy of *Sixteen Candles* that would stay in my Jansport until it was time to come back and try again.

As difficult as it was to rent them, actually returning them was even more daunting. There was no store drop box or laundry chute or rabbit hole or whatever the fuck most other rental stores used. Instead, you'd have to physically hand the tapes over to the clerk, who'd place them in their corresponding video boxes (which were kept underneath the counter while the videos were out) and then place the boxes on a floor-to-wall shelf behind him. And since porno video boxes are roughly the size of a turducken, *everyone* in the store would get a clear view of your debauchery.

The first few times this happened, it was fine. No one except for the clerk and a couple other white guys were in the store. But then it happened on a day a Rihanna doppelganger and her mom walked in. I wasn't quite sure if they ever noticed the copy of *Booty Juice* sitting in the middle of the wall behind the counter, or even that I was the one who handed it to the clerk. I wasn't quite sure that they *didn't* notice, though, and that scare was enough to convince me to never do that again.

To be clear, by *never do that again* I didn't mean that I'd never rent pornos again. I still rented them. My studies weren't complete. I just stopped *returning* them, taking advantage of a loophole in PA's rental policy that allowed you to still rent videos while accumulating late fees on unreturned movies. I became a porn hoarder, stashing tapes under my bed and between the mattresses. When I ran out of space there, I used old shoeboxes. And when I ran out of space there, I used my locker at school. I even began a short-lived bartering service where I'd lend rentals to classmates, exchanging them for cafeteria cheese fries or Karl Kani belts. For two weeks in the fall of 1995, I was Penn Hills Senior High School's thrift shop Larry Flynt.

Of course, video rental stores have an annoying tendency of keeping track of never-returned tapes. After a month, they called Dad, wanting to know what happened to volumes two through six of *Assliciously Delicious*. He had no idea what they were asking about, so he asked me. And I swore on a stack of invisible Bibles that surely burst into flames that I also had no clue. He believed me and told PA Video there must have been a mistake.

This, regrettably, was not actually the worst lie I've ever told. That came a day later, when PA called again, this time with proof that someone with a Young family membership card had rented a dozen pornos and neglected to return them. So when Dad pressed, again, if I had anything to do with it, I finally fessed up:

"I let Brian borrow the card a few times. Maybe he knows."

It's been more than two decades since the PA Video porn heist. Brian Carroll was my closest friend then and has retained that status, serving as my opponent in the hundreds of one-on-one games we played at Pennley Park in the early and mid-nineties, my ride to Whiskey Dick's and Tequila Willies and the rest of the awkwardly titled Pittsburgh-area nightclubs we frequented in 2003 and 2004, and the best man at my wedding in 2014. And because he's my best friend, he will receive an advance copy of this book before it's sold, and he will read this chapter. And he will discover, for the first time, that the reason Dad called his dad in 1995 to ask to speak to him, so that Dad could ask Brian to return the gaggle of pornography he stole from PA Video with my family's membership card, was because I told him that Brian might have.

Naturally, Brian denied this. And when he called me later that night, asking why my dad insisted that Brian had sullied the Young family's good name with delinquent pornography, I told *another* lie, saying that I'd lost the card and perhaps my dad just wrongly deduced that he had it. Now stuck between three separate lies, I did what I could the next day to rectify them and clear my conscience. I collected each of the tapes I'd rented—from my shoeboxes, underneath my mattress, and my locker at Penn Hills—stashed them in a garbage bag, and placed them in a dumpster next to the East Busway Homewood station.

The mystery of the missing pornography was never solved. A week later, Dad joined Blockbuster.

This was far from the first lie I told that required multiple escalating lies to prop it up. I lied about my family's financial status, volunteering that my parents' incomes made us solidly middle class to preempt doubts and concerns about our money and well-being that no one actually expressed to me. I lied about the colleges recruiting me in high school, going as far as to namedrop Pitt and Penn State in newspaper articles and postseason all-star game program profiles despite never having received even a letter of interest from either. I lied about my

SAT score, adding 100 points to jump from the "good . . . for a black kid" 1190 to 1290—the point where I believed such qualifications would be unnecessary. I lied about living at home after college, assigning myself some sort of performative sobriety and thoughtfulness where I'd share that it was a conscious choice I made to help my parents out with their mortgage, when living rent free for four years just helped me shop at Banana Republic and pay off my T-Mobile Sidekick bill. I regularly added a half inch to a question about my penis length that I've still never actually been asked. Any point of insecurity that could be rectified with a lie was. The inherent incentives of truthfulness—which I'm assuming are a clear conscience and a surprisingly thorough spiritual foot massage from Jesus—were often outweighed and occasionally engulfed by lying's clear lack of disincentive. It was just easier to lie and be the person I assumed I was expected to be instead of admitting I wasn't.

Also, I was equipped with an ironic medley of talents that allowed me to be an extraordinary liar. The same shyness and reticence that prevented me from doing the things I lied about doing provided a cover of inherent believability. I didn't speak much. And when I did, my words were so strained and measured and sedate that no one would dare doubt the truth of them. Like, imagine if a basset hound learned how to speak. You'd trust the fuck out of everything it said, right? Of course you would! Because even baby basset hounds look and carry themselves like Thurgood Marshall. Well, quiet niggas with glasses and resting frown faces are like basset hounds with sentences. (And you wouldn't believe a word coming out of a lying-ass shih tzu's mouth, because they're fraud-ass fucking dogs.)

In order for the lies to satisfy some sort of anticipated measure of believability, I'd make them small enough to pass that vet. No one would dare challenge that my SAT score was one hundred points lower than I said it was, because who the fuck would bother making the effort to create, share, and continue such an insignificant falsehood? I'd defy logic by bending reality so slightly that you couldn't see a crease.

Whichever angsts I carried about the inherent immorality of habitual dishonesty were alleviated by the level of morality and self-righteousness I believed I possessed. I was a good guy—a nice guy™—so little white lies here and there were allowed. *Earned.* I *deserved* to be able to be less than forthright when I believed it to be necessary because I was pleasant and chivalrous and would never even consider changing the channel during ChildFund International commercials. Every minute of uninterrupted eye contact with Sally Struthers bought me another gallon of lie leeway. Plus, while other liars lied to get themselves out of hot water or to nick or destroy someone else's character, my lies were merely a function of my own pervasive self-consciousness. My lies were reluctant and pitiful, and this reluctance and pity gave them integrity. My lies were righteous and decent, respectable, moral, and noble. You'd introduce my lies to your coworkers and invite them to dinner with your parents, and your parents would call you the next day to compliment their diction and their table manners. My lies would get on one knee to ask you to the prom, and would gift you with matching and monogrammed corsets even if you declined. If my lies were a place, they would have been Memphis or Norway. If my lies had a face, they would have been Bernie Sanders. But if Bernie Sanders were a black woman. My lies were every song John Legend has ever sung. My lies were a pot roast dinner with carrots and roasted potatoes and a salad with iceberg lettuce and French dressing. My lies were a Buick LaCrosse. My lies had a landscaping guy. My lies *were* the landscaping guy.

Even the lie I told on Brian was excused away because I felt so bad about it. Not bad enough to not do it, obviously. Or even bad enough to admit that I did it. But bad enough to feel really, really, really bad and think long and hard about how bad I felt about it. I thought about how bad I felt about it in the shower, during homeroom, in line at the Potato Patch at the regatta in August, and even once while getting a ride home from Brian's dad. The pain and torment and agony of me torturing myself with the memory of the lie I didn't quite feel bad enough about to not actually tell consumed me, and this was all the penance I needed. I felt fucking punished, man. And brave for allowing myself to receive that pain.

This decades-long liaison with easy and easily alibied lying led to that day in Rooney's office. It's how an embarrassment over my parents' lack of a car led to me lying, in high school, about having a driver's license. And how that lie followed me to Canisius. And how I'd kept that lie alive, despite possessing a very real opportunity to actually learn how to drive when my teammate's Jetta-whipping cheerleader girlfriend taught him and would have happily taught me if I'd dropped the act and just asked. (He was from Harlem, though, and niggas from Harlem weren't expected to have driver's licenses. Or musical tastes outside of Mase, Cam'ron, and Brian Pumper. Or any idea that things like "squirrels" and "tact" and "Michigan" existed. So not having a license at twenty didn't carry the same stigma for him as it did for me.) I'd lug it through young adulthood, choosing then to lie about having a license instead of experiencing what I believed to be the humiliation of learning how to drive in your twenties. And by then the lie changed from "I have a license but just choose not to drive" to "I can drive, but my license is suspended." And I watched the root of that lie morph from embarrassment to abject fear. The thought of getting behind the wheel and driving became such a Thing I Needed to

Do but Hadn't Yet Done that the longer I waited to do it the more it became a Thing I Don't Know If I'll Ever Be Able to Do Because the Thought of Doing It Makes My Teeth Itch.

Of course, the people closest to me knew the truth, and they'd encourage me and sometimes even attempt to shame me into learning how to drive. Which might have worked if it were, say, swimming (which I also never learned how to do). Because I could be bad at it in anonymity. Each step involved with learning how to drive, however, possessed the potential for prolonged public humiliation. Beginning with the act of having to catch the bus to the DMV to grab a learner's permit book to study with, with the added insult of being forced to memorize shit about yield sign height and air bag herpes I'd never fucking need to know after the test. And then taking the learner's permit test when I'd be the only one in the room old enough to buy a beer and grow a beard. And then convincing someone to allow me to practice driving their car while they sat in the passenger seat and pretended to be cool with me bringing them four inches from permanent disfigurement with each left turn. Or perhaps buying a course from Easy Method Driving School, and having to trek through Point Breeze and Squirrel Hill and Schenley Park in a Kia Sedona with a THIS CAR IS FOR OLD-ASS NIGGAS WHO CATCH JITNEYS TO DATES sign attached to the bumper while the instructor pinched her stress ball and yelped each time I tried to merge. And then there was the actual driving test, with the closest course set in the parking lot of the Penn Hills Shopping Center. Which meant niggas I knew could order extra-value meals from Wendy's and enjoy their six spicy chicken nuggets while watching my developmentally arrested ass crash into the parallel parking cones like a goddamn fucking Goonie. Fuck that.

Instead, I reconciled myself to the day-to-day abstract humiliation of not possessing a license, which was so ingrained in my existence that I was able to push it to the recesses of my mind. It was a chronic but not-deadly-at-all condition that was daunting and mundane and complex enough for me to forget about it; an annoying bout of driver's license gout that'd flare up during thunderstorms or pollen season. It also cultivated a re-curring matryoshka doll of procrastination, where I'd tell my-self I was "without a doubt getting a license this year." And then when the year ended, I'd adjust my expectations to "this month, definitely." And when "this month, definitely" came and went, I'd change them to "this week, for sure." And when "this week, for sure" approached, I'd get ambitious and say, "I'm doing this fucking shit TODAY, dammit!" And when today passed, I'd eat an Eggo and watch *The Sopranos*.

Perhaps this is why I pursued the CMU position and ac-cepted the interview despite knowing I'd eventually be outed. Maybe it was an intuitive self-motivational ploy, a way of speaking my license into existence by lighting a fire under my own ass. Only it didn't actually work. I didn't rush to get a license when learning I'd be granted an interview, and I didn't refocus and repurpose the embarrassment of losing the op-portunity into some sort of fuel enabling me to finally jump that hurdle. Just more excuses. More procrastination. And more bus passes.

And then, six months later, while shopping for slightly dam-aged Timberland chukkas at the Gabriel Brothers department store, I happened to run into Rakia Curry, who had sat in my classroom at Wilkinsburg as an appropriately inappropriate fourteen-year-old freshman. Now sixteen, Rakia had a job at Popeye's on Penn Avenue and was beginning to make the tran-sition back to being an actual human. I liked her. She saw me and greeted me the exact same way *every single student* would when they'd happen to see me outside of school.

"Mr. Young! I didn't know you shopped at Gabe's!"

(For the record, I'd also, at various points during my teaching career, heard the following:

"Mr. Young! I didn't know you went to church!"

"Mr. Young! I didn't know you got haircuts!"

"Mr. Young! I didn't know you went to Kennywood!"

Once, while at Giant Eagle, I even heard "Mr. Young! I didn't know you ate food!" Apparently, the students assumed we teachers stopped existing when they exited our classrooms. Like motion sensor lights with sentience and homework assignments.)

Now, Rakia was tiny even for a teenage girl. She was barely five feet tall, and maybe weighed ninety-five pounds. She also spoke in an aggressively delicate whisper. You'd hear the sound of her voice and you weren't sure if it was her talking or a kitten laughing. As I was leaving the store with Brian, she waved at me. From the driver's seat—of a car she was driving. This tiny and mousy little girl who, just two years earlier, once asked to be excused from the room while I showed the class Michael Jackson's "Thriller" video because it was too scary, had a fucking license and was driving a fucking car. All the driving-related tasks I allowed to frighten and overwhelm me were apparently mastered by a girl who still shopped at Kids Foot Locker.

This broke something inside me. Not a levee releasing a new and advanced and hyperspecific strain of shame. But, surprisingly, *relief.* Seeing Rakia's Lilliputian ass pushing a two-thousand-pound Chevy Malibu dissipated all of the daunt I'd attached to doing it myself. If she could do it, I totally, definitely, absolutely could. I also felt, well, stupid. So fucking stupid. Like the dumbest motherfucker who ever lived. I'd allowed this task to become such an albatross that it blinded me to the fact that the source of my shame was also the solution. I, a twenty-six-year-old man, hadn't yet done something that sixteen-year-olds regularly do. Which also meant that this impossible task was something sixteen-year-olds regularly did, so it couldn't be that fucking hard.

Three months later—and five months after that day in Rooney's office—after passing the permit test, buying two lessons from Easy Method, receiving enough private lessons from my doting and patient and encouraging mom for her to seriously consider disowning me, and passing my driver's test on my third try (parallel parking is racist), I had a license. Which I celebrated by driving my parents' Cadillac to the Monroeville Mall the first evening I was able to legally drive, and promptly leaving a nickel-sized dent in a stationary Ford Explorer when attempting to back up while parking. (The owner of said Explorer was sitting in the driver's seat and was remarkably cool about this, possessing a blaséness about the damage that I'd later recognize as the mark of someone who didn't have insurance.)

I also soon found myself on another interview. It was at the YMCA in McKeesport, where I'd be in charge of a teen after-school program, community centers in both the Crawford and Harrison public housing projects, and a youth basketball league for $26,000 a year. There were no edibly plush chairs to fondle and no biscuity hands to shake. The wormhole of whiteness and middle-class-ness and shrimp I'd found myself ensconced in at CMU didn't exist out there, just the 61C (which would take me from downtown Pittsburgh to McKeesport in thirty-two minutes), two Shop 'n Saves, and a distractingly disproportionate number of beige toddlers with unfortunate tornados of berets and oblivion on their heads—which is what occasionally happens when white women have babies with black men and have no fucking clue what to do with their hair. (I still, to this day, have never seen as many interracial relationships per capita in one place as I did there. It's fascinating. *McKeesport* is apparently Swahili for "Mon Valley Miscegenation.") Still, I'd have both a salary and medical benefits for the first time, and the bump in income would be enough for me to get my own place, a six-hundred-square-foot and $565-a-month spot on the corner of Ellsworth and Negley in Shadyside. To complete the moving-on-up-ness of this experience, I outfitted the apartment with all-white furniture; finding an off-white futon at Urban Outfitters, a white dining room table from IKEA, and a stark white couch bed from a Chinese med student on Craigslist, who'd apparently owned the couch for two years but somehow managed to keep it completely and eerily pristine. I'm still not 100 percent convinced she wasn't an apparition specifically sent by Jesus to help me complete my living room set. I have an awkward relationship with the purpose of God.

But before any of this could happen, I needed to answer a crucial question. Running the Teen LEAD program and overseeing the community centers would require me to drive the Y's van back and forth from McKeesport Area High School to the Y and from the Y to Crawford Village and Harrison Village. I'd also need to make occasional runs to Shop 'n Save and the Walmart in North Versailles. So when Mr. Jason, my soon-to-be boss, asked if I had a driver's license, I told him the truth.

"Yes."

# 7

# THREE NIGGAS

For the majority of black men who frequent barbershops, most trips to the barber don't actually involve much hair removed from the tops of their heads. Instead, they're there to get "shape-ups" (also known as "line-ups" or "edge-ups"). Which is what happens when the barely perceptible amount of growth that occurred near the hairline since the last shape-up—which might have happened just last week—is cleaned and tightened up. (In a month's time, it's not uncommon to get three or four shape-ups and only one actual haircut.) For those who don't shave daily, this can also be when mustaches, sideburns, beards, and goatees are beautified.

Although this particular type of hairline maintenance is most common with black men, every so often you'll see a white boy with the same type of sharp and angled edges and closely cropped hair—a sign that he probably gets his hair cut at a black barbershop too. If a white man possesses this, it can also be a sign that he's comfortable enough around black people to willingly frequent a black barbershop; which, next to Patti LaBelle's kitchen and Al Sharpton's activator drawer, might be the single blackest place on earth. Being comfortable enough around black people to not call the cops when surrounded by us is a primary characteristic of the down-ass white boy. (The bar for down white people is pretty low, unfortunately.)

Of course, there are down-ass white boys with hair like Don Draper or Kid Rock. (Rick Rubin, for instance, might be the downest-ass white boy ever, and he looks like Chewbacca.) And, of course, not every white boy who gets his hair trimmed at Donnie's House of Cut-Rate Afro Sheen is down, as there are quite a few perpetuating-ass white boys with cuts like Stephen Curry and politics like Stephen Miller. But, if you were to make a Venn diagram with "white boys with cuts from black barbers" and "down-ass white boys" as sets A and B, there'd be quite a bit of overlap.

(Also, it's important to distinguish the down-ass white boy from the woke-ass white boy. The down-ass white boy, while possessing a comfort around black people, isn't immune to unfortunate bouts of hotepitivity—the strain of performative pro-blackness that conceals its regressive politics and affinity for patriarchy in a pan-African Trojan horse. The woke-ass white boy, however, is conveniently progressive-ish and liberal and knows how to incorporate terms like *intersectionality* and *gentrification* and *Viola Davis* into regular conversation, but the only time you'd find his ass in a black barbershop is if he was actually watching *Barbershop*. Down-ass white boys cite *Hidden Colors*. Woke-ass white boys write two-thousand-word think pieces on *Hidden Figures*.)

Nickolas Booker, the downest-ass white boy I've ever known, got his hair cut at East Liberty Kutz, the same barbershop I frequented. And between his tapered fade and his meticulously kept goatee, he looked so much like Jon B—the late-nineties crooner you might but probably don't remember from that one video he did with Tupac's ghost in 1997—that niggas in the Burgh called him White Jon. I doubt most even knew his real name was Nick, which I suspect is why he got NICKOLAS tattooed on his forearm. Nick also graduated from a predominantly black inner-city high school. *And* played basketball in high school and college. *And* dated sistas. His life was a perfect round of down-ass white boy bingo.

We first met in a spring basketball tournament my sophomore year of high school. He was the only white boy in the gym, but he wasn't actually very good then. He was long (already six foot three as a sophomore) and athletic, but his handle was weak and he needed too much space to get his J off. But, because of an inverse form of affirmative action, where white boys who dared attend and play sports for predominantly black schools are often assigned an elevated status their ability doesn't warrant, Nick had a *name*. He was maybe his team's sixth- or seventh-best player talent-wise, but when niggas would talk about them, his name would get dropped like he actually mattered. Like, imagine someone listing the most vital members of the Jackson family, and saying, "There's Michael, Janet, and, of course, Tito. You can't forget Tito." Nick Booker was Tito. He eventually got better—good enough to get a scholarship to a D-II school. But I could never quite shake the feeling that his white privilege mattered in inner-city Pittsburgh's basketball ecosystem and hierarchy, one of the few places that I'd assumed would be immune to it.

Anyway, when Nick was the sole non-black invitee to an all-male cookout/NBA conference finals viewing party at my man Roger's house in 2007, it wasn't a surprise to anyone there. Because Nick and Nick's goatee were down as fuck. Also, if we made too much noise and the cops came through to break it up, Nick answering the door instead of Nayshawn could buy us a couple more hours and a couple less bullets.

A dozen or so people made their way to Roger's that day. All between twenty-five and thirty-five years old, all former ball players who either still played in men's leagues or coached high school, and all wearing a variant of the circa 2007 version of the perfunctory nigga-chillin'-with-a-group-of-his-niggas-at-his-nigga's-house outfit: a T-shirt or polo (Polo or Lacoste), jeans (Levi's or Sean John), Tims or Air Force Ones, and either a fresh cut or a strategically placed New Era fitted cap to conceal the wolf. Unfortunately, one of us didn't get the implied dress code memo, and inexplicably showed up with a full Harlem Globetrotters FUBU uniform set—the shirt, the shorts, the socks; *everything.* Like an extra on *The Harlem Globetrotters on Gilligan's Island.* But if Gilligan's Island were in Homewood. His name was Terrell, but for the rest of the night—and the rest of the year—we called that nigga Meadowlark Lemon.

After the game ended, the party predictably segued into a night of drinking, Spades playing, shit-talking, and storytelling. The conversations bounced from topic to topic—standout subjects included an impassioned debate about Jay-Z and Nas and a surprisingly thorough take on why Mark Cuban could be president—but eventually settled on women. In a forty-five-minute-long-span, we debated and eventually formed a consensus on who had the fattest ass in the city (the dark brown chick with the braids working at the perfume counter at Lazarus downtown), who was the baddest chick in Hollywood (Halle Berry), who probably had the best pussy in Hollywood (Halle, again, because "a woman that fine and single must be insane," and everyone knows "crazy bitches have the best pussy"), who's the baddest video chick, Esther Baxter or Melyssa Ford (Esther), whether immediate fellatio or eager anal sex was a better indicator of a woman's credit score and willingness to cosign a car loan (don't ask), and how the premarriage ministry workshops at Mt. Ararat Baptist Church really help young couples navigate through the first few months of cohabitation.

The "crazy bitches" bit that began with Halle became a recurring theme and then the dominant one, as the conversation gradually shifted structurally and thematically to each person there sharing his own personal crazy-woman tale. To my lament, I had nothing to offer. I'd somehow managed to avoid dating or sleeping with any women who could be accurately categorized as crazy, and the infrequent bouts of crazy-ish behavior exhibited by women I knew were usually just natural reactions to garden-variety fuckshit that I did. I assumed that I was just lucky. Or perhaps the seemingly ubiquitous crazy bitches somehow intuited that I wasn't quite nigga enough to effectively control them and subsequently avoided me. Maybe it was something about the way I pronounce *mimosa*. Still, without a crazy-bitch story or experience to share, I nodded and laughed along. I wouldn't dare let them know that my crazy-bitch magnet was broken.

When it was Nick's turn, he recalled a time that he hooked up with a black woman who lived in the Northview Heights housing projects, a story choice that subtly shifted the theme from "crazy bitches" to "craziest shit I've done for pussy."

"So yeah, I go over to this broad's house, blahzay, blahzay, and in the morning, before I get dressed to leave, she goes to the door to get her mail or something. A moment later, she comes back in the bedroom all concerned-looking like, 'Nick, there's three dudes out there sitting on your truck.' So I get up and look out her window, to see whether or not she was just fuckin' with me, and lo and behold, I see three niggas sitting on my front hood. So I'm looking out there, debating what to do—"

I'm now going to stop this story midsentence for two reasons.

1. I have no idea what the hell he said next. I was in too much shock. I might have even blacked out.
2. We're gonna play a game!

Considering what you've read already about Nick, and seeing how effortlessly he incorporated "three niggas" into his story retelling, I want you to guess what happens next. I loved multiple choice tests as a kid, so I'm going to give you three options. Ready? Great!

A. The closest dark-skinned nigga to Nick immediately takes a bottle of Heineken Light and smashes it over his head, while two other niggas run to their cars to grab blankets. While Nick writhes in pain on the floor, we douse the blankets in gasoline, wrap him in them, and set him on fire before we toss him out of the house, burning alive, while taunting, "Well, you wanted to be a nigga. You's a nigga now." (Also, during this melee/murder, I suffer a second-degree burn to my left thumb.)

B. After finishing the story, Nick sees the stunned looks on our faces, stands up, lifts his shirt to reveal a fully loaded Desert Eagle tucked in his waistband, and sneers, "Yeah, niggas. I said 'nigga.' What the fuck y'all niggas gonna do about it? Nothing, right? I thought so, bitch-ass niggas." When he's done, he sits back down, finishes his raspberry Alizé, and asks, "Which one of you bitch niggas wants to be my partner in Spades?"

Since Nick is known to be the best Spades player of the group, I happily volunteer, and we beat all comers for the rest of the night.

C. After Nick says "three niggas," Brian and I look at each other for a second, mouths agape, and then look at the faces of everyone else in the room—most of them inebriated, some of them high, and all with similarly puzzled looks on their faces—while Nick continues his story. Brian can't take it anymore, and just starts saying, "End of story, end of story, end of story," over and over again while he and I literally fall out of our chairs in laughter.

The correct answer was C. (Although B would have been the best story and A would have been the best movie.)

The room-wide stunned silence became an awkward collective noise too loud to be a murmur but not confident enough to be a rumble. No one quite knew what to say or how to react. (Except for Nick, who apologized profusely and looked like he just saw the world's blackest ghost.) There are extensive guidebooks, syllabi, curricula, and degree programs devoted to how to react when called a nigger. Plus emergency bags and danger kits devised specifically for this purpose and strategically placed around the hood. Niggas are steeped in "what to do when called a nigger" preparation. So much so that we occasionally even anticipate it, waking up in the morning and stretching, checking our emails, brushing our teeth, and combing our beards while thinking, *Yeah, I'm totally gonna be a nigger somewhere today*. Niggas, as we've seen, have elaborate and cinematic *nigger* fight stories. Preparing for and reacting to *nigger* turns niggas into Jason Bourne.

Nick's three niggas, however, existed in a racial rabbit hole far deeper and more labyrinthine than the mundane and run-of-the-mill nigger. Because *nigga* and *nigger* ain't the same word. And, well, Nick's *nigga* usage was expert and dexterous. He didn't start the story by referring to the three men on his truck as niggas. That would have been unnecessary and sloppy, the type of ostentatiousness unbecoming a veteran *nigga* user. Instead he allowed it to serve as both the punch line and some sort of realness equalizer and authentication. He used *nigga* exactly how each of the rest of the niggas in the room would have. The context, the inflection, and the rhythm were each pitch-perfect. If Nick were administered a *nigga* pop quiz, the professor would use his test as the answer guide in each subsequent class period. He'd even invite him back the following semester to teach a guest lesson.

Sensing the damper of whiteness Nick placed on the party, Roger broke the ice. "Well . . . they *were* niggas, though." Which provided some levity, but not enough to obscure that Nick's *nigga* use was so splendid that it was clear he'd done this before. Many times. Many, many, many, many times. He was a fucking *nigga* maven. Somehow, between the basketball teams he played on, the black barbershops he frequented, and the black project chicks he slept with, he grew emboldened, confident enough in his veneer of blackness to wield its most powerful word. The result: a white boy—a down-ass white boy, yeah, but still a white boy—chucking *nigga*s around like rice at a wedding. So sure of his place in blackness's confines that he brandished *nigga* in a room full of niggas. We could only imagine how many other *nigga*s he retained under his employ, venting them to plumbers, texting them at gas stations, and perhaps even loaning them out to other down-ass white boys to practice with each other. He probably had a *nigga* barter service! Teaching other white boys how to say it while they offered bank loans in return.

It's telling, also, how shocked the room was by Nick's *nigga*, and the juxtaposition of that shock with how chill we were with the racism nestled in Nick's effortless sexism. We were more bothered by his clearly accidental *nigga* than by this down-ass *white boy* matter-of-factly speaking about working-class black women as if their disposability was inherent and assumed. *Nigga* belonged to us. And we were more protective of that word than we were of the "project chick" he was fucking. Most of the men in that room, when in mixed or polite company, referred to black women as *sistas*. Sometimes even *queens*. But we were only familial and revering when it was advantageous to be so. When *sista* made sistas think of us as good *brothas*. The type of good brothas they'd root for and defend and support and stand behind. The type of good brothas they'd recommend for jobs and then promotions at those jobs. The type of good brothas they'd date, hook their homegirls up with, invite to their parents' BBQs, and (maybe, hopefully, possibly) marry if they were a good enough sista. The type of good brothas worthy of *their* protection and mobilization if that good brotha was ever treated unjustly by white people. When sistas weren't around, however, and that performative loyalty and veneration was no longer immediately beneficial, our allegiance was to this down-ass white boy. Who, although a *white* man, was still a *man*. Nick's use of *nigga* offended our sensibilities. His facile misogyny matched them.

For the veteran *nigga* user, the primary focus of employing it is to cut through the shit. The exclamatory "Nigga!", the incredulous "Nigga please," and the dozens of *nigga* variations sprinkled in standard conversation are ways to imply that the bells, whistles, and other bullshit that permeate our daily discourse are no longer necessary or appropriate. It's a reduction machine that removes the pretense by reminding the subject of the stench of our collective shit. It also connects, existing in a singular space impervious to the effect that class markers like income, degrees, and town houses tend to have on someone's regard. When Larry Wilmore referred to President Obama as "my nigga" to culminate his performance at the 2016 White House Correspondents' Dinner—a statement accompanied by the perfunctory closed-fist-to-chest double pound of black male sincerity—it wasn't an attempt to demean or minimize the president's position, as dozens of hysterical and self-righteous responses to that act asserted. Nor *did it*. It was a way of acknowledging their commonalities and histories, a status that transcends status. President Obama—*Barack*, rather—is Larry's nigga. The same way Larry's barber and cousins and (black) neighbors and (black) coworkers are his niggas too. It's praise, not pejorative.

While the experience of American blackness is too varied and motley to feign some sort of universality, none of us are immune to the random and haphazard violence of *nigger*; of being called one, of being treated like one, of being thought of as one. It, like *nigga*, also transcends status and station, as even niggas who believe they've somehow escaped and eclipsed *nigger* are susceptible to the *nigger* wake-up call, of having their blankets of perceived privilege yanked from underneath them, hurling them into space while *nigger*'s savage gravity vaporizes them. It's through this collective fire that *nigga* is *earned*. We've earned the right to be it, to call each other it, to allow it to permeate our thoughts and our taunts, our minds and our music, our sentences and our souls.

This intraracial affinity for *nigga* is not without its black skeptics—many, actually—who believe it either exists as an only slightly less negative variant of *nigger* or is virtually indistinguishable from it. To them, keeping *nigga* alive reminds us of and reinforces our centuries-long collective trauma, and regenerates an ugly word they wish to bury—as the NAACP did in a mock funeral for it in 2007. In an interview with *Parade* six years later, Oprah Winfrey echoed this sentiment, stating, "You cannot be my friend and use that word around me." This apparently was enough to make veteran *nigga*-user Lee Daniels completely relinquish it while they worked on *The Butler* together, as he weighed the benefits of *nigga* use against the complimentary baby Minotaurs and the other amazing perks associated with being one of Oprah's niggas, and chose the latter. (I would have too.) When pressed about her feelings, Oprah explained, "I always think of the millions of people who heard that as their last word as they were hanging from a tree," which is an emotionally resonant and seemingly unassailable defense of her beliefs. And also an indictment of *nigga* and black people who still use it. But it doesn't quite move me.

I know that a person like Oprah Winfrey, who was born in Mississippi and raised in the midwest in the sixties and seventies, has a different relationship with *nigger* and *nigga* than a person like me, who has only been called a nigger to his face once. And I wouldn't dare suggest that Oprah's (or anyone else's) negative feelings toward *nigga* are invalid. It stems from a detonative and byzantine word; one invented by racists to subjugate and antagonize the people they decided to deem "black," cultivated by descendants of those racists to continue that legacy of fulmination and intimidation and hate, and existing today and in perpetuity as both a relic of that era and a reminder of the boundlessness of said era. And if I'm in conversation with a black person I know who possesses an active distaste for it, I'll refrain from using it. I'll even admit that if some nigga I'd never met, seen, or heard of before approached me with "What's up, my nigga?" today, I'd probably feel a certain way about it. Not angry. But not *not* angry. Not because he called me *nigga*. But because *he doesn't know me well enough* to call me *nigga*. *Nigga* is not an introduction. *Nigga* is something you use after the introduction has already happened.

Where people like Oprah and I differ, however, is in that *nigga* as I've come to know it has never not been empowering and sweet. It's what my uncles would call me and each other while drinking Jack and eating chili dogs on my grandma's porch in New Castle. It's what my parents would use in private and hilarious conversations with each other while they were downstairs and I was upstairs in bed listening to them, hoping one day to meet and marry the type of woman I could *nigga*-banter with. It was embedded in the music I grew up on and was an essential fulcrum of all the conversations at basketball courts, barbershops, bus rides, and parents' basements that raised and shamed and educated and entertained me. I am a veteran *nigga* user, and I have the stripes to prove it. So if I'm ever granted the privilege of meeting Oprah—perhaps I'm invited to a Sunday brunch on her lawn—I won't say *nigga* in her presence or while on her property. But the moment I step outside of her gates and I'm ferried off of her lake (I'm assuming she has gates and a lake at her house) I'm going to call one of my niggas. And the first thing I'll say is "Nigga! Guess where I just was? Oprah's! I had brunch at Oprah's! We had peach Bellinis and shark-meat frittatas, and those niggas were delicious!"

Annoyingly, conversations about the non-black appropriation and application of *nigga* somehow find their way back to black people who use it, like a tapeworm tracing back to an exasperated intestine. When a Nick effortlessly and adroitly slips it into conversation, or one of Nick's brethren mindlessly repeats it when voicing the lyrics to Kendrick Lamar's "DNA," or one of Nick's cousins argues that white people should be able to say it, we're blamed for it. Because if we don't want them to use it, we shouldn't. Because all of that *nigga* use by us niggas can confuse and encourage those delicate and oblivious mother-fuckers. *Nigga* is apparently so singularly contagious that white people in the vicinity of it are possessed with an uncontrollable compulsion to use it too. We, the blacks who push *nigga* on unsuspecting whites like crack cocaine and properly seasoned chicken breasts, must curtail its use before these soft-pedal motherfuckers overdose.

I'm not ashamed to admit that I've possessed this thought before. That chiding Nick or any other white person for us-ing a word I use so freely is hypocritical. Even as I recognized and articulated the queasiness I felt when Nick told us about the three niggas on the hood of his truck, I felt guilty. Like our unencumbered use of *nigga*—at that party, in the songs we all listened to, and in the basketball locker rooms and black barbershops he frequented—granted him a pass. A gift for be-ing a down-ass white boy. An implied thank-you for being cool enough to play our sport, date our women, and model our ta-pered fades and shape-ups. The least we could do for him mak-ing the effort to not allow himself to be infected by regular-ass feckless whiteness. This thought exists in the same strain of re-spectability politics that bleeds into blackness like a staph infec-tion, cracking skin, corroding spleens, and convincing niggas to wear suits to Target. It tells us that our salvation is found in a self-induced and performative filtering of our own behavior. Maybe if we stopped listening to Migos and stopped watching *Love & Hip Hop* and started modeling our hair after the compos-ite player profiles on *NBA Live* instead of numbers 16 through 27 on every hood barbershop poster, a white person might no-tice. And might decide to treat us with a conditional humanity; our citizenships and livelihoods and safeties dependent on our newfound affinity for jeans with belts and properly enunciated consonants. And then maybe this white person would be so impressed by our diction and our behavioral deodorant that they'd tell *other white people*. And then the message that "blacks have finally turned a new leaf" would spread through whiteness like a virus or a really jolly casserole. And then racism: solved!

The idea persists because it's romantic to believe that a few superficial etiquette alterations are enough to battle and perhaps even vanquish racism. And this romanticism is cloaked in a terrible and terrifying reality. America has done such a number on us (and me) that I allowed myself to entertain this concept, that it was somehow *our* fault when white people were audacious and bold enough to use a word created by them, used against us, repurposed by us, and now forbidden to them. This conceit was furious enough to temporarily blind me, preventing me from recognizing the truth. If Nick were as down as he wished—and we pretended—he was, he would have been aware of the violence of that word escaping his mouth. He believed his downness gave him a pass to say *nigga*, but him actually saying *nigga* relinquished any passes he might have had by proving he wasn't worth it. Saying *nigga*, a word *we'd earned*, was evidence he hadn't earned the invitations to our spaces. He wasn't worthy. Nick was just a white boy with a nice jump shot and a black haircut. While we didn't kick his ass, that night would be the last time he was invited to kick it with us.

Considering *nigga*'s convoluted definition and complicated history, why even bother? Why continue to use this word when there are so many others at my disposal? I have two answers to this question; one I've given several times before when asked, and one I just realized while typing this sentence. (And the one I just realized while typing this is, naturally, the best answer. Both are good, though.)

1. In the past year, I've referred to each of the following
   things as a nigga:

   Niggas. A Ghirardelli milk chocolate bar sold at Coffee
   Tree on Walnut Avenue in Shadyside. An ice cube. Ice
   Cube. Gravity. My leaping ability. The concept of Wi-Fi.
   The color orange. The future. *Key and Peele*'s "Pussy on
   the Chainwax" skit. Acid reflux. Lisinopril side effects.
   The goal of getting the flat-screen TV in my living room
   mounted by the end of the summer. Amy Brenneman's
   character on *The Leftovers*. My daughter. Hans Zimmer.
   Kanye West's post–*808s & Heartbreak* production. A bowl
   of freezer-burned frozen blueberries. Snapchat. My ACL
   reconstruction in 1998. The regressive politics of the
   international conversation about Pippa Middleton's nice
   but totally not international-conversation-worthy booty.
   The word *nigger*. A panel at the University of Maryland
   on "The Power of Popular Culture." Driverless Ubers.
   The state of Missouri. Rompers.

   I've used it as a noun addressing a *person* ("Come here,
   nigga."), a *place* ("It usually takes four hours to drive to
   that nigga"—referencing the drive from Pittsburgh to
   D.C.), and a *thing* ("Pass that nigga, nigga"—asking a
   friend to pass the hot sauce). It's also been a *verb* ("Yeah,
   I'm totally gonna niggafy that party next week."), an
   *adjective* ("You know Pop-Tarts ain't nothing but nigga
   croutons, right?"), and an *adverb* ("Of course she smiled
   niggaishly. She just got her refund check."). Okay,
   the adverb is pushing it, and may have never actually
   happened before the sentence right before this one. But
   the others are legit!

   The malleability of *nigga* is perhaps its most underrated
   characteristic. It stretches like leftovers a week after

Thanksgiving, its function dictated by the creativity and dexterity and mood of the user. It can serve as a singular exclamation ("Nigga!"). A singular articulation of incredulousness ("Nigga?"). A singular way of confirming the matter-of-fact-ness of a debated point ("Nigga."). It's the English language's boldest, blackest, and best Swiss army knife.

It also contains a rhythmic kick, a poetry within its pronunciation where its inclusion adds a necessary dollop of spice and cadence to vanilla sentences. For instance, while "D.C. dudes love business cards, man" works as a perfectly functional sentence, substituting *niggas* for *dudes* just gives it so much more pop and verve. "D.C. dudes love business cards, man" is the banquet-buffet rubber chicken breast of sentences. "D.C. niggas love business cards, man" marinates that breast in Old Bay.

2. White people can listen to, write, write about, perform, and pass themselves off as experts on hip-hop, R&B, neo soul, the blues, and gospel music. They can move (back) into the inner cities, drive up the prices, displace the residents, replace bodegas and hair salons and Jamaican restaurants with yoga studios and quinoa festivals and gourmet fried chicken stands, and transform historical fulcrums of black culture into appendages of whiteness. They can rock cornrows and twists, Afros and high-top fades, Caesars and Rakims, frohawks with symmetrical parts and pigtails with berets. They can attend Howard and Hampton, Morehouse and Spelman, and they can pledge Delta Sigma Theta and Omega Psi Phi while there. They can dap each other up and dab and do the Nae Nae and the Wobble and the Heel Toe and the Harlem Shake. They can give speeches on blackness in

front of black audiences and write books on blackness and sell them to black people. They can even pretend, for *years*, to be black—stealing opportunities and occupations away from actual black people—and have sociologists coin a new word to synopsize their plight and sympathize with their thievery.

They cannot, however, say *nigga*. It's one of the few privileges unique to blackness that remains sacrosanct, untouchable, and unco-optable. We alone possess *nigga*'s license, and the decision of whether to incorporate it in our language remains exclusive to us. I use *nigga* because I can. And, more importantly, because they *can't*. I enjoy maintaining the exclusionary rights to it and using it freely and intentionally while they covet that liberty and trip over themselves while attempting to reckon with it. I'm the kid on the playground with the *Star Wars* figurines that no one else can play with even if I have no interest in playing with them myself. That's my nigga lying in the dirt over there underneath the swings. And no, you can't see it. No, you can't touch it. No, you can't hold it. Nah-nah-nah-nah-nah motherfuckers.

# 8

# OBAMA BOMAYE

The first time I heard Barack Obama's name was the day after his now-iconic keynote address at 2004's Democratic National Convention. I was teaching summer school English at
Wilkinsburg, a job I greatly preferred over teaching during the
regular school year because the extended classroom hours—
classes were three hours long with breaks at the top of each hour
instead of the standard forty-five-minute period—and relative
lack of distractions created an environment more conducive to
learning. And by *because the extended classroom hours and relative
lack of distractions created an environment more conducive to learning*, I mean *because summer school paid twenty-two dollars an hour
PLUS time and a half for overtime . . . almost triple what I made per
hour during the school year.* This was also the summer I severely
sprained two ligaments in my right ankle while playing basketball, an injury that required me to use crutches for two weeks.

(By the end of my first week with the crutches, "Mr. Young
got hurt while hoopin'" somehow went through the school's

telephone-game rumor mill and morphed into "Mr. Young's ankle got fucked up when he got jumped by some Homewood niggas while walking to the busway." Which resulted in Thomas Hicks—the sincerest and most chivalrous teenage dopeboy at Wilkinsburg High—approaching me after school one day to promise that he and his crew were going to "see" the Homewood niggas who messed up my foot. It's still the sweetest thing anyone's ever said to me.)

Because of my limited mobility, my colleagues spent much more time in my classroom than I would have preferred. I appreciated the help with moving desks and writing lessons on the chalkboard, but that often led to another round of the dreaded "extended small talk with teachers"—the single weirdest and lowest form of regular human discourse. If you're in the wild, and you happen upon two dead-eyed educators talking to each other about GradeQuick or the missing celery tray from last week's in-service day—their faces wrought with exasperation and the long-term existential effects of teacher's lounge masturbation; their breath reeking of coffee, Zoloft, and scotch—shoot them both in the fucking head and put them out of their misery. Sure, you'll probably go to prison. But God'll appreciate your efforts to end their suffering, so you'll definitely go to heaven.

During one of these seppuku-with-a-mechanical-pencil-inducing conversations, Mr. McKinney, one of the other summer school teachers and doppelganger of Chris Bauer in *8MM*, told me about a man who'd captivated him on TV the night before. He was "movie-star handsome and articulate" and "tan-skinned . . . perhaps even bronze" and spoke with a soothing and dangling and commanding rhythm "like a jazz singer." Right when I began to wonder how long this round of racist Yinzer Yahtzee would stretch—and also right when I began to wonder what it was about me that made him comfortable enough to share his Magical Negro fanfic—he told me the man's name (Barack Obama) and that he was some sort of politician in Illinois and would be president one day. Unfortunately for McKinney, America had already given me a healthy cynicism for the type of black people that white people fawn over—he couldn't be that great if McKinney's translucent ass was already on board—and I dismissed him with a "whatever" and continued pretending to read essays.

Four summers later, if you happened to be driving behind my Mercury Mountaineer, you would have seen an Obama sticker on its bumper; the red and white and royal blue adding a touch of sun to the Mountaineer's barf-green tint. If you happened to see me exit the car, you had a one in five chance of also seeing a T-shirt with Shepard Fairey's iconic rendering of Obama's profile on my chest. And if you were invited to my apartment to maybe watch an NBA Summer League game or play Scrabble, you'd see an Obama yard sign fastened to the wall behind my couch. I hadn't simply drunk the Obama Kool-Aid; I had ground it down into a powder and snorted it.

The contrast between how I felt during my intro to him and my ultimate infatuation with him is stark, but predictably so, as I'd imagine most black Obamaphiles who first became aware of him in 2004 followed a similar trajectory.

1. Become intrigued by but skeptical of this gangly redbone with the funny name and the hippie mom who white people with Priuses and Marmot backpacks seemed to flock to and adore like he was distributing L.L.Bean gift cards.

2. Learn about and fall in love with Michelle, whose Chicago-ass, hot-comb-ass, salt-on-grits-and-chitlins-

on-New-Year's-Day-ass, beautiful blackness legitimized
Barack in a way he'd never be able to replicate if married
to a white woman.

3. Hear his name dropped by rappers, many of whom
   would shoehorn contrived analogies about "Osama" or
   "Botswana" or "*Gymkata*" or "a llama" into their verses
   just to find something to rhyme with Obama and possibly
   get invited on MSNBC.

4. Get excited when learning he did real nigga shit like
   smoke weed and play basketball, and have that excitement
   tempered when first seeing footage of Obama hooping
   with a T-shirt tucked into his sweatpants and the same
   Costco Force Ones on his feet rocked by referees,
   registered nurses, and Marge Simpson.

5. Pretend you'd "been on Obama for years" and chide
   everyone for "jumping on the Barry bandwagon when
   it was cool" like your perpetrating ass didn't first hear
   his name when your grandmama's backgammon partner
   asked you how to pronounce it.

What mattered more than his résumé and his studiousness
and his swag was the fact that this nigga had a chance. And not
a "chance" the way Jesse did in 1988. But a real actual chance
that enough of these white motherfuckers would treat him like
a white motherfucker for him to win. Which is all we wanted.
A nigga with a chance. Someone who might possibly maybe
potentially actually win. I could've, in all honesty, given two
fucks about his politics. Once I discovered he (A) was black
and (B) had a black-ass wife and (C) could win, then as long as
this nigga wasn't Strom Thurmond in beigeface, I didn't give a
damn what the hell he was talking about. Raising taxes on the
middle class? Fine! Just raising taxes on awkward Pittsburgh

niggas named Damon? Be my fucking guest. Take my money! Just beat these craven niggas in November.

Sometimes I'd wish that *I'd wish* I was less transparent about Obama. I gave no shits about how clearly and demonstratively I was in the tank for ol' boy. But I'd often feel guilty about not feeling any guilt whatsoever. Like shouldn't I give a damn that I don't give a damn? Shouldn't I feel the least bit bad about caring about nothing other than his blackness? Shouldn't I at least pretend to give a shit about his policies or what hope and change actually meant? And then, right when I'd begin to consider the possibility of giving a fuck about not giving a fuck, I'd watch Sarah "My Arms Are Too Short to Box with Science" Palin claim she could fart on her porch and they'd smell it in Moscow. And I'd remember that John McCain—who was supposed to be one of the *good* ones—chose her as his running mate as an equally transparent ploy to attract voters repelled for some mysterious reason by Obama, and the remaining hint of a fuck about not giving a hint of a fuck would dissolve.

This lack of shame derived from our collective and pervasive political chancelessness, from never knowing how it felt for *our guy* to win. And the fatigue I possessed from either rooting for the Washington Generals or being asked to support the least racist racist and hope they wouldn't be *racist*-racist when elected had congealed. I didn't just want Obama to win. I wanted them—racists, bigots, conservatives, Republicans, rednecks, nationalists, Michelle Malkin, white people with names starting with the letters *M* and *P* and *D* and *C* and *T*—to *lose*. I wanted them to know how it felt to be the team making the walk of shame to the postgame podium, where they'd be asked questions like "*So, when exactly during the game you just lost did you realize you were getting that ass beat?*" and "*What adjustments do you plan to make, since your team's pregame strategy of not fucking losing obviously didn't work?"* and *"Did you wait until you were alone in the shower to cry like a little bitch or did you let those tears fly on the bench?"* I wanted them to feel the sting of defeat; to be triggered and overcome with disgust and shame each time they were reminded of their loss. I wanted them to witness us celebrating, to have our shouts pierce their eardrums, our balloons pop in their faces, and our popped champagne corks smack their foreheads, puncture their skin, and induce allergic reactions. I wanted them, a year later, to still discover faded pieces of confetti that had unknowingly embedded themselves into their parkas the night their butts were whooped. I wanted them to feel hopeless, and that the election was a referendum on their values and personhoods. I wanted them to believe themselves to be irrelevant and anachronistic. And that they didn't belong and would never belong again. I wanted them to be shocked into a prolonged and paralyzing silence where they'd just stand in one place for, like, forty-five minutes while staring off into the nothing and pondering its vastness. I wanted those motherfuckers to be swallowed by the void, and to either doubt the existence of God or acknowledge this as His punishment for sins they hadn't yet committed. I wanted them to feel, for once, that the system wasn't just working against them, but that it was constructed specifically for that purpose. That each level of society was working in concert to ensure their subjugation. That their defeat wasn't evidence of a broken system but proof of its efficiency. I wanted remotes hurled at TVs, doors and drawers accidentally slammed on purple knuckles, toes jammed from kicked couches, and holes dug through punched walls. I wanted them to feel how Cleveland Browns fans always felt and how Qdoba must feel when Chipotle moves next door.

My memories of the night of November 4, 2008, begin when California was called for Obama, cementing his victory. I do not remember anything that happened that day before that moment. I do remember, however, that I was in my living room, watching CNN by myself. After calling Dad (who was at work) and Mom (who'd been in West Penn Hospital for a week dealing with a bout of chronic obstructive pulmonary disease), I spent the next two hours vacillating between phone conversations completely consisting of "OMFG!!! HE FUCKING WON!!! I CAN'T FUCKING BELIEVE IT!!! WHERE THE FUCK ARE MY REPARATIONS AND MY FREE KFC!!! I WANT ALL THE CRISPY CHICKEN AND POTATO WEDGES!!!" and scouring both TV and the Internet for all the Obama-related content I could find. Including, of course, Fox News for a satisfying stretch of masturbatory schadenfreude. I think I actually came when I saw Tucker Carlson's face, and I think I might be the only person who's ever said that.

I eventually stumbled upon a clip of some niggas in some club somewhere rapping the chorus to Young Jeezy's "My President." Which, of course, was my cue to open my living room window, lean my head out of it, and scream it down Ellsworth Avenue, raining the lyrics down on passersby, some of whom even joined with me.

> *My president is black, my Lambo's blue*
> *And I be goddamned if my rims ain't too*
> *My momma ain't at home and Daddy still in jail*
> *Tryna make a plate anybody seen the scale*

I'd never done anything that publicly demonstrative before. I felt—and probably looked—like some rando white boy on spring break in Cancun, lustily screaming "SHOW US YOUR TITS!" from a Comfort Inn balcony while rocking a sombrero and a sleeveless jean jacket. For the first time *ever*, I felt the wave of unbridled privilege and fucklessness and dominion that compels and encourages Connor Kegstand and Dustin Dude-bro to be the way they are. That perpetual sense of boundless possession, of never having to seriously entertain the concept of no, of never feeling unwelcome, that urges them to act as if consequences are a thought exercise and ramifications are a hypothesis, coursed through me as the reality of the blackness of the president-elect—*my* black-ass president-elect—permeated the atmosphere. For the first two hours following the election of Barack Obama, I knew how it felt to be a white American. And you couldn't tell my black ass nothin'. I even began to chant "OBAMA! BOMAYE! OBAMA! BOMAYE!" Which, in that context, made no fucking sense. I didn't want President Obama to kill anything, except for maybe the national debt and the prison-industrial complex. But Obama Bomaye just sounded so fucking cool and so fucking black that it felt like the proper way to revere what I was experiencing.

My nigger wake-up call—the term coined by Paul Mooney to encapsulate what happens when niggas forget they're black and are subsequently shocked back to reality—began to occur moments before Obama was scheduled to give his acceptance speech. My *the president is black and y'all niggas can't tell me shit*–induced high hadn't yet begun to subside, but I began to feel a hint of anxiety, a biliousness beginning to build in my gut. It increased as someone who I think was Wolf Blitzer but may not have been Wolf Blitzer but will just be Wolf Blitzer for the sake of this story remarked that the Obamas would be on-screen at any minute. And it crescendoed when they strode to the stage: tall, beautiful, presidential, and black as fuck with their impossibly cute and perfect replica daughters. All the whiteness I'd felt moments earlier and all the pride I felt in that moment were neutralized by worry, tension, and dread. As each history-making word left Barack's mouth, I pictured that same mouth ripped open by a bullet piercing through the back of his head. I'd glance at Michelle's rakish midnight-black-and-red dress and imagine it covered in Barack's blood while Secret Service agents rushed to her side. I envisioned the heartbroken pandemonium of the crowd and the stunned and devastated shock of Wolf Blitzer as he attempted to stay professional but just kept muttering, "Oh my God. Oh my God."

Often during Steelers or Pens games, I could hear my neighbors in my building and even in other buildings near the corner of Ellsworth and Negley yelp and shout when a touchdown or goal was scored, but now all I could think of were the wails I'd hear from the street when our black-ass president-elect was assassinated.

The bile that had formed in my stomach began to bubble and creep up through my esophagus. The thought of the president being murdered—of this moment, this victory, this life getting snatched away from us—consumed me, and during his speech I began to mumble the same chant after each passage:

*"It's the answer that led those who have been told for so long by so many to be cynical, and fearful, and doubtful of what we can achieve to put their hands on the arc of history and bend it once more toward the hope of a better day."*

Intheeachgitoffdauckinage

*"I was never the likeliest candidate for this office. We didn't start with much money or many endorsements. Our campaign was not hatched in the halls of Washington—it began in the backyards of Des Moines and the living rooms of Concord and the front porches of Charleston."*

Intheeachgitoffdauckinage!

*"The road ahead will be long. Our climb will be steep. We may not get there in one year or even one term, but America—I have never been more hopeful than I am tonight that we will get there. I promise you—we as a people will get there."*

Intheeachgitoffdauckinage!!!

*"America, we have come so far. We have seen so much. But there is so much more to do. So tonight, let us ask ourselves—if our children should live to see the next century; if my daughters should be so lucky to live as long as Ann Nixon Cooper, what change will they see? What progress will we have made?"*

INTHEEACHGITOFFDAUCKINAGE!!!

What I was actually saying—well, mumbling at first, until I was *screaming* at the TV by the end of his speech—was *End the speech. Get off the fucking stage.* Fortunately, President Obama didn't heed my commands and chose to complete his speech instead of doing what I wanted him to do, which would have been to come onstage, say, *"Thanks for this"* and then immediately be whisked away to some subterranean bunker with eighteen feet of reinforced titanium on each wall, where the Obamas would live for the duration of his presidency.

This dread persisted for Obama's entire first year in office, with an ebb and flow. It'd be near nonexistent when he wasn't on live TV. But whenever he had a nationally televised first (his inauguration address, his first State of the Union, etc.), I'd become possessed again with the thought of someone taking this very public opportunity to end his life. It became such a neurosis that I'd refuse to watch any of these events alone, choosing to attend watch parties not to collectively consume and celebrate our president but because I'd somehow convinced myself that the company could serve as some sort of telepathic force field. If enough of us banded together in one place, our psychic energies would be enough to counteract and possibly neutralize whatever threats he'd encounter.

I still haven't forgiven the asshole who spoiled *The Matrix Revolutions* for me during a conversation about fucking corn dogs by matter-of-factly mentioning that Trinity dies, so I hope you'll forgive me for spoiling the President Obama story by admitting that he wasn't actually assassinated in office. My anxieties, acid reflux, and bubble guts were for naught. We *won*. He beat their fucking asses. Twice. And all the things I wished would happen to them—the agony and the shame of losing to him; of waking up each morning in a country led by a mild-mannered redbone with a nappy black wife and kids named after Kwanzaa figurines—did actually happen. (Which is also how the world's rapiest vat of Cheez Whiz somehow managed to become the next president.)

But I felt cheated out of this comeuppance, because I didn't actually want them to feel as bad as I thought I wanted them to feel. This change of heart wasn't due to an actual change of heart. I still wanted those motherfuckers to feel like shit. But the fervor of the moments leading up to the election and the ecstasy of election night temporarily sequestered me from a reality that, unless there was some sort of Caucasoid Rapture, would remain true for as long as I remained an American citizen. White people were still *everywhere*. And still controlled everything.

As much as I felt like one of them when "My president is black!" screamed out of my lungs and through each Shadyside intersection, that privilege and fucklessness and dominion were a mirage. I was reminded of the danger of entertaining that delusion when my black-ass president appeared on my screen and the only thought I could muster was *Please don't let these motherfuckers kill him*. I still itched to receive satisfaction from their anguish. I just didn't want them to feel *so* devastated and defeated that this conspicuously negro affront to their violent fucking whiteness would compel one to assassinate him. So I wanted them to kinda, sorta feel these feelings. But only for like an hour. Or at least until the Obamas made it back to their core-of-the-earth bunker. My president was black. But for my sanity's sake, I wanted him to be invisible.

In the year following Donald Trump's election, there were calls for the Obamas to return to public office. And by *there were calls for the Obamas to return to public office* I mean *niggas begged them to come back and save us from that motherfucker*. I felt some of this desire for them to return too. Especially in early 2017, when it seemed like we'd see a different picture of the Obamas vacationing or brunching or surfing or judging slam dunk contests each day. But then I remembered election night. And how the stress I felt in Pittsburgh, 460 miles from Grant Park in Chicago, where Obama gave his acceptance speech, must've paled in comparison to the stress *they* felt that night and for the next eight years, as they were under the international spotlight as both the most famous family on earth and the most disrespected family to live in the White House maybe ever.

That in mind, I want them to get (and stay!) as far away from us as possible. They already gave us enough. I want them to deep-sea dive and spelunk; to parasail and learn to practice kundalini yoga; to spend an entire year milking cows in Aruba and eating fistfuls of Frosted Flakes straight from the box; to binge-watch *Atlanta* and barbecue butt-ass naked. The paparazzi photos and Instagram updates of them doing exactly that are nice, but I don't even want that. Fuck a postcard, I don't want to know where they are. I don't even want *them* to know where they are, because they're too gone off the genetically engineered molly Barack has access to and they're finally allowed to take to give a damn.

I want to feel like Ben Affleck at the end of *Good Will Hunting*. I want to pull up to the Obamas' driveway, climb the steps, and knock on the door, and I want no one to answer. I want to peek through the window and see tumbleweeds and hangers and maybe a discarded package of Swisher Sweets. And I want to know that they got the fuck out and away from us and didn't bother leaving a note.

# 9

# BROKE

Wilbur and Vivienne Young raised me to be a Christian, but I wouldn't necessarily say that we were *practicing* Christians. I mean, we were Christians, technically, and they both grew up as regular Baptist churchgoers like most other decent and respectable black folks in the fifties and sixties. But Christianity in the Young household felt like more of a benevolent and perfunctory guide for proper Jesus-living than any sort of concretized edict. Like perhaps Jesus had given us the keys to His condo while He spent a weekend in Myrtle Beach, and just hoped we didn't set His kitchen on fire. Christianity was a reasonably priced Airbnb.

I was taught to pray before every meal—a ritual I still follow today. (The efficient and immature "Jesus wept. Amen," was my go-to food prayer until I graduated from Canisius, and switched to "Lord, thank you for this food that we are about to receive, through thy bounty through Christ our Lord, Amen," which I hoped was appropriately pious enough to convince bougie black girls they could introduce me to their aunts.) The Lord's name was never to be said in vain. And there were Bibles around, somewhere. Not a swarm of Bibles, but just maybe two Bibles, which were mostly used to store birth certificates. But we never actually went to church ourselves. The only time I went was for funerals and weddings and if I happened to be spending the night at Brian's house or one of my grandparents' houses. (Also, I'd attend Mass at St. Barts on holy days and holidays and Wednesdays and Kennywood days and whenever they decided it was Mass-attending time there.)

We did, however, worship at the church of Kool-Aid, and our devotion was fanatical. If you were to randomly peek into our refrigerator at any point, searching for something to drink, you'd likely find orange juice and you'd probably find milk, but you'd definitely find a half-gallon container of Kool-Aid, made with a sugar-to-granular-Kool-Aid-powder ratio of 18:1. We used so much sugar that you could plant a serving spoon in the bottom of the pitcher and it would stick straight up, and you'd need the force of five Thors to pull that nigga out. If there was no Kool-Aid in the fridge, it was because it was currently being made. And if it wasn't currently being made, there was definitely a conversation happening somewhere about who drank the last of the Kool-Aid because that person was slacking on their Kool-Aid replenishing duties and needed to step the fuck up. "Who drank the last of the Kool-Aid?" was both the most asked question in the Young household and a threat.

We were so zealous that I can tell you which flavors go best with certain types of meats. For steaks and burgers and other types of heavier beef, grape is the best choice. If you're eating seafood—such as Mom's fried whiting, which I used to split in half, lather with ketchup, and make Giant Eagle white bread sandwiches with—orange Kool-Aid works best. And if you're eating fried chicken (the blackest entrée), you'll need a glass of red Kool-Aid (the blackest nonalcoholic beverage) to best wash that bitch down.

My Kool-Aid fever stretched into adulthood. Because I loved and was addicted to the way it tastes. But also because it's cheap as fuck. You can cop 29,000 packets of it for a nickel. Not only did I buy the perfunctory grapes and oranges and reds, I also bought the slightly off-brand flavors like red cherry and raspberry and the shit they clearly only sold as an experiment to see if niggas would buy it, like bacon-blueberry and pistachio. In my first apartment, the only things you'd always find in my fridge were bacon, eggs, creamy Caesar salad dressing, orange juice, and Kool-Aid.

And then one day, in the fall of 2008, everything changed.

In my apartment were Jessica and Marguerite, two women I'd known, at that point, for a little over a week. I'd invited them over to watch one of Barack Obama's debates against John Mc-Cain. Which was actually a ruse for me to eventually, during a commercial break, play a VHS tape of me in high school dunking a basketball because Jessica didn't believe that I could. Soon after they arrived, I asked if they wanted something to drink. Marguerite asked what I had in my fridge. I told her Kool-Aid. She scoffed:

"Nigga, you still drinking Kool-Aid?"

As we've discussed, and as skilled *nigga* users know, *nigga* is not a word that you use haphazardly with black people you just met. It's a term of familiarity—not something you say when answering an innocent question from a nigga you've known for a week. But that *nigga* used by Marguerite articulated exactly how disappointed she was that I was drinking Kool-Aid, *and* how annoyed she was that I had the audacity to offer it to her. Basically, I was Kool-Aid shamed.

So I lied. "Sometimes."

Sensing the tension and attempting to provide me an out, Jessica then asked if I had any bottled water. I didn't, because of course I didn't. There is literally *zero* overlap between "niggas who drink five gallons of magenta sugar water per day" and "niggas who keep cases of lukewarm Dasani in their cabinets." After realizing her homegirl had convinced her to spend an evening in a Kool-Aid-chugging nigga's tiny apartment, Marguerite sighed at Jessica, rolled her eyes, and sat on my couch.

By the end of that year, Marguerite's Kool-Aid shaming had worked. I was so embarrassed by her vehement disgust that I gradually weaned myself off the habit. Within two years, it was no longer a part of my daily consumption. I stopped buying it and would only drink it when I visited my parents.

The series of events that led to Jessica and Marguerite in my apartment that night and my consequent Kool-Aid detoxification began in October of 2007, eleven months into my job at the McKeesport YMCA. I was scheduled to meet with our executive director (Mr. Jason) and a human resources representative from the downtown Pittsburgh YMCA mothership to discuss some "imminent changes within our organizational structure." I assumed that this would be when they'd inform me that my position had been eliminated, and my assumptions were proven to be correct. Our Y was hemorrhaging money; the only consistent source of revenue was a rapidly dwindling and rapidly aging membership base who'd come to the Y five days a week to argue about Luke Ravenstahl and durable toilet paper. It also needed extensive equipment upgrades and some sort of building-wide atomic fumigation to combat the Jurassic cockroaches who'd occasionally pop up to remind us they worked there too. I think I even saw one complete a timesheet once. So nonessential positions were to be consolidated or phased out, and my $26,000-a-year job—where I spent (at least) two hours every day in my office scouring the Internet for Frou Frou and Massive Attack tracks to autoplay on my Myspace page—was the very definition of nonessential. To quote early-twenty-first-century poet/Ultimate Wine Flute Fighting Champion Evelyn Lozada, I was a non-motherfuckin'-factor.

Jason and I had become friendly during my time there, so when I entered his office to face the guillotine he looked like he'd just received an order to literally chop my head off. "Damon, I have some news for you," he said with the weight of a fucking sperm whale. Which I recognized as him genuinely feeling bad and exaggerating his misery to communicate to me how hard this was for him. I appreciated the effort and couldn't stand to see him in such conspicuous agony much longer, so I preempted his pity party with some news of my own. A month earlier, I'd applied for an open site coordinator position for Duquesne University's Career Literacy for African American Youth (CLAAY) program. Two interviews had followed, and the day before my meeting with Jason, I'd learned I'd been hired. I was to start at the end of the month. Jason looked both elated for me and somewhat disappointed he wouldn't have the opportunity to follow through with the script he'd surely practiced to himself in his driver's-side visor mirror that morning. I almost felt bad enough to offer him a hug.

The move to CLAAY was a substantial upgrade. The jump in pay, from $26,000 to $36,000, was tremendous (for me); enough to finally buy a car and some necessary forks. (I only owned one.) Duquesne's campus was a seventeen-minute drive in rush hour traffic from my apartment, a welcome contrast to the fifty-minute-and-two-bus-ride-long commute to McKeesport. The perks of being a Duquesne employee were immeasurable.

(These niggas even had their own credit union!) And I wasn't exactly heartbroken over ditching my current roach- and angry-octogenarian-infested work environment for an office on a college campus.

Most importantly, the work—connecting volunteer mentors (grad students, doctors, lawyers, retirees, etc.) with high school students to help them create a feasible path to postsecondary education, and facilitating the hour each week that the mentors would meet with the students at their respective schools—was legitimately interesting, fun, and important-*feeling*. I'm still not quite sure if it was actually important, but I know I felt like King Shit of Philanthropy Fuck Mountain while doing it. Site coordinators were also required to help recruit the mentors, which meant a generous portion of my job comprised me sharing coffee at Borders, Starbucks, and Crazy Mocha with grad students, recent Pittsburgh transplants, and young professionals who'd heard about what we did and wanted to "give back to the community" and "make a difference." Since women are somewhere between 80 and 192,000 percent better people than men are, most of these interviews were with women. One of these women, a neuroscience PhD candidate at Pitt named Jessica, was my neighbor. She lived on Ellsworth and Ivy: a thirty-second walk from where I lived. Despite the closeness of our addresses and us existing as the only two black people under sixty on that block, the interview was the first time we'd ever seen each other. We only discovered we were neighbors after I asked which part of the city she lived in.

After the interview, we added each other on Facebook, and made plans to "hang out or something sometime." A week later, she invited me to her apartment for Boston Market rotisserie chicken breasts and exactly one bottle of refrigerator-chilled Trader Joe's strawberry lemonade. I remember it was exactly one bottle of refrigerator-chilled Trader Joe's strawberry lemonade because when we finished it, I asked if she had any more, and she said, "Yes, but it's in a cupboard, so it's lukewarm." Which, as I discovered months later when she remembered this story while hosting a Spades party, was her attempt at dissuading me from drinking the last of her lemonade, assuming I'd pass on consuming the eighty-degree bottle. She was wrong. I am a human garbage disposal.

We repeated this hangout contrivance—one of us provides food and the other assists with eating it—three or four more times. And on the third or fourth hangout, we followed the food with the worst sex I'd had since 1997, which also happens to be the year I first had sex. The shittiness of the sex was entirely my fault. A collection of anxieties about my performance, derived from an obsession with inducing multiple orgasms, left me unable to maintain a full erection. Which meant the condom loafed on my *maybe*-almost-as-hard-as-a-microwaved-banana dick like lazy spandex on a tube of Jell-O. Which meant I kept slipping out of her. Which meant I grew even more self-conscious. Which made me even softer. Which gave my dick the consistency of a bowl of Campbell's clam chowder left on the kitchen counter for, like, a day. Which I still attempted to place into her still (!!!) somehow patient vagina. Which was like shoving three scoops of soft-serve chocolate ice cream into an open bottle of Aquafina. My fingers helped, I guess, the same way an umbrella might help when kayaking. But after an hour of attempting to reenact the saddest Penthouse Letter ever, we gave up and watched *Lost*.

Fortunately, this wasn't enough for her to delete my number, unfriend me on Facebook, quit CLAAY, and Molotov-cocktail my apartment. Jessica and I continued to see and sleep with each other for the next couple of months, and eventually found ourselves in an exclusive relationship, which was my first since Teresa.

During this time, I was also introduced to her collective of friends—a dozen or so twenty-two-to-twenty-eight-year-old niggas who'd recently moved to Pittsburgh; there either to get an MBA or PhD from Pitt or CMU or because of some high-paying gig that brought them there. They called themselves the PhDeez.

Of the crew, I grew closest to Camille, a twenty-five-year-old CMU MBA who (A) was shacked up with Rondell (an engineer) and (B) was the first woman I personally knew with her own luxury sports car (an Infiniti G35 coupe), and Marguerite, a twenty-six-year-old Spelmanite from San Diego who was also in Jessica's PhD program and was the de facto alpha of the PhDeez.

I knew niggas like this existed. I'd see them in the McDonald's spots that'd run during BET awards shows and NBA games, and I'd wonder where Mickey D's would find these jolly niggas with perfect teeth and *my credit's as bomb as my pussy* bone structure sharing Filet-O-Fish and orange drink in late-model Land Rovers while singing along to some Jennifer Hudson song. I also knew that certain parts of the country bred and cultivated black people like this. You'd find them in Atlanta and Houston; in Harlem and D.C.; in Chicago and Philadelphia; in Dallas and Columbus, Ohio. Basically anywhere with a robust black middle class and/or a nearby HBCU existing as that city's black professional feeder system. But knowing they exist and reading about them in *Ebony* and *Jet* wasn't the same as playing flag football with a bunch of niggas younger than you whose résumés and lists of accomplishments and earning potentials dwarfed yours. And I wasn't a fucking slouch! I was twenty-nine when I met them, and I had a decent job at a university. A college degree. An apartment with a private parking lot and white neighbors. A truck. No STDs or children (that I knew of). And I'd always have really nice haircuts. I was Pittsburgh Young, Black, and Successful. Pittsburgh Young, Black, and Successful meant Friday evenings downstairs at Savoy in the Strip District, and perhaps a table upstairs if it was your birthday. It meant Alpha and Que boat rides, NEED Scholarship dinners, and Ronald H. Brown Leadership Awards galas. It meant a stint on the Urban League Young Professionals executive board. It meant brunches at the LeMont on Mother's Day and the Grand Concourse when you wanted to stunt. It meant frequent pictures in the *Post-Gazette* and the *City Paper* and on the First Friday Facebook page. It meant 40 Under 40 recognition from the *Courier* if niggas knew who you were, and 40 Under 40 recognition from *Pittsburgh Magazine* if white people did too.

For the PhDeez, however, Pittsburgh was just a stopgap. A temporary conduit on their roads to world domination. They didn't give a shit about being Pittsburgh Young, Black, and Successful because they'd lived in Atlanta and L.A. and Baltimore and Brooklyn—cities that actually matter to black people and have enough black people living there to convince us sometimes that they treat us like we matter too. They were here to get a degree and/or some money, and bounce as soon as that task was fulfilled without even bothering to collect their security deposits from their landlords. Because who gives a shit about a bougie Pittsburgh boat ride when you've summered in Singapore?

They all became my friends too. And we'd brunch and birthday BBQ and game night together. I even introduced them to the Burgh, sharing wing spots they hadn't yet discovered and Pittsburgh niggas they hadn't yet dismissed. But I always felt like a Mazda parked in a lot full of Maseratis. A Mazda that hadn't even seen a Maserati in person until a car hauler full of Maseratis pulled up next to him and asked for directions to Squirrel Hill.

Jessica and I had a genuinely good and fun relationship. She was outdoorsy and attempted to break me out of my urban housecat shell. The very first picture of me that she posted on her Facebook page was a shot of my back and my straining neck muscles as I was attempting and failing to scale a wall at an indoor rock climbing spot in Point Breeze. (Underneath the picture, Camille commented, "Why does it look like he's holding on for dear life? He's three feet off the ground!") She was from Boston and an avid sports fan, and if the Steelers would lose and Ben Roethlisberger would fuck up somehow, she'd taunt, "Well . . . they can't all be Tom Brady." She'd always make the trek out to the Penn Hills YMCA with me to the men's basketball league I was in, but got tired of being the only person in the bleachers—9 P.M. Wednesday night games at suburban YMCAs ain't exactly a *Hamilton*-level draw—and started inviting Marguerite with her. I'd return the favor and would get up at the asscrack of dawn to cheer her on in 5Ks and half marathons. When the crew would gather to play flag football, I'd usually be a quarterback and one of the captains, and she was such a great athlete that I always picked her first and *still* would've even if I weren't contractually obligated to as her boyfriend. Despite all of this, I couldn't shake the feeling that I was her Pittsburgh stopgap too.

This was not her fault. She came from money. Her mom and stepdad lived in Maryland, and their finished basement was the size of my parents' entire house (yard included). The first time we visited them, after Jessica and I had been together for six months, I was awestruck by how many conversations her parents had that revolved around money. Not in an obnoxious way. They were very kind and sweet people, and they seemed to want to make as good of an impression on me as I hoped I would on them. But they'd have these discussions about interest rates and investment properties and the motherfucking Dow Jones that I knew people had but just never heard in person before. They watched CNBC the way I watched ESPN. When Jessica's stepdad asked what my parents did for a living, I replied, "Oh, my dad is in sales and my mom is in health care"—my way to replicate the manner in which I believed people with money and parents with *careers* and not *jobs* talked to each other.

Still, Jessica never acted too good to be with a working-class Pittsburgh nigga. Perhaps because she wasn't as accustomed to money as I thought she was. Her neuroscience PhD work was centered on the science of addiction, which fascinated and frightened her because of how crack had damaged her family. She was terrified that she might possess the same traits that had allowed so many of her cousins and aunts and uncles to suc-cumb to drugs, and she wished to learn as much about addiction as she could to prevent that from happening to her and other families. And while her mom and stepdad were doing well, these were not people with generational wealth. They were those special perfect lucky niggas for whom a series of right de-cisions (perfection) and a two-decade-long tsunamiless stretch (luck) enabled them to climb out of the working class and make pit stops at middle and upper middle before settling into the 1 percent. I learned all of this over the first eighteen months Jes-sica and I were together. But the bougie first impression was so strong—and my anxieties about my limited financial ceiling so pressing—that I suspected, despite all evidence to the contrary, that she was slumming.

After twelve months at CLAAY, I was called into the office of our director, Kim, who told me I'd be receiving a $2,000 raise, to $38,000. Forty thousand dollars at twenty-nine in 2008 was Pittsburgh Nigga Rich. I was $2K away from Pittsburgh Nigga Rich! Jessica and I celebrated my Pittsburgh Nigga Rich adjacence with buttermilk pancakes, applewood bacon, and frozen mimosas that Sunday at the Harris Grill on Ellsworth. Four months after this meeting, I was called to another meeting with Kim, but in the third floor conference room at Fisher Hall instead of her office. The dean of Duquesne's school of business and three of my colleagues were also there. A year and a half after jumping to CLAAY, I once again had the experience of learning that my job would be eliminated. We no longer had enough in our budget to continue and CLAAY would cease operations at the end of the month.

This wasn't a shock. Although we were Duquesne employees, most of our budget came from grants and foundations such as the United Way and the Heinz Endowments, and the recession made those already tenuous dollars even less reliable. By the summer of 2009, we barely had enough to print and distribute the annual report I'd spent the entire spring collecting data for and editing. I knew CLAAY wasn't built to last. Still, I was tired of jumping from soon-to-be-eliminated job to soon-to-be-eliminated job, like a frog anxiously hopping from one sinking lily pad to another. I had a special talent for applying for and receiving shit that wouldn't exist in a year. A gift for deferred irrelevance.

I pursued a few similar positions at Duquesne, Pitt, and Point Park and even landed a couple of interviews, but none panned out. The recession meant that the only Pittsburgh niggas with solid job prospects were Steelers and morticians. As each jobless month passed, my delusions of Pittsburgh Nigga grandeur slowly dissolved into a puddle of brokeness. First came the nonessentials: Brunches were cut from thrice a month to maybe once. Haircuts from biweekly to bimonthly. The

American Apparel two-toned spandex minidresses I'd occasionally surprise Jessica with before parties cut to "maybe if it's her birthday or something." Then came the bills. The recession-specific extended unemployment benefits were enough to cover my rent, my car payments, and all the grape Kool-Aid packets I desired. Cable, though? Gone. Internet? Gone. Health insurance? Gone. Car insurance? Gone. Inspections and emissions tests? Ha! Regular oil changes? Are you shitting me? On the bright side, after a year of driving with expired registration stickers, I mastered the art of cop car evasion, an immeasurably valuable skill for a black man. I was fine, I surmised, as long as I didn't allow one to get directly behind me. So even when alone on the street, I'd scout for right turns I could quickly make and parking spots I could immediately slide into if they happened to appear. Winters were great, because strategically placed snow was a crucial obscuring agent. I was the only nigga in Pittsburgh who wished for blizzards so I could *relax* while driving.

This gradual dissolution was exacerbated by the soon-to-be-upper-middle-class niggas partnering with me at Spades tournaments, dancing with me at First Friday, riding with me to Eat'n Park, and sleeping with me in my bed. We'd share bowls of guacamole and bottles of Honey Jack, and I'd listen to their plans for their post-escape-from-Pittsburgh lives—the six-figure job offers they'd already received, the 1,600-square-foot lofts they planned to lease, the BMWs and Audis they'd cop with their first checks, the vibrant and vital cities they planned to move to—while I remained possessed and paralyzed by thoughts about whether I'd paid the past due balance on my electric bill in time. And whether Duquesne Light had posted one of those multipage shutoff notices on the entry door of my building while I was out. And how hard it was to scrape that scotch tape off the door. I'd think about that Cam'ron line from

"Losin' Weight" ("*Can't get paid in a earth this big? You worthless, kid / Niggas don't deserve to live.*") And I'd wonder what the fuck happened to me. How the fuck did I end up a broke thirty-year-old nigga? A fucking scrub? What was wrong with my wiring? Why couldn't I just fucking *be*?

The only saving grace was that, since most of the PhDeez were in grad school, there weren't many financial distinctions between their day-to-days and mine. We all placed somewhere on the broke spectrum. We'd all get to parties at the Shadow Lounge and Ava disturbingly early to catch the free Long Island iced tea before 11 P.M. deals, we all had either roommates or roommate-ish romantic situationships, and we'd all regard a Costco membership card like it was one of Willy Wonka's golden tickets. When hanging out with them, I could convince myself this was just an extended version of college. They were the precocious and overachieving sophomores, and I was the seventh-year super senior. The only difference was that my brokeness was metaphysical too, written into my HTML with no foreseeable way to hack it out.

Also, I had Very Smart Brothas. I started blogging in 2002 as an extension of my bomb-ass-poetry-writing-ass-nigga phase in college. My cousin Sarah Huny Young—who, unbeknownst to me at the time, was already a big-ass Internet deal—offered to build me a website to archive my poems and introduced me to the concept of a blog. At first it began as something I'd update once or twice a month with stream-of-consciousness thoughts about dating, pop culture, and work. As one of the few men in the black blogosphere then, I started to develop a following, and began to update more regularly. In 2004 I met Panama Jackson, who lived in Washington, D.C., and was also a black male blogger. (I think there were seven of us then.) We were fans of each other's work and became friends. In 2008, while I was working at CLAAY, Panama and I and Liz Burr (a mutual friend) came together to start Very Smart Brothas (VSB)—which began as a platform for our tongue-in-cheek dating and relationship advice, to position ourselves as the hipper, wittier, and more progressive versions of Steve Harvey and the dozens of Harveyites dominating those conversations. Panama and I combined our respective followings and VSB grew in popularity each month. By the time I was laid off, we'd expanded our content to pop culture, politics, and race, and that growth continued. We grew from 1,000 unique visitors a day to 10,000. VSB was beginning to matter. And I could make my brokeness less conspicuous by telling people I'd made the conscious decision to "write for a living"—adding a shake of nobility and laudable self-determination to the reality that I'd only decided to write for a living because I got laid off and couldn't do shit else and couldn't get hired to do shit else and could use this stretch of unemployment benefits to temporarily subsidize my listicles about chicken wings and Kanye West. So, while the PhDeez were working on MBAs and actual PhDs, I was "working" on my blog, and using it to distract them and everyone else from the irrepressible shame emanating from me.

After a year of unemployment, I even had a consistent daily work schedule.

8:30 A.M.: Wake up in Jessica's bed. We always stayed at her place because her apartment was nicer than mine. She had hardwood floors, cable, and Wi-Fi. And no pesky landlords rattling her door at 7:45 to interrogate her about a bounced rent check.

That she even stayed in a relationship with me during this stretch should've deadened any anxieties I had about her possibly slumming. It didn't, but it should have. I also believe that the collective but temporary brokeness of the rest of the PhDeez affected her feelings about my situation. My particular brokeness wasn't as notable then, and thus was easier to ignore. If we'd been dating four years later, after Jessica and the rest of her friends had all graduated and secured six-figure gigs, this wouldn't have worked. Even if it still worked on her end, I would've done something to sabotage it. The differences between me and them would have been too stark for me to handle.

8:45 A.M.: Go home to shower, eat breakfast, and change clothes. If we didn't have sex that morning, masturbate while looking at porn clips downloaded on the old MacBook Jessica gave me when she bought a new one.

(Also, just to be clear, the masturbation happened *before* the shower and the change of clothes, not after. I am not an animal.)

11:30 A.M. to 6 P.M.: Walk to Crazy Mocha on Ellsworth Avenue. Write a piece or two for VSB and perhaps my relationship advice column at MadameNoire. Also, edit and curate old VSB pieces for a self-published relationship-advice book Panama and I had talked about creating for years but I finally had the time now to address.

To broadcast to everyone within earshot that I was WORKING ON AN IMPORTANT WRITERLY BOOK BECAUSE I'M A PROFESSIONAL WRITER WHO WRITES FOR A LIVING, I'd bring a dog-eared copy of Chuck Klosterman's *Sex, Drugs, and Cocoa Puffs* with me, and I'd set it on the table next to my laptop. Every half hour or so I'd open it up, read it, nod my head in performative epiphany, and then type furiously. In hindsight, while I meant to communicate that I was WORKING ON AN IMPORTANT WRITERLY BOOK BECAUSE I'M A WRITER and using Klosterman's as a guide for how to structure chapters, I think I just looked like I was plagiarizing.

6 P.M.: Go back home again, take a ninety-second ho bath in my bathroom sink, change into workout clothes, and either

play basketball at Central Catholic's open gym or use one of the dozens of free three-day membership passes a friend who worked at LA Fitness hooked me up with.

9 P.M.: Link back up with Jessica and have a late dinner at her place. She'd tell me about her day—the way her monkeys were reacting to the experiments, the neuroscience conference in San Antonio in October she was preparing for, the new house her parents just closed on in Silver Spring—and I'd tell her about some treatise on Arby's curly fries I'd written for VSB that got six hundred comments and a retweet from someone who maybe used to work for *Salon*.

"So you had a good day too?" she'd ask. And I'd remember that my good day standard had become so low that a Twitter like from Someone in Media Who Might Have Mattered at Some Point was all it took for a day to qualify as good. A like *and* a retweet? That was a holiday. My goddamn birthday.

To celebrate, we'd drink an eleven-dollar bottle of South African moscato, watch *Basketball Wives*, and debate who was the Evelyn of the PhDeez. We'd be in bed by midnight, and I'd wait until she was asleep to climb back out of her bed, go into her living room, crack open the laptop she'd given me, and browse xHamster for an hour while her two cats, Utz and Mr. Peepers, sat next to me. And then I'd be ready for that great fucking day to finally end.

# 10

# HOW TO MAKE THE INTERNET HATE YOU IN 15 SIMPLE STEPS

1. As your blog (VSB) grows in audience and relevance, use this as an opportunity to have it completely subsume you, piggybacking off of its burgeoning status to stem the shame of your unemployment. Print T-shirts with either VSB's logo or *Very Smart Brothas* written on them and wear them *everywhere*. Reggae nights at Ava Lounge, family reunions in New Castle, Gateway Clipper boat rides, Kennywood, Sneaker Villa, Coffee Tree, airports, church . . . it doesn't matter. And do this so that you're not just recognized as you from VSB, you're synonymous with it. There's no you apart from VSB, and no VSB apart from you.

2. During a nearly two-year stretch of unemployment—
from July 2009 to April 2011—spend much of 2010
compiling, compressing, and editing approximately fifty
different VSB pieces to create a book. Title this book *Your
Degrees Won't Keep You Warm at Night: The Very Smart
Brothas' Guide to Dating, Mating, and Fighting Crime*,
print and publish it through Amazon's CreateSpace, and
release it on January 31, 2011. Watch the book's existence
give VSB (and you specifically) a leap in relevance and
attention, as having a book—even a self-published
one—adds some sort of metaphysical legitimacy to your
work. Begin to get book-related mentions and profiles in
national publications.

   (Also, at the book launch/VSB three-year anniversary
party in Washington, D.C., in March, meet Panama in
person for the very first time.)

3. In April, get invited to a meeting at the August Wilson
Center for African American Culture (AWC) with several
prominent Pittsburgh writers to brainstorm on a digital
magazine to be launched by the AWC that fall. Volunteer
to lead it because, three days before the meeting, a friend
who worked at the AWC told you that whoever signs
on as the editor in chief will receive a $3,000 monthly
stipend starting in May.

   Have this decision become especially fortuitous
because your unemployment benefits—which you had no
plans of giving up (the $3,000 a month *plus* benefits would
have placed you squarely in Pittsburgh Nigga Richness)—
run out that month too.

4. With your newfound wealth, rent a town house with your
girlfriend, finish paying off your Mercury Mountaineer,
and trade that in for a bone-white 2011 Dodge Charger, a

car which (1) could be accurately categorized as the Peak
Nigga Purchase and (2) you're only able to buy because
your mom cosigns on the loan—which makes the Peak
Nigga peak even sharper.

5. In October, during a conversation with your soon-to-
be-graduating-and-getting-the-fuck-out-of-Pittsburgh
girlfriend about the future of your relationship, suggest
that she should make whichever post-PhD plans she has
to make without you in mind—a pseudo-considerate offer
filled to the brim with skanky fuckboy that effectively
ends your three-year-long relationship and complicates
the fuck out of cohabitation. Tell yourself that you're
doing this because you just never quite got over the
economic insecurity you felt when comparing her and her
family's financial status to your own, and you didn't see
an extended future between you two. Don't tell yourself
that you're also breaking up because you want to be single
more than you want to be in a relationship, because this is
the first time you've been able to live the life you've been
wanting to live since you were twenty-one. You finally
have a driver's license and a Peak Nigga car. A name and
a following and fans. A cool gig and enough income to
live on your own. You'd been single before, but you were
never single with any sort of the flexibility and status you
associated with singledom, and you wanted to see how
that felt.

6. Get invited by *Essence* magazine to New York City for
a photo shoot and magazine feature on relationship
bloggers. While in Manhattan and walking to *Essence*'s
building, literally run right into Jamilah Lemieux and
Geneva Thomas—two writers you've met before—who
ask why you're in town, chide you for not wearing a coat

during this seasonably and predictably chilly fall day,
and share that they were recently hired by *Ebony*. *And*
also that they've just left a meeting where your name was
mentioned.

Call Jamilah later that night when you're done with
the *Essence* shoot and learn that *Ebony*'s interested
in hiring you as well. When she asks if this interest
is reciprocal, pretend to have a thought in your
head other than *OH HELL THE FUCK YEAH I'M
FUCKING INTERESTED IN WORKING FOR
MOTHERFUCKING* EBONY *MAGAZINE* and tell her
you'll get back to her.

7. Accept the *Ebony* gig, where you'll be required to write
a couple of pieces a week and edit the breaking news
section. Marvel at how, in less than a year, you've gone
from an unemployed scrub with a bottomless cadre
of Spreadshirt-printed VSB paraphernalia and an
aggressively illegal truck that would shake and stutter
and Dutty Wine whenever you'd pass thirty-two on the
speedometer to a professional fucking writer working
for fucking *Ebony* magazine and launching a magazine
at a multimillion-dollar African arts center named after
Pittsburgh's most iconic writer *and* the founder of a
popular and increasingly lauded blog *and* an author of a
book *and* driving a fucking Charger. Which, although it's
the base-model Charger—your cousin Michael jokes that
it has a minivan engine—allows you to speed from Crazy
Mocha and Coffee Tree to Trader Joe's and Panera Bread
like Dominic Toretto.

8. Begin looking for a new place and have this search for
a new place complicated by not receiving your monthly
check from the AWC.

**9.** Learn in late November that the AWC ran out of money,
which means the magazine project is a wrap and your
$3,000 a month is gone. Since the *Ebony* gig doesn't start
until January (and you won't get paid until the last week
of January at earliest), you'll have no income for two
months. Lament that this is the third fucking time in four
years that this has happened to you. Begin to believe you
might be cursed and that something keeps tripping you
up and holding you back each time it seems like you're
set to make some sort of permanent leap into adulthood.
But continue driving around and being seen in your
car to give everyone the impression that you're doing
much better than you actually are. Basically, do what
you've always done, the thing you do better than you do
anything else: pretend.

**10.** Move back in with your parents, keeping some essentials
and putting the rest of your shit in the same storage
facility your parents used when they were homeless in
2001. And do this a week before their house in Penn Hills
is foreclosed on. Something you had no idea was going to
happen until the day before they had to leave.

**11.** During an ice storm (and with two Penn Hills sheriffs
parked outside the house to make sure you get the fuck
out) help move all of your parents' belongings from
their three-bedroom ranch to a considerably smaller
two-bedroom rental a quarter mile away. And vacillate
between mediating, witnessing, and instigating explosive
arguments your parents have with each other during
this move. Since your dad is currently unemployed (the
recession swallowed his job in 2010), and your mom's
COPD requires her to sometimes carry an oxygen tank,
presume (wrongly and unfairly) that his unemployment

is why this shit is happening, and take your mom's side at every opportunity. Seethe the same way you seethed on Papa's Barcalounger when it was your bed for two weeks in 2001.

12. Start the *Ebony* gig, which requires you to be up at 7:30 A.M. to write, edit, and publish breaking news stories. Since your parents' new house doesn't have cable or Wi-Fi yet, get up at 6:45 every morning to drive five miles to a Starbucks in Monroeville to work. Believe that doing this—getting up early to go to work—gives you some sort of transcendental canonization. Like you doing what every other nigga with a job does every day makes you specifically committed to writing—to being a WRITER—and deserving of laudatory fellatio. Believe that niggas need to recognize how committed and invested slaving away each morning in a fucking Starbucks while eating a snickerdoodle makes you.

13. Later that month, and inspired by the success of *Shit Girls Say* (the viral web series created by Kyle Humphrey and Graydon Sheppard and featuring a man in drag spouting phrases *white* women are stereotypically prone to say), write a piece on "Shit Bougie Black Girls Say," using the PhDeez crew as your bougie cheat sheets. Have it receive 35,000 unique visitors in twenty-four hours, a VSB traffic record at the time.

Three days later, ask the homies JRuss and Emmai Alaquiva to help you create a video based on the piece. Have JRuss don a blond wig with the tag still on it and feed him lines to read while Emmai records. Upload it to YouTube, and watch it receive 850,000 views.

14. Begin to believe you're the Black Blog King Kong. That your words are unassailable and exquisite; your thoughts

and opinions sanctified and eternally righteous; your freedom to share them—regardless of topic or tone— indubitable and concrete. Allow your twenty-seven consecutive weeks of moderate successes to unlock your dormant Diva Dude; an irrepressible hubris you now finally have the platforms and external validation to unleash. Be the nigga who believes his shit smells like Nabisco factories and Carol's Daughter Cactus Rose Water.

15. And then, read "Stop Telling Women How to Not Get Raped"—an *Ebony* piece from Zerlina Maxwell, a woman you've become friendly with over the past year. And decide, on a reckless, illogical, and triflin'-as-fuck fucking whim, to pen a response to Zerlina's piece with the same flippancy and impudence you'd apply to a debate about Ray J or buffalo wing dings, because you think it will be a trollish but good discussion prompt for the next day. Implied, also, is that you're the levelheaded pragmatist— the *man*—imparting sage wisdom to this smart but silly woman who clearly has no idea how the world really works.

Begin the piece by patting yourself on the back for being progressive and brave enough to admit that rape is wrong, and then intimate that women like Zerlina— herself a rape survivor who's written about her own assault—may wield some responsibility for the crimes committed against them.

Include nuggets such as *"What's stopping us from steadfastly instilling 'No always means no!' in the minds of all men and boys AND educating women on how not to put themselves in certain situations?"* and *"It seems as if the considerable push back against victim-blaming has pushed all*

*the way past prudence and levelheadedness, making anyone who*
*suggests that 'women can actually be taught how to behave too'*
*insensitive or a 'rape enabler.'"*

Title it "'Rape Responsibility,' and the Fine Line
Between Victim Blaming and Common Sense." Hit
publish.

———

It's July 2002. I'm at the Monroeville Mall and I see a cute girl
with her friends. We walk past each other. I smile. She smiles
back. I tell myself that I'm going to approach and talk to her if I
ever see her again. Twenty minutes later, I'm in the food court,
waiting in line at Chick-fil-A, and I see her, by herself, in line
at Flamers Grill. We make eye contact again. I smile again. She
smiles again. I freeze and stay in line. She gets her food and
leaves.

"This can't fucking continue," I say to myself while angrily
dipping a waffle fry in Chick-fil-A sauce. I'm so disappointed in
myself for not talking to her that I pledge to talk to the next attractive woman I see, regardless of the circumstance. Two days
later, I'm on a bus downtown, headed to Shadyside. An attractive woman gets on by herself. "Here's your chance," I tell myself, aloud, "to stop being a pussy."

I'm in the back and she's seated near the front. To talk to
her, I'd have to move up and sit or stand next to her. While I'm
attempting to gather the gumption to do this, she gets up and
gets off the bus in the Hill District. "Fuck this," I say to no one
in particular, and I jump up, race to the front of the bus, and get
off at the next stop. I walk a block and a half back down Fifth
Avenue to maybe catch up to her. I see her waiting to cross a
street. It's 7 P.M. We're the only people on the block.

I walk toward her. She's possessed with her thoughts and doesn't see me coming. When I'm within her line of vision, I speak.

"Hello."

This startles her, slightly, and she says "Hi?" back in a way that's both a question and a polite way of communicating her irritation with my introduction.

I can feel her bracing herself. I put both of my hands up, with my palms open and facing her, to communicate that I'm not a threat. "I'm sorry. Didn't mean to scare you. My name is Damon, and I saw you on the bus and just wanted to say hi." I extend my hand. She grins (slightly), looks down at my hand, looks at me, looks at my hand again and shakes it.

"I'm Tiffany. Nice to meet you. Wait . . . you were on the Seventy-One too?"

"Yeah. Near the back."

"Okay."

"Well . . . I just wanted to talk to you and see if I could call you sometime."

"Oh . . . I'm sorry, hun. I'm engaged."

She smiles and shows me her left hand. Sitting on her ring finger is, in fact, a ring. It's sparkly.

"Oh shit. My bad. I'm sorry. Didn't know you were taken."

She laughs. "It's cool. Well, it was nice to meet you, Damon."

"Nice to meet you too."

She crosses the street, and I walk back to the bus stop.

It's June 2017. The decision to not support Nate Parker's *Birth of a Nation* when it is released—a reaction to Parker's response to and behavior following the spate of news stories in 2016 about his 1999 rape trial (and the subsequent suicide of the woman who accused Parker and then-roommate Jean Celestin of raping and harassing her)—is not a difficult one for me. I do not see many movies at the theater. And when I do, it's usually the type of action and/or science-fiction fare that's best appreciated on the big screen. I see *maybe* five movies a year. And with the controversy surrounding Parker, it just so happens that the push against him aligns with my politics *and* my viewing habits. My act is less a boycott and more a converging of convenience.

I do, however, catch twenty minutes of it the week after it premieres on HBO. As I flip through the channels on a Wednesday evening, I land on a scene where Aja Naomi King's Cherry Ann Turner is approached, surrounded, kidnapped, raped, and beaten to within an inch of her life by three white men. The rape is implied and not shown; all that's seen is Cherry Ann's disfigured face afterward and the seething rage of her husband, Nate Parker's Nat Turner. As devastating as this scene is to witness, that devastation exists in concert with knowing that this rape—and a subsequent rape featuring Gabrielle Union's character soon after—was inserted by Parker as a historically inaccurate narrative device whose only function was to provide a cinematic motivation for Turner's revolt.

Of course, the rape of enslaved women by the men who owned them was common during American chattel slavery. Even now, in the twenty-first fucking century, these rapes are still often spun as consensual sexual relationships by those either wishing to minimize the realities of slavery or oblivious to how ownership obviates sexual agency. But from what we know of Nat Turner, rape was not the impetus behind his revolution. Instead, he believed he was instructed directly by God, a message communicated not through sexual assaults but by a solar eclipse.

Without the context of Parker's history, him writing and filming those scenes becomes merely a tone-deaf directorial decision, one which depicts a world where women exist only to be victimized by evil men and to motivate great ones. It makes the scene bad, but bad in a remarkably unremarkable way. (And, to Parker's credit, creating a world where black women are victimized and black men fight for them allows black women the opportunity to be seen as able to experience pain *and* worthy of defense—a counter to how black women and girls are often treated in cinema and within our general culture.) But as he continued to dig his own grave during his pre-*Birth*-release press tour—giving interview after interview expressing self-righteous indignation when pressed about his trial and the death of his accuser—it became impossible to divorce Parker's relationship with sexual violence from the movie's. Maybe Nate Parker put some fucked-up rape shit in his movie because Nate Parker (allegedly) did some fucked-up rape shit in college and (definitely) still refused to reckon with the consequences of it. He—and, by extension, his picture—do not deserve the support and the praise he undoubtedly expected when creating a film about America's most famous slave revolt. So I do not give it to him.

Also, the way he acted during his press tour reminded me of me.

It's January 2012. Our custom at VSB at this time is to publish new content at midnight. We do this to become a part of people's nighttime and early-morning routines. I also enjoy falling asleep soon afterward and waking up the next morning to see dozens, sometimes hundreds, of comments already. It gives me a rush. After publishing "Rape Responsibility," however, I make sure to stay up and witness the initial conversations it provokes, because I know they will be good.

The first response—a tweet calling it "disgusting"—comes a few seconds after midnight. Which means that the commenter hasn't even read it—or doesn't need to read it—before making that assessment. The title is enough. Variants of the message conveyed in that tweet flood VSB's mentions on Twitter and Facebook and in the comments for the next hour. I read them all.

Realizing that I need to do *something*, I sit on the love seat in the living room of my parents' house—my de facto bedroom while I stay there—to type a response that I first leave in the comments and eventually attach as an addendum to the piece.

So, although I realized while writing this that it may be a touchy subject, I admittedly underestimated exactly how potentially explosive it was going to be. I read some of these responses late last night and early this morning, and I'm genuinely shocked at the level of anger and hurt this entry has caused. I really did not expect this to happen. And while I don't apologize for expressing my viewpoint, but I do apologize about being so flippant and not being more careful to articulate exactly what I meant to convey. Considering the subject matter, leaving lighthearted footnotes and links to my appearance in Essence at the end of the entry was a very bad idea.

Anyway, as far as the actual article and responses, my intent wasn't to imply that any victim of rape should be held "accountable" for what happened to them. I also realize that the majority of rapes are done by people who know their victims—boyfriends, co-workers, friends, dates, etc.—making it almost impossible to defend against, and in no way did I want to spread the message that staying sober and out of shady situations is all a woman has to do to avoid being raped. All I was trying to do was respond to a theme—men always have to be hyper-vigilant, hyper-careful, and possess the ability to read women's minds; women, on the other hand, can do whatever the hell they want—I got from Zerlina's article, the comments attached to it, and the Twitter convo it sparked. And, I still believe that this is a dangerous way to approach things. I'm aware that all the education and conversation in the world about learning how to protect yourself and stay out of harms way and properly vetting men isn't going to prevent men from raping women. A woman can do all of that and still get sexually assaulted. I'm also aware that the onus of responsibility falls directly on the shoulders of the rapist, and nowhere else. But, my whole point is that young men AND young women need to be taught how to behave around the opposite sex, and I don't see how saying that suggests that I think women should be held responsible for their own rapes. Perhaps I'm being too obtuse, tone deaf, or insensitive, but I just don't see the connection between "everyone should be educated and learn how to take responsibility for their actions" and "rape is the woman's fault."

You know, before logging on and leaving this comment, I called up a friend to ask her to read the post and let me know if people were being way too sensitive or if I was crazy in thinking "what the hell is everyone so upset about?" Her (paraphrased) reply: "Yeah, I think you should have left this topic alone. Any time a man writes about rape and even puts women and accountability in the same sentence, you're going to anger people and come off as either completely tone deaf or dangerously insensitive, even if you don't actually say or feel that women need to be held accountable for what happens to them. Maybe you could have worded your feelings better, but there's really nothing you could have said besides 'rape is wrong, the end' that would have made much of a difference."

I think she's right.

Although this piece and the reaction to it have remained fresh in my mind since 2012, I forgot that I'd added that edit, something that only came back to me after rereading the piece to prepare to write this. And perhaps it escaped to the recesses of my mind because that 554-word-long screed of half-assed penitence was so terrible that I convinced myself to eradicate its memory. It somehow managed to be worse than the original piece.

I begin with a sentence referring to rape as a "touchy subject," and I follow by expressing surprise and thinly veiled dismay at those who had the audacity to be outraged and/or hurt by my article. I end this *paragraph*—remember, this is only the first fucking paragraph—by making sure to preface an apology with a "sorry, not sorry" in the *same fucking sentence*. And I admit that my biggest regret wasn't explicitly declaring that rape is (paraphrasing) "somewhat y'all bitches fault" but that my articulation wasn't explicit *enough*.

The two following paragraphs are a pasticcio of hotep fuckshit best synopsized by *"Raping is bad. But . . ."* And then it decrescendos and ends with a paraphrased conversation with Marguerite where I make myself the victim for having the balls to dare challenge the idea that the onus and blame of sexual assault exists firmly with the criminal, and that the placement of this responsibility exists without caveat or condition.

Neither this edit nor the near 1,200-word-long apology that comes a day later makes much of a difference. Tweets and Facebook status messages disparaging me continue to pile up.

Women I know email and text me throughout the day, some checking to see if the outrage maelstrom has killed me yet, and none able to contain how disappointed and hurt by me they are. Women I know and women I don't know begin to leave accounts of their own rapes in the comments. Some expressing that they had considered VSB a safe space to bond and build with like-minded black people, but my words triggered and refreshed memories and thoughts they wished to escape. Articles about my article begin to surface. One published by Huffington Post is still on the second page of results when I google my name three years later.

When I'd been particularly embarrassed or depressed before, my inclination usually was to burrow myself indoors. There was a stretch at Canisius, for instance, when extended melancholy about my lack of playing time and my situation with Tracey kept me in my apartment for a month. I left only for class, practice, games, and food. Showers were optional. But because my laptop was my accomplice, I spend as much time out of the house and away from it as I can. It is a symbolic and useless gesture. I still carry my phone, and my phone still buzzes for each new comment and whenever I am mentioned in a tweet. VSB has become so unextractable from my life that I can't fathom even a temporary Internet disconnection. So I pout outdoors for a week, and the pout becomes more exaggerated and incredulous with each alert. I can't believe these people are saying these things about me. Do they not know who I am? They don't know about my hilarious book that pokes fun at women *and* men (and mostly men!) and my gig at *Ebony* and my wit and my politics? Have they forgotten that I was one of the dudes who actually embraced it when someone called me feminist? Which is what women had begun to call VSB (and, by extension, me). *A feminist blog.* Don't they realize that my accepting the feminist label is proof of my feminist bona fides? Sure, maybe I fucked up. But I am one of the good guys. Doesn't that earn me some slack? Do they not know that most of my closest friends in Pittsburgh now were women? And that I am such a great fucking guy that my ex-girlfriend still invites me to game nights and house parties and I am still friends with her friends? I don't deserve this fucking shit. Fuck them. Fuck those motherfuckers. They don't fucking know me. What gives them the right to say that shit about me? Fuck them.

I still believed that what I initially said was valid. The execution might have sucked, but my intent was justified and my message crucial. My only crimes, I thought, were not being articulate enough to express that message and bothering to express it in an environment unwilling to grapple with those hard truths. I wasn't interested in any type of honest reckoning. I just wanted a fire extinguisher and some sort of unearned absolution. This incredulousness bleeds through my responses, which is probably why the published responses to my responses are even sharper and less forgiving than the responses to the original piece.

I am reminded of this order of feelings now each time some public figure does or says something terribly stupid or just terribly terrible and is forced to jaunt through the public contrition gauntlet over the ensuing days and weeks and (sometimes) months. Thorough confessions and reparations are rare. Mostly, the mea culpas are mealy-mouthed and self-involved; pretentious pablum disguised as penitence. Snoot in sheep's clothing. And this happens, and will continue to happen, because, like how I was that first week, they're not really sorry. And they're not really sorry because they're still unable to be.

The apologies possess the veneer of contrition—they look and sound and smell and taste sincere—but they're apology seitan masquerading as steak, falling short for the same reasons mine did and the same reasons Nate Parker's did. Whatever was lurking within them to do or say the terrible thing they did or said is still inside them. The converging thoughts and beliefs leading to that act—possibly brewing for years—don't automatically dissipate when facing outrage. Especially not in a *day*. If anything, the initial instinctual reaction to the push-back is defense. You believe you're being attacked and scape-goated, and while you know penance and some performative self-flagellation are what people want and what you'll probably need to do, you do it through clenched fangs.

But if your desire to avoid continuing to disappoint and hurt the people affected by your words is deep enough—if your lament about the pain you spearheaded is sincere—this is also where the work starts. This is also where that incredu-lousness and anger begin to transmute, eventually shifting to full-fledged embarrassment. And then fear. Where you pledge to never do this again. Because you don't want to hurt people like that again. People you know and love and people you don't know and don't even like. And also because being the very de-serving source of the Internet's outrage *fucking blows*. (If you've ever been a member of this fucked-up club and you possess even a semblance of a conscience, you know you'll do whatever the fuck you can to prevent yourself from experiencing that again.) So, instead of continuing to circle your wagons, you use the shame as fuel to excavate and examine whatever's existing inside you so you can understand why you said the things you said. And not why you thought it was cool to say it aloud. But why you *thought* the shit you thought was cool to say aloud.

And it wasn't until I was able to do this, that I was able to see exactly how problematic my interactions with women had been—specifically women I was romantically interested in. And how my "Rape Responsibility" piece didn't live in a vacuum but was formed over a lifetime of experiences. How I believed and internalized that women were a code that needed cracking or a safe that needed breaking; that they were these beautiful and ethereal fortresses containing unlimited supplies of kisses and sex and validation if you could somehow game your way inside of them. How I hadn't thought about how my contrived efforts to approach them and talk to them and meet them and dance with them at parties and get their phone numbers and kiss them and ask them to come over and ask them to spend the night and somehow get them to believe that sex with me wasn't the worst way to spend their evenings may have felt from their end. Like the time in 2002 I followed Tiffany off of that bus. When I was so possessed with what *I* wanted and how good she looked to *me* and how approaching her and maybe getting her number would validate *me* that I didn't consider that some nigga creeping toward her while she's standing alone and distracted could be scary as a motherfucker. I'd devoted so much energy and effort to impressing them and convincing them and winning them instead of *knowing* them that I didn't have much use for the type of empathy that would allow me to realize how fucking dangerous the world is for a woman and how I'd added to that danger. That I maybe was the reason why a woman felt unsafe enough to pretend to be on the phone while I happened to be behind her while we both walked down the block. That maybe a vibe I'd given off at a club made a woman leave the dance floor and search for her homegirls sooner than she'd planned to. While I was used to, was annoyed by, and even made fun of the white women who'd enter an elevator with me and clutch their purses with ridiculous intensity, I hadn't considered the very real danger often felt by the black women I saw and knew and liked and loved, when I (or someone who looked like me) noticed them and wanted them to know I'd noticed them and wanted them to notice me. I wasn't the black boogeyman white people assumed I'd be. I was—I *am*—just a man, and in the right context that's scary enough.

It's November 2017. #MeToo, the movement first created by Tarana Burke in 2006 to demonstrate the ubiquity of sexual assault, and popularized by Alyssa Milano in October, soon after the numerous accounts of Harvey Weinstein's alleged sexual misconduct and abuse went public, is dominating the news cycle and our collective cultural consciousness. More and more men (some famous; some not so famous) are outed as either secret abusers or men whose pattern of abuse has been an open secret that was never quite on the record until now. More and more women (some famous; some not so famous) are coming forward with their stories. Even men are offering their stories. Terry Crews, a man so physically imposing that the flexing of his pec muscles is a punch line in one of the Old Spice spots he starred in, reveals that he was groped by a Hollywood executive during a party with multiple witnesses present; one of many now-public acts that enunciate exactly how deeply entrenched rape culture is. The presumed dominion over others' bodies that too fucking many men possess is so goddamn deep, so goddamn *conventional*, even, that it allowed a man to be brazen enough to saunter up and snatch the dick of a six-foot-three, 250-pound ex-NFL linebacker and be sure enough of that privilege to anticipate no consequences.

#MeToo was (and is) a mass indictment. It was (and is) a reckoning. It was (and is) a purging. It was (and is) a tearing and a burning down. It also was (and is) a mind-meld. A reverse lobotomy, if such a thing were possible. Or something similar to what happens in *Inception*, where your subconscious is infiltrated and your memories and feelings about those memories are forever altered. Interactions you may have believed were benign and mundane when they occurred are now considered through a different lens and assessed with different criteria. What was then pedestrian and banal is now problematic and abusive. Of course, these things that are all of a sudden considered problematic and abusive and violent after #MeToo have always been. Shit always been fucked up. It's just that in the fall of 2017, it becomes incrementally less dangerous for the victimized to admit this publicly, because they now have company and platforms and mediums and a movement behind them.

It's May 2014. It is my bachelor party. We're at a day party at Ozio, a club in D.C. We have a reserved table, and the bottles of liquor are never-ending. Honey Jack. Hennessy. Cîroc. Champagne. When each bottle is finished, another magically appears. I'm walking around the club with a bottle in my hand. I think it's champagne, and I swig it like it's champagne, but it tastes like whiskey. I don't give a shit. I'm drunk as fuck.

I remember dancing with a woman I met at the club. I forget her name—I'm not sure if I ever even knew her name—but I remember that the Fatman Scoop remix of Faith Evans's "Love Like This" is playing. I remember still holding that bottle. The next thing I remember after that is my friends and I walking down the stairs of the club. It was still light outside, so I'm thinking it was six thirty. The next thing I remember after that is waking up in a hotel room at 4 A.M. I was, according to my friends, at least semiconscious up until around 11 P.M. But the memory of it is either gone forever or stuck in a part of my brain I haven't been able to access.

That memory gap exists as one of those nostalgic *I can't believe I got that fucked up!* memories because I was with my niggas and I trusted they'd take care of me. And they did. When I woke up in that hotel room, I was in a bed, and my pants were off. I assumed I must've taken them off or one of them did for me. Either way, I didn't wonder if anything bad happened to me while my pants were off. Because there'd be no reason for me to consider that. No memory rife with stories about the bad things that happened to men I knew who also woke up pantsless and confused. No historical and cultural and sexual and personal context for that concern. I was protected. I was safe.

I told myself, in the weeks after "Rape Responsibility," that my overpowering sense of decency was what separated me from men who were actual abusers, and it wasn't fair to lump me in with them. And I believe that I'm decent. I believe that I'm *good*. And I want to believe that to be true. No. Fuck that. *I fucking believe that to be true.* It has to be true. But if this is true—and, again, it *must* be fucking true—why did I write that? If this decency actually exists inside of me, why didn't it asphyxiate the thing that's also inside of me that compelled me to think and write that?

Of course, thinking about and stressing over how I felt instead of how I made people feel is natural. Selfish, but understandable when considering that, well, they (the people hurt by my piece) are not me. But this is what rape culture does. This is one of the things that rape culture does. It places the wants and feelings and desires and fears of men on a pedestal, where the thoughts of men are the only thoughts worthy of consideration, and the thoughts of women are only to be considered if men are kind enough to grant them some space, and we construct our interactions on that imbalance. This is why rape culture is a misnomer, because *culture* doesn't go far enough. It's not just a culture, it's an atmosphere. It's not just an atmosphere, it's an amniotic fluid that soaks and brines and feeds and shapes us. And with this surrounding us, and with us sloshing around in it, and with us swallowing it and choking on it, what does it even mean to be a good man? A *decent* man?

Merriam-Webster says that to be decent is to conform to "standards of propriety, good taste, or morality." By that standard—which would be based on our established standard—I am a decent man. I am, by our standard, a good man. I have never been accused of a crime. I'm the type of man seasoned black people would say was "raised right." I'm chivalrous in a way that grants me an inexhaustible alibi. "*Oh, no. Damon would never do that terrible and violent and criminal thing that other man did.*" Which is what, I think, *our* decent means. To consider yourself to be decent is to act in a way that removes yourself from culpability and blame, and that's it. You are a decent man if you do nothing. You are a decent man if you keep *yourself* safe.

It's April 2012. I'm playing flag football on the grassy stretch next to the baseball fields at Mellon Park with Jessica, Marguerite, and the rest of the PhDeez. Altogether there are twenty-two people there, enough for a good game with subs. Later that night, there's a game night/potluck at the town house Marguerite and Camille share in Crawford Square in the Hill District. Everyone will be there. It starts at nine. I get there on time because I have to leave early because I'm driving to D.C. the next morning. I'm the first one there. I bring wings from Hook Fish & Chicken in Homewood. Camille is upstairs getting dressed, and Marguerite and I are in the living room, talking.

"D-Money, I'm glad you brought wings this time, 'cause those pancakes you brought to the last potluck were trash. Also . . . who brings pancakes to a potluck? And no bacon? Nigga, where was the bacon?"

"You talking shit now, but you ate them too! You always trying to act lightskint on me. Stop playing."

"I'll stop playing when you do better."

This back-and-forth continues for a few more minutes, and then it settles into a conversation about our respective futures. What I have planned for VSB, and where she is looking to do her postdoc. She will officially be a PhD soon.

"As much shit as I talked about Pittsburgh, I'm going to miss it."

"Yeah, I know. It's gonna miss you too."

My embrace of decency is a safe and nice little lie, like the ones I used to tell about my driver's license. I could always distinguish myself from them other niggas because I was better. I didn't do the things that the men who weren't as good as me did. They were just dudes. I was *decent*.

But decent was (and is) a baseline. Decent was (and is) the threshold. Decent was (and is) a standard WordPress template. Decent was (and is) a practiced and careful passivity. You are *decent*, not because you do things that actually matter and actually help, but because you don't do shit. Decent ain't shit, really. Fuck decent. What mattered and still matters most is being *worthy*. Worthy of the friendship of Marguerite and Camille and Jessica and my homegirl Taaliba and my cousin Huny and the rest of the women I knew who still loved me. Worthy of the bus that Kierna Mayo and Jamilah Lemieux and Genese Cage and the rest of the women at Ebony.com *didn't* throw me under when they were asked to (and had good reason to) do so. Worthy of the readership and the follows and shares and retweets and comments of the thousands of black women who continued to engage with and amplify my work.

None of these women were bound to me by blood or through sex. They'd just extended me the same empathy I denied them when I wrote that their sexual assaults might have been their fault, and I needed (and still need to) earn it.

# 11

# BANGING OVER BACON

To call the last fistfight I was in a "fight" requires a generous definition of the word *fight*. As well as a favorable understanding of what it means to be *in* something. And a serious conversation about whether *fist* is really a necessary qualifier.

I was twelve years old, shooting by myself at the courts behind Peabody High School, practicing bank shots from the foul line extended and doing the thing that boys do in Gatorade commercials and *Nightline* specials about latchkey kids. I'd shake invisible defenders, provide my own play-by-play (*"Young goes baseline, spins into the lane . . ."*), count down loudly and dramatically (*"four . . . three . . . two . . . one . . ."*), and hurl buzzer beaters toward the hoop with the accompanying appropriate announcement if I made the shot (*"Swish! Young wins the game! And here comes his girlfriend, Tatyana Ali from* The Fresh Prince of Bel-Air, *leaping from the stands to give him a kiss! And some nachos. Boy, that Damon Young sure loves his nachos!"*).

I was so invested in my fantasy that I hadn't noticed that

Ricky "Bumpy" Nelson—then fourteen-ish; now serving a life sentence for shooting and killing the new boyfriend of his ex-wife in 2006—had joined me on the court.

I'd met Bumpy two years earlier underneath that same basket. I'd envied his rattail, and he knew how to make a layup, so I'd invited him to my house to play *Contra* and *Double Dribble*. I remember him being so aggressively mannerly when he met my parents that I felt embarrassed, like they'd judge me behind my back for befriending someone so uncool. I also remember the conversation I had with Dad later that night:

"Son."

"Yes?"

"Be careful around that boy."

"Who? Bumpy?"

"Yes."

"Why?"

"He's too . . . polite."

Months later, when ten dollars disappeared from our kitchen counter during my birthday slumber party, Dad believed it was Bumpy and forbade me from inviting him to the house again. We'd already begun to grow apart by that time. I was into high-water Bugle Boy jeans with multicolored cuffs and Wiffle ball home run derbies in the alley behind our house. He was into throwing Frank's RedHot sauce–filled water balloons at PAT buses and flashing his dick at school janitors and fat squirrels. The only reason he was even at the party was because he happened to come over the night the rest of my friends were there, and this nigga just *stayed*.

Bumpy also had a reputation for having hands. I'd never seen him rumble before, but it wasn't hard to believe he could. Some dudes just carry it like that, and Bumpy was one of those dudes.

Anyway, I wasn't exactly happy to see him when he crept up behind me at Peabody. Mostly because this nigga was a perpetual creeper. You'd never see this sneaky motherfucker coming. He'd just *appear*, popping up at courts and popping out of couches like he was playing hide-and-go-seek with gravity. His nickname was Bumpy, but we should have called that nigga Poltergeist. And he'd always ask you to do something that existed in the gray space where legal ended but illegal hadn't quite yet begun. Like "No, Bumpy, I'm not gonna go pee on the bleachers with you today." That day, however, Bumpy was interested in my bike, which was leaning on the chain-link fence with my lock linked within the wheels so you couldn't ride it without the combination.

"Yo, Dame, lemme ride your bike."

"Naw, man, I'm busy." (Which was me saying, "Fuck no. If I let you ride my bike today, I won't see it again till Wednesday.")

"You a lame for that. Aiight, I'm out."

He turned and walked back off the court and toward the gate's entrance. I turned my back and continued doing Mikans. Twenty seconds later, I sensed an unease in the atmosphere, a disruption in my space-time continuum, and I stopped and turned toward the gate and saw that gravity-bending motherfucker sneaking away with my bike. Since he couldn't ride it, this delinquent nigga was *carrying* it away and cracking the fuck up. I chased toward him, caught up to him, and pulled the handlebars while his hands gripped the down tube and the chainstay. Still thinking it was the funniest fucking thing ever, he pushed me away, and I tripped over a crack in the pavement and fell. At this point, I convinced myself that when I got back to my feet, I was going to sock him in the face. Both I and the mortified neighborhood squirrels had had enough of Bumpy's supernatural shenanigans. Apparently this nigga could read minds too, as a right-hand cross landed on my cheekbone when I began to lift myself up. Thwarted and back on the ground, I responded the only way I was equipped to: lay there and cry like a baby.

Bumpy never actually stole my bike. He took a couple more steps toward the gate, passed through the exit, saw I was more interested in pretending I'd just seen the last twenty minutes of *Marley & Me* than chasing him again, and lost interest, leaving the bike splayed on the sidewalk. After enough time had passed to ensure he was out of eyeshot, I inched around the fence to retrieve my bitch-ass second-place prize.

Remembering this story always makes me feel like a wuss. Not because I lost the fight. Or how I lost the fight. But because it's a reminder that I've gone twenty-five years without getting in another one, and saying that aloud makes me believe I've neglected a baptismal rite of passable blackness. I feel like I should have been in more fights between then and now. Especially since I never really snagged a *nigger* fight story. Which makes me wonder why I haven't been in more fights. And then wonder if the embarrassment of the Bumpy beatdown was so traumatizing that I'd vowed to never go through that again, and lived the rest of my life skirting physical confrontations.

This is partially true. Aside from random and unavoidable basketball-related skirmishes peppered throughout my life— usually comprised of pushes, raised elbows, really determined pointing, and aggressively enunciated cuss words—learning how to detect and eschew potential rumbles became a vital part of my personal ethos. But not necessarily because I feared getting my ass kicked. I just really enjoy staying *alive*, and randomly fighting niggas in East Liberty and Garfield and Homewood and Larimer when you didn't know if those random niggas—or those random niggas' cousins/friends/brothers/girlfriends—were packing would have been an efficient way of ending my still untarnished streak of consecutive years lived.

In an irony that much of America still hasn't quite realized yet, it's assumed that black people from the hood emerge equipped with fighting bona fides. The thought being we wouldn't have survived long enough to make it out of the hood if we didn't know how to handle ourselves. But while we've all been around fights, seen fights, heard about fights, and known niggas who can fight—and niggas who *itch* to fight; niggas who can't wait to finish doing whatever they're doing right now just so they can fight again—you escape the hood bullet-wound-and-criminal-charge-free by learning how to *look like* you can fight; accomplished by walking around like you'll stab a nigga if necessary and possessing a resting Stanley-from–*The Office* face. And having a sense of humor. And being too busy to loiter and hang. And being friendly with enough fight-compelled niggas that they wouldn't want to fight you. And then learning enough *they about to fight/brawl/stab/shoot up in here* context clues to sniff out and evade fights.

Also, I constructed and existed in a reality where I'd never have to fight. I hooped and played football, *and* was taller and heavier than the average kid, *and* was from East Lib—each granting me the presumption of ass-whipping proficiency. Plus, I'm at the darker end of the color spectrum. And everyone—even other black people—assumes that the darker-skinned you happen to be, the tougher you are; like our skin is only dark because it was left on the stove too long. (Which accidentally creates a paradox where the most willing fighters often happen to be light-skinned black dudes. They're aware light-skinned niggas are presumed to be soft, so they get extra super-duper tough sometimes just to prove they ain't. Hell hath no fury like a scorned nigga with gray eyes and freckles.)

My lack of postadolescent fighting isn't even all that rare. Most adults exist on the far ends of the fighting spectrum. Either you've been in somewhere between 0 and 2 fistfights since you were thirteen, or you've been in 214, and you just fought in a Waffle House parking lot last night. No one has been in, like, 8 fights. But this doesn't change how I feel. I don't want to be in more fights. I'd just like to know how it feels to be in one—and whether I'd be able to handle myself in it—and I'd prefer retaining ownership of that feeling without actually doing it. I also still relish opportunities to *seem* tough. I don't actually possess a need to *be* tough. That ship has sailed. My life is too tony to be fighting niggas in bars and on the street, and it's hard being a legitimately tough guy when calling Suitsupply tech support while clutching a Green Machine Naked Juice. Looking tough and having other people (particularly women) witness this grandiloquent toughness is enough for me.

I *knew* this was bullshit. I knew that no one I knew gave a shit about how many fights I'd been in (and won) as an adult. With the niggas I knew and hung out with in my twenties and thirties, fighting would probably just get me deleted from group texts and disinvited to brunches and bachelor parties. ("Yo, you didn't invite Dame to the housewarming?" "Nah, man. That nigga just be fighting too much. Can't have him up in my new crib breaking all my IKEA plateware.") But even though I *knew* it didn't matter, and *knew* that fighting and the toughness associated with it only mattered to me because of those mythical benchmarks of sufficient heterosexuality that *I knew was a sham*, I still gave that lie a home. I still had investments in it, and I couldn't let it go just yet.

Fortunately, on May 14, 2012, the stars aligned and allowed me to do exactly that.

One of the PhDeez had a birthday, and the entire crew

planned to celebrate by caravaning to Savoy, where we'd reserved two tables upstairs. Altogether there were eleven of us;
nine women and two men. And since a table at Savoy is a big-ass
Black Pittsburgh deal—it's the place in Pittsburgh where niggas
go to show off—the women each had their freakum dresses on,
and I was wearing my finest and shiniest two-button Sean John
suit. (Did you know that Sean John sold suits? I didn't either
until I saw this one on a discount rack at Burlington Coat Factory. When I bought it, the sales clerk suggested I also buy a few
of the slightly damaged Trump ties sitting behind the counter.
They were five for ten dollars. I declined.)

Our section at Savoy was a din of doctoral iniquity. The
PhDeez had mostly eschewed the partying and bullshit associated with college life when undergrads, so if out together
and in a relatively safe environment, they'd release all of those
suppressed twerks and lap dances on unsuspecting couches
and crotches, caged birds finally free to be Bougie Black Girls
Gone Wild. Every so often, a nigga would clutch his nuts and
inch over to the section, attempting to maybe get a phone number or a grind partner or just a closer look. First he'd pound
up and brown-nose me as if I were the PhDeez's bouncer or
handler. And then he'd just stand there like the Strip District's
horniest scarecrow, waiting for one of the women to engage
him. And then, after five to seven minutes of not being engaged or even fucking noticed, he'd walk all sad and slow and
shit back to the bar.

After Savoy, the entire crew drove to the twenty-four-
hour Eat'n Park in Squirrel Hill, where the midnight breakfast
buffet is a popular and crucial sobering agent for Friday- and
Saturday-night club-hoppers in Pittsburgh. Our crew of eleven
had expanded to near twenty. And all of the extras were either
niggas who were currently hooking up with one of the PhDeez

or niggas who really, really, really, really, really, really wanted to. We asked one of the servers to put two long tables together, and we squeezed our asses into them. I sat at the head of one of the tables, flanked by the PhDeez, while the thirsty niggas all crowded together at the second table. I knew and was friendly with everyone, except for one stocky Kappa nigga I'd never seen before. He was wearing a bow tie and oxfords with no socks, so I hated him and his ankles immediately.

The buffet's food—while hot and plentiful—was usually terrible. The bacon was flaccid and annoyed, the eggs despondent, the pancakes in need of a spa day and a therapy session, the French toast sticks trapezoidal and impenetrable, the fruit fishy, the fish fruity, and the sausage gravy looked too much like spunk to even try. You'd see it and you'd wonder how many East End sperm banks were missing samples. Fortunately, I was too tipsy and hungry to give a fuck about any of that. So while the PhDeez ordered from the bougie-ass menu—which meant they'd have to wait like eleven whole minutes for their food—I ravaged the lamp-heated nutriment, packing green sausage patties and woebegone grits into my mouth like a taxidermist stuffing sawdust into a dead walrus.

When drunk, I usually eat how rabbits fuck—angry, sweaty, and looking over my shoulder for falcons. I made multiple bacon runs to the buffet. Too many bacon runs. Like eight bacon runs. I ate twenty-seven slices of bacon that night. As I'd walk back to the table, the PhDeez seated near me would snatch a slice or two off my plate while I pretended to try to stop them. It was both one of those drunk-people games that's only funny to other drunk people and subtly intimate. They were comfortable taking food off of my plate and I was comfortable allowing them to do that (as well as taking food off of theirs when it came). These were my girls. My homies. My *niggas*. And *they* could do that. Random stocky sockless Kappa niggas couldn't. But that didn't stop the random stocky sockless Kappa nigga there from trying, as he reached his random stocky sockless Kappa hand up from his seat and tried to grab a slice off of my plate during one of my runs.

There are few social crimes worse than an anonymous nigga taking food off of a nigga's plate. I'm pretty certain the nineties East Coast/West Coast rap feud started because Suge Knight snatched an oxtail out of Biggie's bowl during a house party in 1994. I wasn't actually upset about this breach in decorum. But I knew I had to address this clear affront to my masculinity and my appetite. And I was fucking elated that this random stocky sockless Kappa nigga gave me a prime opportunity to look tough. I'd waited twenty years for something like this, to be a tough nigga in front of a crew of women. I could have kissed that random stocky sockless Kappa nigga for the gift.

I went back to my seat and sat down, placed my plate and my hands on the table, stared down to the opposite end of the connected tables (where he sat), and spoke calmly and forcefully with the deepest voice I could conjure.

"Yo, what the fuck is wrong with you?"

"Huh?"

"You heard me, bro. What the fuck is wrong with you?"

At this point, you could see the expressions on everyone's faces changing from *Wait. Damon's not serious, is he?* to *Um, yeah, he's serious. This is getting uncomfortable. And entertaining. This is uncomfortably entertaining,* and finally landing on *Wait, we're not about to witness a couple niggas in suits fight over some bacon, are we?*

Random stocky sockless Kappa nigga finally replied.

"It's just bacon, bro. My bad. I didn't realize Pittsburgh niggas got so heated over bacon."

Now, I knew I wasn't going to fight this dude over some

buffet bacon. But *he didn't know that*. And I was perfectly fine with allowing him to continue to wonder if I was actually that bacon-brawling-ass nigga.

"Really? You got jokes now? Come on, bro. You don't wanna go there."

Holy shit! It worked! As soon as I finished talking, I could see an inkling of fear form and then pass through his eyes. He really believed that, wherever the fuck "there" was, I was more than willing to go "there." He thought I leased beachfront property "there" and was just elected mayor of "there." And no one wants to go "there" with a nigga willing to go "there" over some bacon.

"I'm just saying, man, I saw them take some bacon and I thought it was cool. I didn't mean any disrespect."

I went in for the kill.

"It was cool with THEM because I know THEM. THEY are my niggas. I don't know YOU. I've never seen you or your shoes before in my life, dog. Plus they're women. Niggas don't take food off of other niggas' plates, man. It's whatever, though. I'm cool."

This, officially, was the most badass thing I've ever said. Or done. And I knew immediately it was the badassest thing I've ever said or done because of the muffled laughs that followed. They were the type of laughs that happen when you shame a random stocky sockless Kappa nigga who needs shaming. And the type of laughs that happen when bougie black girls are relieved that no niggas fighting over emasculated pork are going to stain their freakum dresses. And if they're relieved no fighting is going to happen, it means they believed there was enough of a possibility of a fight to be relieved by it not happening. THEY BELIEVED THERE WAS ENOUGH OF A POSSIBILITY OF A FIGHT TO BE RELIEVED BY IT NOT

HAPPENING. WHICH MEANT THEY BELIEVED, FOR A MOMENT, THAT I HAD ENOUGH TOUGH NIGGA IN ME TO FIGHT A PLUMP NIGGA IN A SUIT OVER SOME BACON.

The random stocky sockless Kappa nigga apologized again. And Marguerite said we needed to hug it out. So we got up from our opposite ends of the table and embraced to sarcastic cheers. World War Swine had been averted. And finally, after two decades, I exorcised those Peabody High School basketball court demons. The ghost of Bumpy was (finally) dead, and I could ride my bike back home.

I sat back down and tore through my fifth plate of bacon. And then I went to the bathroom and threw up.

# 12

# YOLO

My wife, Alecia Dawn Young—the woman I married in 2014, thirty-three months after I had pledged in October of 2011 to stay single as long as I could—has many talents. Among them are her four separate laughs. One for when she's genuinely shocked by how funny something is, a manic cackle that explodes out of her mouth like a Dodge Hellcat engine revving, startling babies, scaring yogis, and making Uber drivers miss right turns. A subdued one for when she's in a polite space and wishes not to stun people. A silent one where her face freezes in laugh formation for five seconds like the *Scream* mask and, if she's sitting next to me on the couch, she hits me and I'm not quite sure if she's having a stroke. And one she usually reserves for midday phone calls with her homegirl Tara. From what I've observed, most people only seem to have two consistent laughs in their wheelhouses. When I learned she had three, I knew I had to date this three-laugh-wielding woman. And by the time I found the fourth, I was ready to commit to a lifetime of gluten-free baked goods and haphazardly constructed Fabrikör glass-door cabinets repurposed as TV stands.

Her sense of smell is annoyingly accurate. If pilots and marksmen and singles hitters are supposed to have 20/10 vision, she has whatever the equivalent of that is for noses. It's so great that she smells things that haven't even happened yet. She can walk into a room, sniff, and discern that someone is going to spray some Scrubbing Bubbles Multi Surface Bathroom Cleaner in seventeen minutes. This nigga can smell into the future.

She shares my general philosophy about white people, which exists as a repetitious vacillation between bemusement, annoyance, fury, and pity, and is a vital core value for any appropriately aware black person to possess. Admittedly, this sounds quite a bit like racism. And perhaps it would be, if black people could be racist toward whites. (We can't, btw. We can be prejudiced, but actual racism is bias plus *power*. The only "reverse racism" is when white people wear Confederate flag snapbacks backward.) But even if we could, Alecia and I wouldn't be *racist* racist. We don't *hate* hate white people. We watch *Game of Thrones*. We each have white people we're friendly with. Sometimes it's even the same white person. It's just nice to find someone who understands and appreciates private conversations and comments about viruses white people catch because they're never wearing weather-appropriate clothes, and who also knows what "that's some white-people shit" means without exposition.

She also loves to dance, and she thinks she's a better dancer than she actually is. Which is an ironic statement for me to make, since paraplegic spiders move on the dance floor better than I do. I dance like a nigga who both is hyperconscious of every move his body makes and believes everyone else is just as hyperconscious of every move his body makes. I was once told in middle school that I dance like I'm scared of pussy. I hope I've gotten better since then, but my optimism has limits.

We actually first met on the dance floor. It was 2008. We were both at Ava Lounge in East Liberty for Reggae Night; her with her homegirl Robin, and me with a couple of my niggas. She was (and still is) tall and lean and somehow still curvy, built like a college volleyball player spotted at a mall and asked to be the cover model for a Harambee Ujima Black Arts Festival brochure. She had (and still has) long locs stretching to the end of the small of her back, the type of Citizens Bank–commercial smile that made you self-conscious of your own teeth, and eyes like a Disney princess specifically commissioned and created for a Black History Month special on NBC. And she also seemed completely . . . unaffected. Like she lived in a world with no mirrors or thirsty men with easy and nasty compliments and had no clue how striking she was. She knew, of course. But she didn't act like it. She'd dance with whoever wanted to dance with her. Which is rare for good-looking women. And decent-looking women. And just women, generally. Who are usually (and justifiably) discerning about who they decide to dance with, as everything from looks and odor to (lack of) rhythm and inappropriate erections can be eliminating factors. Basically, this is an awkward and vaguely problematic way of saying she was fine as fuck and might dance with me!

So I bided my time while two-stepping with my homegirl Taaliba, watched Alecia politely smile and drift away from the guy she was dancing with—the universal *this was cool and nice, but we're done dancing now* communiqué—and continued talking to Taalie for the duration of another song because I didn't want to look like I was waiting for an opening to pounce (which I totally was). And then, when Tanto Metro & Devonte's "Everyone

Falls in Love" bled through the speakers, I finally approached her (in rhythm!), locked eyes, and reached for her hand as she allowed for me to grab it. We danced for two songs. By the middle of the second song, I'd gathered the nerve to speak. I introduced myself, learned her name and that she was in grad school at CMU. I'd already assumed she wasn't from Pittsburgh because she looked and moved and felt more Northern Virginia or Prince George's County than Pittsburgh. Niggas like her just weren't from the Burgh. And the grad-school-at-CMU thing cemented this assumption. I also asked for her phone number, because I possess zero chill. She smiled and told me she had a boyfriend. I said, "Ah, okay," and grinned with sad eyes. We continued dancing to the Roots' "Sacrifice" until the song ended, and she excused herself and went to the bar. On the way there, I watched her catch eyes with Taalie, do the "Hey, girl!" thing that black women do when they're happy to see each other, and hug. After a brief conversation, Taalie walked back to the side of the dance floor I was on. Of course, I had to ask about Alecia.

"How do you know her?'

"We went to high school together."

"She went to Schenley?"

"Yeah. And she's from the Hill."

"Word?

"Damn, nigga, you thirsty."

"Whatever."

"You talk to her?"

"Yeah. She told me she has a dude, though."

"Hmm."

"What?"

"I don't know if that's true."

"So she lied?"

"I'm not saying she lied. But I'm just sayin'."

Whether she had a boyfriend was irrelevant. She wanted me to believe she did, and that was enough for me to pretend I was never actually interested in her. Which I did for the next three years, as I kept sporadic tabs on as much of her Facebook page as I could without sending a friend request. It was there I learned that we had fifty-seven mutual friends, and that she was an intern or something at the August Wilson Center (AWC), and that she was part of some black runners group that practiced at Schenley Park. She also seemed to really enjoy wearing comfortable pants, had a dog, and actually did have a boyfriend. After doing some quick reconnaissance on *his* page, I learned he had a master's degree *and* an Audi. Which was disheartening. I was just barely a nigga with a 2003 Mercury Mountaineer that I copped from one of those "no credit, three felonies, no nipples, no problem" lots on Rodi Road in Penn Hills. I couldn't compete with niggas with Audis and advanced degrees. This nigga probably had sculpted abs and good credit too. Shit, he probably leased that Audi because it was a sensible financial decision. His ass probably lived in a loft. With furniture he probably actually bought from a furniture store and not Craigslist. With plastic hangers and tasteful, oxygen-generating plants and enough silverware and plates and condiments and shit to host dinner parties and parents. My cabinets were filled with ramen noodles, grape and wild cherry Kool-Aid packets, empty boxes of Frosted Flakes, and serving spoons repurposed as eating utensils, and this nigga probably made scratch risotto for Alecia's mom. Fuck. She was just out of my league, and this nigga—her nigga—was proof.

We crossed paths again in 2011. She was still at the AWC, but a full-time employee now, and I was asked by them to host a signing party and reading for the book I wrote with Panama.

We were introduced to each other by her boss, Erica, who told us that we'd be working on this project together.

Erica: "Hey, Alecia. This is Damon. Y'all are going to be working on this event together. I'm sure you know each other though, as small as Pittsburgh is."

Alecia: "Actually no, we've never met. Hi, I'm Alecia!"

This was not an act. I (probably) knew which flavor Sanpellegrino her now ex-boyfriend copped from Whole Foods (pear—he looked like a pear Sanpellegrino-ass nigga), and she genuinely thought this was the first time we'd met each other. I'm sure she'd been approached in random clubs dozens of times, and to her I was just some random and forgettably thirsty club nigga. Which was great because all that awkwardness from 2008 was erased. But not so great because I was so easily erasable.

Of course, I fucked this up too: "I'm Damon. And actually, we've met before."

This is where I discovered another one of her talents. Instead of making this conversation more awkward and admitting she didn't remember me, she just said, "Oh, okay. Well, it was nice meeting you . . . *again*," smiled, and walked out of the room. She had (and still has) an uncanny ability to defuse random bouts of public weirdness. Which I know is an arbitrarily specific talent to have, but a marriage to someone who's attuned enough to social cues to always know the right thing to say in public is a gift for someone who's probably somewhere on the spectrum.

We became friends while working on the event and bonded every Friday over half-priced fried calamari and shrimp at Savoy's happy hour. That summer, we were both approached to join the Urban League Young Professionals (ULYP) and encouraged to run for positions on the executive board, and we urged each other to ignore our mutual aversions to joining clubs and proceed. We both served on the board for a year—her the community engagement chair and me the communications chair. I became friends with her new boyfriend, Andre, the only man in Pittsburgh with locs as long and a smile as bright as hers. When together, they looked like the niggas propped up when white people need to lie about diversity. You could totally see them on a billboard for a college or a pamphlet for a luxury loft complex. They fucking *matched*.

On New Year's Eve, I helped Alecia and Andre with the soft opening of the ice cream shop Alecia started downtown. She'd received a small-business grant from the city to open it, and Andre worked there during the day while Alecia was at the AWC. The freezer broke and the ice cream melted, so instead of cones and shakes we served customers vanilla ice cream soup plopped into cups of hot cocoa. (It was fucking delicious.) After the ball dropped, we closed the doors, locked ourselves inside the shop, and the dozen or so of us there drank Moët and danced and rapped and shouted to Drake's and Weezy's verses in "The Motto" until 4 A.M.

*Now she want a photo*
*You already know though*
*You only live once—that's the motto nigga YOLO*

As 2012 began, our respective romantic relationships became the fulcrum of our relationship. I'd pick her up from work once or twice a week for lunch, and we'd trek to Hokkaido Seafood Buffet in Homestead or Robert Wholey's in the Strip, and we'd sit in my car in the parking lot or maybe on Tenth Street behind the AWC, our stomachs bursting with lobster mac and cheese and precarious buffet sashimi, and I'd tell her about the women

I was dating. She'd listen and offer advice. And then some days we'd see each other again at happy hour or after a ULYP event. Maybe even at a mixer at 720 in Lawrenceville or a First Friday gallery crawl on Penn Avenue in Garfield. And we'd repeat the process. Laughs about white people attempting to Wobble. Laments about Wobbling and too-comfortable white people in rapidly gentrifying Garfield. Expeditions to Yelp-recommended taco trucks. Updates about the women I was dating and the progress she was making on the ice cream shop. And everything between us existing under the umbrella of Alecia's unceasing availability. We both knew that we were spending an inappropriate amount of time together, even as still platonic friends. And we both knew that we were able to because she wanted to. And were able to because Andre didn't seem to care that much about where she was, who she was with, and how much time she was spending away from him. And we both knew what this bilateral apathy communicated about the state of their relationship, but we never talked about that.

And then, in September, we drove to D.C. to celebrate our mutual friend Raymar's surprise thirtieth birthday party. The original plan was for Andre and our homegirl Carmen to also come, but Carmen got arrested or something and Andre had planned a biking trip to Erie with a group of niggas who bike to Erie, so it was just Alecia and I, together, for an entire weekend.

We drove down Saturday morning, made it there in time for Raymar's surprise brunch that afternoon, day-partied afterward at Ozio with Raymar, his girlfriend (Alicia), and his niggas from New Jersey, and then, that night, separated from the rest of the crew and bar-hopped on U Street. Dancing, drinking, laughing, and flirting but never actually touching each other— both intuiting how volatile our relationship dynamic was becoming and how quickly it was happening.

We drove to Raymar and Alicia's apartment after our night on U Street, and slept on opposite ends of the pull-out couch bed in their living room; both of us in sweats and T-shirts, my head at the foot of the bed and next to her feet, her head at the head and next to my feet. As we lay there together, I considered what might happen if I rubbed her thigh or nuzzled her shins. But mostly I just hoped that my feet didn't smell like hot dog water, and I was elated that hers didn't either.

We woke up in the same position, making it through the night with no accidental dick rubs, and no exaggeratedly poked-out and spoon-ready booties. We took turns showering, left with Raymar and Alicia, and joined the rest of the birthday crew at Sequoia in Georgetown for brunch. We sat next to each other, and I began not to mind at all if Raymar's niggas from Jersey assumed we were a couple. Two hours later, we hopped back into my car and drove back to Pittsburgh.

Soon after we got on I-495, headed to Breezewood, and after we'd relived and laughed about our weekend, Alecia got quiet. And then asked the question that changed our lives.

"You know, a few months ago, Andre said that if me and him weren't together, he could definitely see us dating each other. What do you think about that?"

What I thought, immediately after hearing that question, was that her asking me this meant that she was attracted enough to me to reveal that she'd already considered the idea of us together. She was just attempting to glean if we were on the same page. I also thought it was odd that Andre had observed we had romantic chemistry months ago, and was still fine with us spending so much time together. It didn't make sense.

"I'm surprised he'd say that. But yeah, I can see that. And I've thought about it too."

For the next three hours we talked about what the revelation

meant for our relationship, ultimately agreeing that we couldn't
and shouldn't hang out as much because it would definitely be inappropriate now. We promptly ignored that ambition for the next
month. We continued seeing each other, making the same lunch
and happy hour runs to Savoy and Hokkaido and Wholey's, attending the same gallery crawls and ULYP mixers, and having
the same debriefing sessions in my car. Only now we talked about
how wrong it was for us to be talking.

And then, while working together at Panera Bread in Bakery
Square on Columbus Day—her writing the script for a speech
she was scheduled to deliver that evening; me pretending I had
work to do just so I could hang out with her—we started playing footsie. Which sounds, well, who gives a fuck about footsie?
But we hadn't as much as hugged since the D.C. trip, so this
was the most intense fucking footsie ever. This was erotic footsie. Pornhub footsie. She was wearing corduroys, still possessing that affinity for comfortable pants. The Panera was mostly
empty, but some guy three tables down from us was pretending
not to watch, so we stopped and left. She'd driven her own car
there, so she didn't need a ride, but I asked her to come to my
car with me. She did, and we drove up from Bakery Square's
ground-level lot where I was parked to the adjoining parking
garage. I circled up until I found an empty floor, pulled into a
space, and put the car in park. I motioned for her to come here.
She took her seat belt off, climbed over the console, and sat on
my lap. Her face facing mine, her long legs still stretched over
the armrest and dangling on the passenger seat. She asked what
I wanted, I pulled her closer, and we began to kiss. It lasted for
thirty seconds. She tasted like Ultra Mentha Mentha Lip Shine
and the cream of chicken and wild rice soup she'd eaten an hour
earlier. When we came back up for air, we stared at each other,
seeing each other from that angle for the first time. She looked

terrified. I presumably looked however *HOLY FUCKING SHIT I CAN'T BELIEVE THAT JUST FUCKING HAPPENED I JUST FUCKING KISSED ALECIA FUCKING SHIPMAN* looks. Her talk was in an hour, so she climbed off of my lap, got back in the passenger seat, and asked me to take her back to her car. I dropped her off and wished her luck. She smiled, climbed into her car, and sped off. And I sat there, hoping the fireworks I felt weren't self-contained.

She called me at ten the next morning, and from then until noon, we talked about how wrong what happened the day before was, and how we needed to seriously mind our now month-old edict of allowing a distance between us to exist. I agreed, because it was the right thing to do. And then, as the call wound down, she mentioned that Andre had taken her car that day, and she was planning to walk a quarter mile down to the light rail next to Heinz Field to get downtown to the AWC. I was also on my way out, so I offered to drive from my apartment in Point Breeze to her place on the North Side to pick her up. (For context, Point Breeze is on Pittsburgh's East End, which means I offered to drive twenty minutes across town just to give her a five-minute-long ride downtown. In hindsight, Taaliba was right. I *was* thirsty as fuck.)

I arrived at her place a half hour later and sat in the car, expecting her to be waiting on her porch and ready to leave. She burst out of the door soon after I arrived, not to jump in my car but to walk her dog. She'd been on the phone with her mom after she got off the phone with me and didn't have much time to get ready. I got out of and stood beside the car, waiting for them to make it around her block. When she got back, we were both greeted by a white woman who'd just moved into the apartment below her. Although Andre is a half inch taller than me, two shades lighter, and was clean shaven (I had a beard) with locs

(I had a Caesar), this woman apparently couldn't tell the difference between us, and addressed Alecia as if I were him.

"Sorry to make so much noise moving the couches in last night. Didn't mean to keep you up if I did. I'll bring you two a cake this week! Do you like cake?"

"Um, yes. We like cake."

"Great! See y'all later!"

Alecia didn't correct her because what would she have said? "Oh, he's not Andre. Just a random nigga in gray sweatpants chillin' at my house with me at noon while my boyfriend isn't here. Nothing weird about that at all." I'd never been so thankful for gentle racism in my life.

To continue the ruse, Alecia motioned for me to just come back upstairs with her and wait. I followed her and her dog up the stairs, and then through her kitchen to her living room as she stuffed her MacBook in her attaché. While performing that motion, her blouse lifted on her right side, exposing a half inch of skin above her hip in the space where her shirt ended and her comfortable slacks began. I reached out and laid my right hand on her skin. She inched back, pressing her ass against my pants and arching her back, her face brushing mine and her locs tickling my neck. We paused in that moment and locked eyes, as if we were both agreeing and accepting that what was about to happen was about to happen.

And then we had sex.

It wasn't the best sex ever. It was too frantic and anxious for that. It reminded me of what happens when you're hungry for hours and finally eat but can't enjoy the food because scarfing it down gives you a stomachache.

Also, although I knew he was at work, I kept picturing Andre leaving the ice cream shop and sprinting up the steps, perhaps because he thought he accidentally left the stove on and wanted to make sure. In another dramatization, Andre knew Alecia would still be home, and thought to surprise her with a bouquet from Harold's Flower Shop on Fifth. I kept glancing toward the door, anticipating and dreading him bursting through while clutching a dozen roses, a bottle of rosé, and a teddy bear with her name on it. No man has ever been a better boyfriend than the boyfriend Andre was inside my head.

We were silent during the five-minute ride to the AWC. And then, when I parked on Liberty Avenue outside the building, Alecia turned to me:

"Well I guess that just happened, didn't it?"

"Yeah, I guess it did."

"I don't know what we're supposed to do now."

"Me neither."

"I'm going to need some time."

She jumped out of the car and walked into the AWC, exactly like the dozens of other times I'd dropped her off or picked her up from work.

We didn't see or talk to each other for the next two days. I feared that her ask for space was a kind way of communicating that our tryst was cool, but not cool or good enough for her to risk uprooting her entire life. Even though we'd bonded over the stories of the women I was dating and sleeping with, and even after the orgasms she had when we had sex, I still doubted I could satisfy her. She was just so much—so tall, so curvy, so confident, so successful, so funny, so pretty—and I wasn't sure if I was enough.

Nigga neurosis has been my existential state of being since first becoming aware of what it was supposed to mean to be black and that being black was supposed to mean something; a ceaseless wonderment that existed in concert with the concept of whiteness and my proximity to it. *Is this white store clerk following me because I'm black? Did I win this scholarship because I'm black? Did I lose this job because I'm black?* It hasn't been debilitating— it's less like a pebble in my shoe and more like a patch on the elbow of a blazer—but it's always there. As I've grown older and more fuck-deficient, I've learned to embrace it. By my thirties, *Did I get this promotion because I'm black?* became *Shit, I hope I got this promotion because I'm black, and I don't give a fuck if you care because these white niggas got a four-hundred-year head start.* Of the dozens of competing and intersecting and self-sabotaging anxieties I carry, a worry about whether I'm using my blackness as a crutch ain't one of them. I will mine every morsel possible out of this blackness thing while I still can, and I'll eat those morsels with fried chicken and watermelon juice.

I hadn't, however, been able to escape the fear of not being what I considered to be "black enough" where it mattered most to me: in the bedroom. When faced with any sort of romantic ambiguity—even something as slight as a text not received within a reasonable period of time—I still reverted back to the fifteen-year-old too scared of girls to even raise his hand in a classroom a cute girl happened to be in. None of the evidence I'd acquired since then that I might actually be good at sex—including women literally telling me, "Hey, you're actually good at this"—mattered. I developed a sexual dysmorphic disorder that I'd been unable to shake. Ironically, this unending desperation to impress is what led to the cultivation of that "talent." I tried to fuck each woman I slept with like she'd put my name on a hot air balloon if I didn't put it down. (A sign, perhaps, reading "Amon Young . . . because the D is silent.") I needed to hear them scream my name because I'd convinced myself that was the only way they wouldn't throw mud on it when we were done.

A by-product of this strain of self-consciousness was that

it assumed the worst of black women. I'm sure there are black women who have kicked and laughed men out of bed for not satisfying them. I know there are black women who've shared emails, phone calls, and texts with each other about underwhelming partners, perhaps even spending entire happy hours or drinking entire bottles of Apothic Red on couches while roasting each excruciating detail. And perhaps, maybe, I've been the cause of one of those gatherings. I don't know. But I was terrified of and bracing myself for an in-person cruelness that never actually came. The black women who I was sexually intimate with, the black women who chose me and were also chosen by me, were the antitheses of the merciless succubi I feared they'd be.

Still, I knew I was falling in love with Alecia, and I dreaded doing or not doing anything that would encourage her to reconsider the change in our relationship. And I think that this was, considering how preposterous some of my anxieties were, a relatively *normal* hang-up. (Imagine that?) These fears were slightly alleviated that Friday afternoon, when she called and wanted to come over after work to talk. She came through at seven, with blue Levi's and a vintage *Super Mario Bros.* baby tee, a pair of red-and-white high-top Chuck Taylors, her black leather Coach attaché, and her locs pinned up in a bun. She also brought an ounce of weed. It felt like I dreamed her up; a Manic Pixie Bougie Black Girl conjured from twenty-five years of fantasy. We sat on my couch and talked about the past week—how she was feeling, how I was doing, and mostly how surreal it had been. And then we smoked. She's a much more experienced smoker than I am, and when I struggled to inhale properly she offered to shotgun me. And so for the next fifteen minutes, she'd take a pull from the blunt, press her full and glossy lips an inch away from mine, and blow the smoke into my mouth.

It was the sexiest thing that ever happened to me. So sexy that I felt like I should have had a sexy stunt double; a Wilhelmina Model on standby, waiting to get tagged in for scenes too sexy to be believable.

And then we had sex again. It was perfect. She was perfect. And she told me I was perfect.

As our affair continued, I learned that her relationship with Andre was broken beyond repair, and had been before my involvement. But even after we both professed that we were in love with each other, and even after I told her, while lying in my bed after I finally convinced her to watch *Inglourious Basterds* with me (she hated it), that I was going to marry her, she still couldn't leave him. Not yet. She felt stuck. They had so many intersecting parts of their lives—a home, a car, a business, and mutual friends—that she felt trapped. She couldn't leave because she didn't know how to.

I did not enjoy being the side nigga. Sneaking around with this woman I loved provided me no rush, inspired in me no tingles, and indulged me no thrills. None of the sexiness of secret sex that I'd read about in books and saw in movies starring Michael Douglas applied here. I hated spending the evening with her only for her to go home to sleep in a bed with another man. I had no interest in taking her from him. I just didn't want him to exist. I wanted them to not be and us to be able to be. But since he did exist, I did allow myself to feel not quite good but not quite *terrible* about being so much *enough* for Alecia that she chose me because I fulfilled her more than he could. It wasn't exhilarating. But it felt absolving, like I'd finally be able to release that sexual self-consciousness I still humped around with me. Even if doing this confirmed that I wasn't as good of a person as I believed myself to be, I was willing to trade that self-righteousness for self-assurance. I'd be less of what I considered to be authentically *good* if it made me more of what I considered to be authentically *black*.

After we'd been seeing each other in secret for a month, we etched out a plan: She'd tell Andre it was over, and we'd scale back with each other—allowing her an opportunity to mourn the end of their relationship and get the shop and her living situation in order. And then, a few months later, we'd start "dating" publicly. I'd likely be seen as the rebound—and perhaps even a bit of an outcast for dating the ex of a guy I was cool with, like she'd forever be his property—but I was fine with that as long as I had her. She left for a week on a cruise with her girls, planning to have the talk with Andre when she returned.

Only she left her MacBook behind. And Andre used it one night to do some shop-related books in Excel. And Alecia's Gmail tab was still open. And I saw, on my Chromebook, Alecia's Gchat light turn green, which meant she was available. Which made me think she was back from her trip. And I messaged her "Hey." Which is usually innocent as fuck. You can't get more whitebread and Shirley Temple than "Hey." You say "Hey" to grandmothers on Facebook and work colleagues on Slack when you're pretending to be enthused about collaborative projects. Except this happened at one in the morning. Which naturally alerted Andre's spidey senses, and he did some light investigating and discovered a few explicit emails Alecia and I had exchanged. Fuck.

I know all of this because Alecia told me the day after she got back. And Alecia was able to tell me because Andre told her the night she got back, before he told her he forgave her and wanted to work things out. Also, the day after she returned from the cruise, he shared a picture of a flower and some candles and a bathtub on Facebook, revealing to 3,500 of his closest friends that it was their two-year anniversary and implying that they were celebrating it. I saw this bizarre status and thought he was having a nervous breakdown and that Alecia was unsafe, and I pleaded with her to not go back to their apartment until he'd moved out. Especially because when that status was posted, Alecia was actually with me, sitting in my car parked in the lot attached to the Shadyside apartment complex I used to live in— one of the few places I was certain we'd be able to go and talk and not be seen. She felt like shit for hurting him, for creating such a sudden and brutal and public fracture in their lives, for not having the opportunity to collect herself and mourn, and for being a person who does what we did. She was also furious at me for being a person who does what we did, and for doing this with her. We were complicit in creating the fuckshit avalanche her life would soon be wrecked by, and I should've just allowed her to end things with him peacefully and organically instead of forcing her hand. But mostly she was annoyed.

"Why would he even want me back after reading what he read?" she wondered. "How . . . just . . . this shit is so fucking . . . fake."

We were now forged into coupledom because we had to be. There was no point in not being. We'd have no months of separation while we pretended not to be together. No hard but run-of-the-mill breakup where Andre and Alecia had weeks and months to detangle themselves from each other. No space for Alecia to just chill and breathe and break by herself. No opportunity for Alecia to introduce me to her family after a reasonable and appropriate amount of time after her breakup with Andre. During our affair, we talked frequently about marriage. Now, if our relationship ended with anything but a marriage, we'd be seen as homewrecking motherfuckers *and* idiots for doing all of this just for a few months of fucking and some calamari.

I braced for the inevitable social fallout we'd face when our new status was made public, but something happened I should've anticipated but didn't. *We* didn't face it. *She* did. I'm tempted to attribute the distinction in how we were regarded to our roles in what happened, and that if I were the person in the relationship and Alecia the mistress, I'd be the one receiving the brunt of the social ostracization. But nah. The blame when a man and a woman decide to participate in an affair mostly falls on the woman. Men are easily forgiven for doing dirt, because we're expected to be dusty—like we emerge from the womb caked in mud. All a man has to do is say "I fucked up" and lines stretch around the block, offering waves of praise for his growth and maturity and the chance he took and the nuts he grabbed by doing the fucked-up thing. It gets lauds, it gets applause, and in Jay-Z's case with *4:44*, it gets Grammy nominations. Alecia, however, was made to feel by the people who were no longer her friends as if she destroyed him, for no reason other than because that's what black bitches do. Destroy good men for sport and clink goblets of moscato while bonding on couches about the niggas they forever ruined. They treated her as if she were one of those merciless succubi that existed in my head. On at least three occasions, niggas who were friends of Andre's approached her in public and pleaded for her to reconsider, as if Alecia's agency was a psychic threat to their own relationships with women.

(And it turns out it was. Over the next few years, several different women confided in Alecia that what she did convinced them to stop allowing themselves to wallow in uninspired relationships, investing in and staying with men who hadn't invested as much in them. Although she was made to feel like Hester Prynne then, to her friends and a few admirers, she secretly became Diana Prince.)

After Andre moved out of Alecia's place, she found a bigger and much more expensive apartment a half mile away in Manchester. When the lease on my apartment expired, I moved in, and we hid and hibernated for the next year. If we wanted to see a movie, we'd drive out to Pittsburgh Mills or Waterworks—where it was less crowded and we were less likely to run into people we knew—instead of the Waterfront or Southside Works. No more happy hours at Savoy or parties at the Shadow Lounge or 720. If we possessed the urge to club-hop and dance and drink, we'd spend a weekend in D.C. Or maybe we'd just invite a select group of people to our place for Spades tournaments. We'd limited our regular Pittsburgh outdoorsing to work, Giant Eagle, LA Fitness, church, Alecia's mom's house, and visits to Hillman Cancer Center to see Mom, who was diagnosed with lung cancer in October of 2012. In March we drove to Austin, Texas, for SXSW, ate the best shrimp tacos that have ever existed in the history of shrimp or tacos, and saw the Roots live, standing fifteen feet from the stage as they performed a forty-five-minute-long version of "You Got Me." If I hadn't fallen in love with Alecia already, I would have on that trip. In April, Alecia relinquished control of the ice cream shop to Andre, who then proceeded to tell people around Pittsburgh that he'd founded and funded the shop himself, with Alecia helping *him*. The shop closed three years later.

The ostracization and fallout Alecia felt began to pass after that first year. People really don't give a shit about who and what you're sleeping with unless you're sleeping with someone *they're* sleeping with. If not, the fucks they give about who you're fucking slowly wither away until they're eventually swallowed by more pressing thoughts about car payments and couscous and whatever the hell else people think about when they're done pretending to care about what you do.

When Mom died in October of 2013, Alecia sang "Amazing Grace" at her funeral. I forget sometimes that she can sing. She has too many talents to keep track of them all. She can't *sang* sing. She ain't Aretha or Adele. But she'd definitely blow Alicia Keys the fuck out of the water. Alicia Keys ain't got shit on Alecia Dawn.

I proposed to Alecia the Saturday after Thanksgiving, three months after she'd already picked out the ring she wanted at a store in the Clark Building downtown. We got married twice the following summer: once on the summer solstice in a private ceremony at my cousin David's church in New Castle, and then a month later at the Grand Concourse in Station Square with 120 guests, a brunch buffet, and complimentary mimosas. Only a few people there knew we were already married, and even fewer knew of the circumstances behind our start.

The girl with the locs at Ava Lounge, the one who danced with me for two songs and then forgot about me for three years, is now my wife. We have a daughter now too. She was born on November 30, 2015, and her name is Zoe Vivienne, after Mom. She is sublime and surreal. She exists now and didn't exist before and only exists now because of us, and that's still *fucking insane*. I've literally told her, more than once, as I hold her in my arms in disbelief, that she is fucking insane, and I say this to my baby daughter because I am possibly a bad father. And she stares confused, and then asks me to turn on *Elmo's World*.

When people we're not particularly close with—a new neighbor, perhaps, or a couple we're introduced to at a brunch, maybe—ask how we met, we usually tell them we met at work. If they probe, we might share the Reggae Night story, which Alecia only slightly remembers. ("I remember dancing with a nigga who kept trying to talk to me," she said during a Spades party at our apartment in 2014. "And I remember thinking, 'Please stop talking because it's dancing time, not talking time.'")

I'm tempted sometimes to tell them the full story, so they'll know that we're real niggas who did and went through some shit. I've lived my entire life risk- and confrontation-averse. I don't turn right on red lights. I've actually prayed thrice before meals because I forgot whether I already blessed the food. My idea of risky and ballsy is to drink milkshakes without Lactaid. But I enjoyed learning that I had that in me—whatever *that* is—and don't mind much if others know too. But I'm just not as compelled anymore to prove those things to people. And it's not that I believe that I now possess the validation that has been so elusive to me, that external sanctioning of sufficient and vigorous heterosexuality that I sometimes almost convince myself doesn't matter anymore. I'm just no longer as interested in making the effort.

# 13

# LIVING WHILE BLACK KILLED MY MOM

Assuming of course that he dies before I do, when Dad passes away, I'll have a stockpile of entertaining stories to share about him at his funeral. So many that I've already begun vetting them for time and clarity and (assumed) audience, and practicing the cadences of the ones that have made the first cut. I'm even leaning toward incorporating a song—Leon Thomas's cover of Horace Silver's "Song for My Father." I plan to begin and conclude the eulogy by singing, *"If there was ever a man who was generous, gracious and good, that was my dad. The man."* This song, by the way, also includes an extensive yodel. And all the Everclear in State College wouldn't convince me to do that too.

One of these stories took place when I was in sixth grade, a month before basketball season at St. Barts. We learned that the school had ordered new uniforms for us. Instead of the extra smedium nylon nut-huggers they rocked the season before—we called them Stocktons (a reference to Utah Jazz point guard John Stockton, whose shorts were so famously short that he was practically hooping in a jockstrap)—the new shorts were to be baggy and the shirts reversible and personalized with our last names on the back. Which was fucking awesome. Unfortunately, a bout of strep throat kept me out of school for a week when the uniforms came in, which meant that by the time I got back to school, all of my teammates had already chosen the large and extra-large shorts. Which meant I had to squeeze into a medium, which fit my disproportionately juicy booty like spandex.

I was distraught by this. I was already annoyingly self-conscious about everything, and wasn't looking forward to an entire season of breaking zone presses in an adolescent thong, my ample butt cheeks flapping in the wind as I led three-on-two fast breaks. I might have even cried when going home that day and sharing my laments with Dad—who, to his credit, seemed to be trying really, really, really hard to care (and not laugh). Convinced that parents just don't fucking understand, I retreated to my bedroom, watched *MacGyver* and the Weather Channel, and pouted myself to sleep.

Still recovering from the strep, I woke up in the middle of the night and went downstairs to grab some orange juice. Dad was still up, sitting at the kitchen table listening to Miles Davis and doing a crossword puzzle. He was wearing a Sunday Morning Warriors basketball league shirt and some hoop shorts. *My* hoop shorts.

My dad was six foot two and weighed close to two hundred pounds then. If the shorts fit me like spandex, they glued to his thighs like spray paint. I still have no idea how he even managed to get them on without a quart of olive oil and a sheet of Reynolds Wrap. But I knew immediately *why* he was wearing them. He knew how upset I was about the shorts, so he was do-ing what he could to stretch them out for me.

He noticed me noticing the shorts, and he nodded his head at me and continued his crossword. I went to the kitchen, poured a glass of orange juice, drank it, went back upstairs, and wondered if he was going to wash them before giving them back to me.

When Mom died in 2013—the culmination of an excruci-ating and goddamn fucking tragic five-year stretch where she (1) discovered in 2008 that she had chronic obstructive pulmo-nary disease (2) lost her house in 2011 to foreclosure, (3) experi-enced debilitating and mysterious back pain from 2010 to 2012 that doctors tried to remedy and diagnose with everything from steroid injections to a fucking spinal tap, and (4) discovered, in 2012, that she had stage four lung cancer—choosing the topic of the twenty-two-minute-long speech at her wake the day before her funeral didn't require the same extensive submissions pro-cess. I just didn't have as many cute and meaningful stories I was comfortable delivering, choosing instead to opine on how "while everyone loves their mom, not everyone has a mom who every-one loves." I also shared that the reason why I always turned the bacon, eggs, and toast she'd make for breakfast into sandwiches was because I never liked her eggs that much, and putting them in a sandwich made them easier to swallow.

This lack of compelling and entertaining stories wasn't some sort of metaphorical exemplification of a strained relationship with her. Mom and Dad were my two favorite people. Mom and I even had a secret handshake. We'd greet and leave each other by shaking hands, then rubbing the tips of our index and pointer fingers together, then pressing our thumbs together, then bouncing our (right) elbows together, then snapping our fingers. We'd developed it when I was nine or ten. And the last time we did it completely was the day of her discharge from the hospice on Fisk Street in Lawrenceville. We tried again a day later when she was back home, lying in the hospital bed stationed in my parents' living room—three days before she died—but by then she was too weak to follow through.

Instead, my archive of repeatable stories about Mom was limited by circumstance, tact, and love for Dad. The "Your Turn" story, for instance, when my parents were homeless for a few months and staying with Nana, couldn't be told the way I'd want it to be told—and the way it needed to be told—without indicting Dad.

I remember the multiple buses Mom would catch to and from work when we didn't have a car—the 94A or the 71A to the East Liberty bus station, and then the EBA to town—and the work bag filled with UPMC insurance verification binders and her lunch (usually an apple, a turkey sandwich, a salad with French or Italian dressing, and a pack of ToastChee peanut butter crackers) and the purse she'd lug with her, and how the weight of each would make her left shoulder lean like a tree permanently bent by wind. I remember how annoyed with Dad she'd be if she came home from work and the dishes weren't done or the trash wasn't emptied. And I remember how sometimes if it was 5:45 and Mom was due home at 6:00, Dad would morph into a middle-aged nigga Quicksilver; doing twelve thousand chores in fifteen minutes to escape her wrath. And I remember getting annoyed at Mom for getting annoyed at Dad and ruining our fun, a feeling I'm still ashamed to admit I felt.

The bulk of those eulogy-worthy memories of Dad occurred during my adolescence, when I was developing as a basketball player and spent countless evenings and weekends with him as he shepherded me from court to court and neighborhood to neighborhood. And, once I got good enough, from city to city, state to state, and school to school. Simultaneously serving as my drill master, coach, instructor, one-on-one opponent, hype man, financier, adviser, protector, bouncer, dietitian, jitney, critic, vision board, sponsor, and parent. Willing to challenge each and every entity, real or imagined, standing between us and our ultimate goal—a college scholarship. Sometimes, his was the only black face in the gym (or the league) besides mine on the court, his presence ensuring that "these white people" didn't try to mess with his boy. And I have so many great stories.

There's the two hundred shots a day we'd take on the courts behind Peabody High School the summer of '89 to upgrade my shot from a slow-release, appropriate-for-a-ten-year-old set shot to a full jump shot released over my head and at the peak of my jump. The basketball magazines and almanacs he'd buy me when I professed an interest in devouring as much about the game and its history as I could. The mornings I'd watch him play in the Sunday Morning Warriors basketball league at the Homewood Y, where I'd sneak on the court at halftime to shoot foul shots. Even today, his Facebook page is home to several snapshots of those moments. Usually me receiving some award from some camp or league or game, and him behind the lens, making sure my trophy was facing the camera. But I also remember that he was so available to me because, during this time, he wasn't working. This Dad-specific nostalgia might not exist the same way without the bricks laid by Mom.

I do not know how I should feel about Dad. I do not know how I should feel about myself. I know I love him. I know Dad isn't just my dad. He's my homie. My partner. My dude. My *nigga*. I know that the relationship I have with him is rare. I know this because I've seen it and my friends and family have told me, many of whom have confided that they wish they had a relationship with their fathers like the one I have with mine. It's a relationship ensconced in tenderness. I've been taught by Dad that emotion and emotions and emoting aren't just time-consuming annoyances to keep stashed away in a vault, pressure compressed, until they're released as hypertension and acid reflux. I have seen him cry in front of me, over the deaths of his mother and father; the deaths of his best friend Jim Payne and his closest cousin, Ron Hambrick; and frequently after the death of Mom. And when Francisco Cabrera's single and Sid Bream's slide and Barry Bonds's terrible fucking throw allowed the Braves to beat the Pirates in 1992, and Mom told me to go upstairs because she didn't want me to see him like that. And when recounting the story of the summer after his freshman year of college when he worked at the Crane Company in New Castle—where his father had worked for a decade and would continue to work until his retirement decades later—and how terrible and terrifying and goddamn fucking *hard* that work was. And the recollection of his dad doing that terrible and terrifying and goddamn fucking hard work for decades brought Dad to tears.

And while I wasn't there to see it, I know Dad cried when he saw me take the court at Canisius the first time. He and Mom made the drive up from Pittsburgh to Buffalo to watch us play the University of Kentucky. "When you guys left the locker room and ran on the court for your warm-ups," Mom told me a few months later, "your Dad was so overcome by emotion that he couldn't even look. He just stared at his popcorn."

I will not have to wait for his deathbed confession to finally hear that he loves me. I've heard it more times than I can count, and I've known it since I've known what love is. We greet each other with hugs (sometimes) and pounds (mostly). When I was a kid, we'd watch everything from Connie Hawkins Summer

Basketball League games to *Miller's Crossing* together. And now I'll drive past his house and pick him up to go watch NBA play-off games at BRGR in East Liberty or perhaps *Sicario* or *Black Panther* at the mall. I still believe his pancakes are the best I've ever had. (I once asked him what his secret recipe was. His answer: "I follow the directions on the box.") And he'll still make them at the drop of a hat if I ask him to.

Dad is a sweet man. Dad will also fight if he believes he or someone he cares about has been disrespected, a trait he picked up as the second oldest in a family with nine kids (five brothers and three sisters). Along with *nigger*-hurling and machete-clutching teens working at now out-of-business ice cream shops in Squirrel Hill, I've seen Dad challenge and/or fight (1) the entire security team at the Marine Midland Center in downtown Buffalo when I was at Canisius and they wouldn't allow him back to the locker room after a game against Loyola, (2) a six-foot-forever and six-hundred-million-pound man whose pit bull chained to the fence at Pennley ate my basketball when it rolled next to him, and (3) a seventy-five-year-old man in front of the Homewood House. (They got into an argument about door-opening etiquette, and Dad tackled him after he believed the man was reaching for a switchblade. My dad is a character in *Luke Cage*.)

He did not pass the fighting gene on to me. Perhaps because he knew how dangerous our neighborhood was, and knew I had better things to do than fighting potentially lethal niggas over perceived disrespect on Mellon Street. Or maybe because he was equipped to do all of my fighting for me. But much of who I am today can be traced back to him. We have the same walk. We have the same voice. We have the same shoe size. We are the same height. We both consider *The Godfather* to be our favorite movie, New Castle chili the best hot dog condiment, and

Marvin Gaye's *What's Going On* the best LP. His presence has enhanced my life in a way that's beyond mortal comprehension. But I am haunted by the possibility that this enhancement of my years on earth snatched years away from my mom.

Mom's cancer diagnosis wasn't a surprise to me. She'd been a pack-a-day smoker for thirty years; stopping cold turkey in 2008 after a doctor said that her lung situation was so tenuous and dire that the next cigarette could literally kill her. In 2009, she began to need regular oxygen treatments. And from then until the day she died, pain was a constant, a brick-filled knapsack slung around her shoulders like a sash. If anything, I was surprised that they didn't find her tumors sooner. Considering her symptoms and her history, lung cancer just seemed to make sense. But it wasn't discovered until the discovery made death a formality. She was given six months, took those, and stole away six more.

I think she might still be alive today if she had been a white woman from Mount Lebanon or Fox Chapel or Morningside or Bloomfield or wherever the fuck upper-middle-class white women are from instead of a working-class black woman who grew up in a brownstone co-op at the top of the hill on Tilden Street in Belmar Gardens. I am not sure of this. I will never be sure of this. But the thought remains stuck in my mind. Maybe the doctors would have taken her back pain more seriously. Maybe they would have done better tests. Maybe they wouldn't have shoved as many needles and stents inside of her like old business cards and receipts stuffed into an empty shoebox. Maybe they would have paid more attention to her. Maybe they would have tried a thing they didn't try, or recommended a specialist she didn't see, or suggested a diet she didn't take. But maybe, because Mom was a black woman, her discomfort didn't register the same way it would have if her skin were paler and her hair were straighter. Maybe she wouldn't have developed an addiction to nicotine. I am aware that white people are also susceptible to addiction. But they're not *as* susceptible. Their world isn't *as* stress-inducing. The myriad things to get addicted to aren't *as* easily found where they live, aren't *as* prominently advertised, and the resources to overcome those sicknesses aren't *as* hard to find. And when addiction does cripple white communities, as it has with the opioid epidemic, they don't get America's fire and fury, as black neighborhoods devastated by crack did. They get pillows and twenty-three-minute-long *Nightline* profiles.

White privilege—the idea that whiteness, for white Americans, provides an imperishable benefit of the doubt and a flexible and perpetually renewable get-out-of-jail-free card—is often dismissed by critics and even spoken of by believers in it as an abstract and academic term with no basis in reality. But it doesn't exist without the cultural, social, political, and legal reinforcement that white people's feelings, thoughts, desires, and opinions matter more than the feelings, thoughts, desires, and opinions of non-white people (black people, specifically). It's not so much that blacks are thought to be subhuman—although that belief festers too. It's that the humanity of whites is the only humanity that matters. Their humanity is the standard all other humanities are judged by. This ceaseless homage toward whiteness also affects how physical pain and discomfort are assessed and treated. In both East Harlem, New York, and Columbia, South Carolina, today stand statues of iconic doctor James Marion Sims, colloquially known as the "father of modern gynecology." Sims is most famous for inventing the speculum and finding a cure for vesicovaginal fistula—landmark discoveries he made after hundreds of experiments on purchased and borrowed black female slaves. And since Sims either believed black women were unable to experience pain or just didn't give a fuck about it, local anesthesia was never used. He ripped these women open—gashing their vaginas like old newspapers torn and twisted to light charcoal grills—and this motherfucker has *monuments*.

While this particular grade of gynecological terror no longer exists in America, the feelings behind it and the effects of it still linger. In April of 2018, the *New York Times* published an extensive feature on black maternal mortality, revealing that black women are four times more likely to die from childbirth and other pregnancy-related causes than white women are. *Four times.* A University of Virginia study published in the *Proceedings of the National Academy of Sciences* showed that doctors, in *two thousand fucking sixteen*, still believed black people possess a supernatural tolerance for pain. Our pain just doesn't matter as much because our humanity doesn't either. The privilege of experiencing pain—and the privilege of that pain mattering—is exclusive to whiteness.

And I think about that year before Mom learned she had cancer, when the pain from her back would radiate down her spine, through her thighs, and then burst out the soles of her feet, making her wince and grunt and grit and cry while standing and sitting and walking and showering and shitting and getting up and lying down. I think about how she remained warm and sweet and kind and Mom through all of that fucking shit—still whipping up her world-famous and diabetes-inducing French toast, still rocking and changing and collecting the dozens of sterling silver bracelets she wore on her wrists like medieval chainmail, still inviting me over to watch *30 Rock* with her—almost as if she was trying to win a bet. Like someone wagered two hundred bucks that she could remain sane through excruciating pain, and she needed the money for a White

House Black Market shopping spree. I think about how Mom might still be here if she were white. Or maybe just a fairer-skinned black woman, with caramel brûlée latte skin instead of the Snickers-tinted pigment she possessed and I inherited from her. I think about how Mom might still be here if she'd decided to stop smoking after twenty years instead of thirty. I wonder if the stress and the pressure from existing as our family's only stable income for a decade permeated, consumed, and overwhelmed her, and I think about whether that drove her to smoke for thirty years instead of twenty. I think about how she fed me with her body, and how I ate from and off of her like she was a transubstantiating deity instead of a person, a flesh and vessel and marrow and blood human being. I think about how she had the world's fluffiest Afro in the seventies and the world's juiciest Jheri curl in the eighties and loved Michelle Obama and Tina Turner and reading Toni Morrison and listening to Steely Dan and Jill Scott and Ivan Lins and going to shows at the Manchester Craftsmen's Guild when Pat Metheny was in town. I think about how she just gave gave gave gave gave gave gave because life took took took took took took took. I think about how I took took took took took from her. And I can't discern if this parasitic relationship was typical—if sons take from their mothers because that's just what we do—or if our relationship was unnaturally pathogenic. I think about how neither of those options is good. I think about how black women are socialized to be enduring and steadfast and forgiving and giving giving giving so much that there's nothing left of them but dust. I think about how this dynamic exists both within America's general white dominating culture and in black American culture. I think about how its existence in black American culture is perhaps even more hurtful and dispiriting, because there's no deliverance from it in what should be your home and your people. I think about how black women are praised for their strength the way you'd praise a mule or a swarm of ants or a handshake or a really expensive garbage bag. I think about how praise of black women reads like a word association game where someone just placed *strength* in a thesaurus and found the synonyms. Black women are stout. Black women are unyielding. Black women are stable. Black women are durable. Black women are stalwart. Black women are firm. Black women are poised. Black women are reliable. Black women have grace too. But grace is just another way of praising them for being strong for everyone else while also juggling and then ignoring the urge to firebomb the entire fucking planet.

I think about how that continued, even in death, as the $7,500 Dad gave me from the life insurance settlement he received after Mom passed allowed me to finish paying for the engagement ring I bought for Alecia and put a deposit down for our wedding seven months later. I think about how I wished so badly that Mom were at that wedding, that she would have been able to experience that day, that I've invented memories of her there at the Grand Concourse in Station Square, her visage psychologically Photoshopped into each wedding album. And then I think about how her specifically not being there made it possible. If she were still alive, I wouldn't have been able to afford it.

I think about all the things I wanted to be able to do for her that I wasn't able to do for her when she was alive. Like for instance fly her to D.C. when the cherry blossoms were in flower and have Sunday brunch on the river at Sequoia in Georgetown, because I know she would have fucking loved that. Or maybe just buy her a new kitchen table or an updated Kindle. I think about how I can do these things now, and that I can do these things because she traded her life for mine. I think about how cigarettes killed her. How metastasized cancer killed her.

How white privilege killed her. How racism killed her. How blackness killed her. How being a black woman killed her. How being strong killed her. How America is a serial killer of black women.

Dad did not expect to outlive Mom. She was six years younger than him, and he assumed that he'd eventually make her a widow. I did too. He said this to me six weeks after her funeral, the day after I told him I asked Alecia to marry me. He's repeated it several times since. Perhaps more. I know he's said it to me, to his sister Betty Jean, and to the grief counseling group he's in that meets once a week at Mt. Ararat. He's also more into church now than I've ever seen him be. Along with grief counseling, he's part of a mentorship group, a Bible study group, and he attends Mt. Ararat's Saturday-evening service every week. There are nights now when I'll call him, and he'll share a Bible verse he just read. I learned from one of these calls that David didn't just kill Goliath. He decapitated him too, and then taunted the Philistines with his head, like O-Ren Ishii threatening the Yakuza dons with Boss Tanaka's head. I would have paid more attention in religion class at St. Barts if Sister Roberta shared tidbits like that.

Sometimes I join him at church. And I'll glance over at him while the choir's singing "Goin' Up Yonder" and his eyes will be closed, but the space on his face from his eyelids to the peaks of his cheekbones will be damp. And I'll know he's thinking about Mom. And it'll remind me of the last time we were all at Mt. Ararat together. Alecia and I decided to join the church. But in order for me to become a member, I'd have to get baptized first. So I did, with twenty other soon-to-be members, all wearing the stark white gowns Mt. Ararat provided, waiting in the church's basement to be called to the altar and dipped into the baptismal pool.

The pictures of Mom and me in Mt. Ararat's lobby after the ceremony were the last pictures we'd take together. Chemo had stolen away her hair and much of her body weight. But she was still active. On her good days, sometimes we'd drive out to Monroeville Mall together and just walk around. This was one of those good days, and she was alert, energetic, and beaming. I remember how smooth the top of her head was. She'd begun to grow some fuzz back, and it grew and spread evenly, making it feel like the cover of a couch too expensive for me to afford.

Two months later, my parents also joined. Mom was in hospice care by then, so two associate pastors came to her room at Family Hospice and Palliative Care to perform the ceremony there. Mom cried. I recorded it on my iPhone.

She died six weeks later. Dad called me at home to tell me she'd passed. It was 8:15 A.M. The last time I saw her was twelve hours earlier, at my parents' house. She wasn't dead yet. Not technically. But she was already gone.

Dad, however, is still here. Crying in church while thinking about his departed wife. I wonder what he thinks about when he's crying. What exactly induces those tears? Is it just because he misses her? Is it because of how she suffered? Or does he feel guilty? Should he feel guilty?

I never ask, and I never will. It's not that I don't want to know. It's just that I believe I'm culpable too—and I don't believe I possess the right to demand an answer.

# 14

# EAST LIBERTY KUTZ

If you happen to encounter Dad while he's sitting on a couch somewhere, and you fill him with enough Good & Plenty and A&W Root Beer, he might share the story about the first time he took me to the barbershop. I don't remember any of this happening, but apparently I was four years old, and he took me to a shop on Frankstown Avenue in Homewood to get rid of the fluffy and happy and nappy baby fro I'd been rocking since birth.

According to Dad, for a week he hyped this as a big day for me; a *big boy* day. And I anticipated going to the barbershop for the first time like I was going to Chuck E. Cheese's. When that Saturday morning finally came, I got up, got dressed, brushed my teeth and combed my hair without being reminded to, and even made myself breakfast. (Pop-Tarts, but still.) When we drove to the shop, I hopped out of the car, sprinted through the entrance, sat down, and started reading a *Jet* magazine splayed on one of the coffee tables. I was a big boy about to get his hair cut and you couldn't tell me shit. And then, when it was time for me to get into the chair, I started crying. And not just tears, but a shrieking and piercing and terrifying wail of torment. I cried like my dog just died and my parents were forcing me to eat him. *And the barber hadn't even started cutting my hair yet.*

The screams intensified once the cut began. Everyone else in the shop stopped what they were doing to witness me having an exorcism in the barber's chair. And then they'd look at Dad and shake their heads in disgust for raising such a pussy-ass little boy and bringing his bitch ass to their sanctuary. When the barber was done, Dad approached his chair and apologized, even offering to pay double. The barber nodded his head, blinked, and said, "Don't bring that boy back to me again." This clear disrespect immediately put Dad back into Dad mode, and he sized up the barber, looked him dead in the eyes, and said, "Don't worry, nigga. I won't."

We returned to the shop three months later. But we avoided the same barber's chair, and Dad urged me to sit in an empty chair near the back exit. This is something I'd never do now when entering a new shop, as I've learned that a pristine chair on a busy Saturday is a reliable sign of a shitty barber. We were beggars, though, in no position to be prissy. The chair belonged to a twentysomething woman named Miss Jackie, who'd just graduated from barber school and struggled with getting customers because she was new and a woman. As a result of this latent sexism, I've also learned, in the three decades that I've been getting my hair cut at black barbershops, that if a shop employs a female barber, she's likely the best barber there because they wouldn't allow a woman to man the chair—and she wouldn't be trusted by us to sculpt our line-ups and fades—if she weren't. It reminds me of how Dad said there were no black bench players on his New Castle Red Hurricanes high school basketball team in the early sixties. If a black guy was on the team, his ass better be a fucking starter.

Miss Jackie apparently did a commendable job with my hair—and I made it through with no tears—and she officially became my first barber. Six years later, when she moved to Wade's Barber Shop on Kelly Street, I followed her there. Four years after that, when I was old enough to catch the 86A or 77B and go to the shop by myself, I stayed with her. We were together long enough for her to witness and participate in creating the gamut of black male hairstyles modeled on my head during that time. A glance through my class pictures from second to twelfth grade is a carousel of trendy and silly and (mostly) rapper-inspired styles.

From second grade to fourth I had a taper, which was, well, imagine a Kid 'n Play–esque box, but with the top rounded like a crescent moon instead of flat, and the sides bald. In fifth and sixth grade, the taper morphed to a Rakim, a derivative of the style Rakim from Eric B. & Rakim rocked, a shorter but still quite voluminous box with a part above my left eye extending all the way back, splitting the box into two asymmetrical rectangles. I loved the Rakim, but the hair I most desired belonged to MC Hammer, who had a juicy and perpetually sweaty S-curl and (at least) three separate parts stretching lengthwise from ear to ear, wrapping around the back of his head like yellow traffic lines. In hindsight, his hair made his head look like a caramel Blow Pop dropped onto a barbershop floor, but twelve-year-old me wanted that shit and begged my parents to allow me to have it. (They didn't). As I reached my teens, my hair got more conservative. While many of my peers, influenced by niggas in movies about niggas from California and then Bone Thugs-N-Harmony, were allowing their hair to grow so it could be twisted, braided, plaited, and cornrowed, I had a bald fade with a half inch of hair sprouting from the top of my head. The type of hair that communicated I had a Jansport filled with Trapper Keepers and lunchboxes stocked with cups of deliciously syrupy fruit cocktail and ham sandwiches made with love. It was the Honda Civic of hair. If that hair existed today, it would watch *NCIS*—shit, it would own the *NCIS* DVD box set—and it would refer to Mark Harmon as "the Harm."

Then, in eleventh grade, I saw *Above the Rim*, still arguably the best movie ever made about street basketball tournaments on nine-foot-rims and one-on-one games played on high-rise rooftops with no railings. Duane Martin's Kyle Lee Watson had hair that was close-cropped and the exact same length on every part of his head. Later that year, Allen Iverson grew his bald head out and modeled the same style at Georgetown. In Pittsburgh and in other parts of the country, this is called a Caesar. In some other parts of the country, it's called an "even" or a "regular." For the next *nineteen years*, this would be the style I kept.

The first year of the Caesar, I kept a brush on me everywhere I went, and I'd brush in homeroom, on the bus, in the bathroom between classes, between pickup games at Mellon Park, and while watching *NYPD Blue* at home. I wanted—shit, I *needed*—to get waves and brushing my hair with a furious and manic obsession was the only way it would happen. By my senior year, the waves were complete. My waves were so deep and wavy that niggas got seasick looking at the top of my head. My hair gave niggas vertigo. Unfortunately, while Miss Jackie was great at sculpting the boxes and tapers and Rakims I had before, she never gave me the sharpest line-ups. When your hair is as short as mine was, maintaining a sharp and perfectly symmetrical hairline without pushing said hairline back to the crown of your head is your barber's most vital job. You don't want to go full LeBron before nature decides it's time to go full LeBron. She remained my barber while I was on breaks from Canisius, but I'd return home every time disappointed that I'd have to sit back in her chair after receiving the sublime shape-ups from my barber in Buffalo—D at Sean's House of Masters on Delavan Avenue a block away from school. Each time I left his chair I felt an inch taller and 1.75 points cuter, and going back to Miss Jackie was like eating steak all year and then coming back home to Steak-Umms.

So I started cheating on her when I was home. Well, not *cheating* cheating. I wasn't hopping in nigga's chairs all willy-nilly and unprotected, or meeting them in highway-side motels or at dusk in deserted Kmart parking lots for quickie shape-ups and sideburn trims. I did, however, begin asking my boys about where they got their cuts from and if their barbers were monogamous or allowed to have "friends." And then, while going to hoop with Brian and his boy Haston one Saturday afternoon in July of 1998, we stopped at East Liberty Kutz, a shop in a sketchy alley off of North Sheridan between Penn and Centre Avenues in East Lib. Brian's barber—a sloppy fucking dickhead named Mo—first worked at a shop in Oakland when Brian was a student at Schenley. When Mo's bitch ass was kicked out of the Oakland shop for stealing niggas' pickles or some other triflin'-ass shit, Brian followed him to East Liberty.

As I sat in one of the plastic chairs near the door, waiting for Brian to get done, one of the barbers asked if I needed some help. I *did*—I'd been home for a week, and hadn't had a cut since two weeks before I came back—but telling the truth wasn't that easy. Saying yes and getting a cut there in a shop two miles away from my home shop would be a clear and unambiguous act of barber infidelity, and despite my lack of fulfillment at home, I wasn't sure I was ready to possess a new barber nigga mistress.

So I lied. "Nah, I'm good." And then sat there for the next five minutes, watching happy nigga after happy nigga receive exquisite lines from the other barbers in the shop while I stewed and visualized and dreaded the flaccid shape-up I'd get if I returned to Wade's and Miss Jackie. Chris Rock once said a man's only as faithful as his options, and after ten minutes of sitting in a bottomless buffet of superior barbers, I finally relented.

"Hey, man. Can I still hop in your chair?"

That chair belonged to Dre, who I'd later learn was the owner of the shop. I'd also learn, in the sixteen years that Dre remained my barber after that day, that he graduated from Wilkinsburg High in the early nineties, and had opened East Liberty Kutz a year before I sat in his chair. He was the only person I ever met who owned a car with hydraulics like the niggas in the West Coast rap videos, and he'd drive it once or twice a month each summer so niggas could marvel at his gravity-defying Cutlass with twenty-eight-inch wheels popping wheelies down Penn Ave. He dabbled in competitive bodybuilding years before he opened the shop, and still possessed remnants of that body. His forearms were larger and veinier than any six-foot and 190-pound man's were supposed to be. Like Popeye, but after Popeye hadn't been to LA Fitness in three months. Between his body and his curlyish hair and his light-skinnedness—he was basically the dieselest DeBarge brother; Kimbo Slice DeBarge—he was very popular with women. Some of whom would come into the shop and proposition Dre while other niggas were there. One woman even offered me five dollars to get out of the chair while Dre was cutting my hair so he could sit in it and she could give him a lap dance. (She was "joking," but I think she would have done it if I accepted.) This interest persisted despite Dre making *zero* effort to engage any of them—he'd treat them like little sisters he was annoyed with for eating the last of his Doritos. He also wore the same thing every day: a black T-shirt, baggy blue jeans, and the type of ratty and ashy black sneakers uncles wear to mow lawns and fry whiting.

We'd argue about sports, and he'd tease me—for months—about opinions he thought were foolish. Before one college football season, I'd read something on ESPN.com about a phenom freshman quarterback at the University of Illinois named "Juice" Williams. I mentioned his name to Dre one Saturday morning before that day's games were set to start. Just *one* time. And for the next *three years*, whenever it was college football season, Dre would needle me with shit about Juice.

"What's up with your boy JUICE WILLIAMS today?"

"You want some grape juice to drink while watching JUICE WILLIAMS?"

"I'd take JUICE WILLIAMS by himself against the entire Ohio State team. Cause JUICE WILLIAMS is that nigga, right, Damon?"

"I know Michael Vick is good, but wait until Damon's boy JUICE WILLIAMS gets to the league. They ain't even gonna call it the NFL no more. Gonna be the National JUICE WILLIAMS Football League."

In 2011 during a debate about college basketball, I told him Kyrie Irving was better than Kemba Walker and would be the first pick in the draft. He responded with a repetitious incredulousness, asking the same question forty-seven consecutive times.

"Kyrie over KEMBA?"

"Kyrie over KEMBA?"

"Kyrie over KEMBA?"

"Kyrie Irving over KEMBA WALKER???"

Still not satisfied, he took out his phone and made me repeat, on camera, what I'd just told him. He even made me state my name like I was a hostage.

"Hi. My name is Damon Young, and I'm saying today, February 17, 2011, that Kyrie Irving will be the first pick in the NBA draft. Also please wire one hundred and fifty thousand dollars to Western Union account 269-27312 if you want to see me alive again."

We also watched the neighborhood change together. The first day I sat in Dre's chair, Brian and I were on our way to the basketball courts behind Reizenstein Middle School, which were separated from the courts at Mellon Park by two baseball fields, and together served as the nexus for Allegheny County pickup basketball. Anyone who wanted to be anyone made their bones in that corridor. Reizenstein sat on Penn Avenue. On the opposite side of the street sat a Nabisco plant. If at the 'Stein past dark—which was common in the summer because it was one of the few courts in the city with reliable lights—you could smell bread baking. The Nabisco plant closed in 1998. And then some redistricting and school population reshuffling shut Reizenstein down too. And then the Reizenstein building was vacant for a year. And then Pittsburgh Public Schools used it as an administrative building. And then, in 2008, it became the home of Schenley High School after the former Schenley High School building was discovered to have asbestos. In 2009, Schenley changed its name to Pittsburgh Obama. In 2012, Pittsburgh Obama moved a mile away to the building that once housed Peabody High School, leaving Reizenstein vacant again.

The Nabisco plant was bought in the late nineties, and then the ownership of it changed hands several times, until the building was declared blighted by the city, which allowed rental and redevelopment behemoth Walnut Capital to purchase and "revitalize" the Nabisco space. In May of 2010, Bakery Square—a hundred-million-dollar shopping and business space featuring a Panera Bread, a Free People, a Marriott, an Urban Active (which would soon be LA Fitness), an Anthropologie, a PNC Bank branch, and a Google office—opened. By 2013, the Reizenstein building and the basketball courts next to it were completely gone, demolished by Walnut Capital, which planned to transform that space into luxury apartments. By 2014, if you had $3,400 to spare, you could rent a two-bedroom loft there. And if on a high enough floor, you could probably see Homewood—the predominantly black neighborhood a quarter mile east of Bakery Square—from your window. If ambitious, you could drive down Frankstown Avenue or Bennett Street in Homewood and use a year of that rent money to buy a house.

We also saw the three-hundred-foot-tall Penn Circle high-rise—which housed low-income residents and stood where Penn and Centre Avenues intersected—demolished. The space where it once existed eventually became a two-story Target. When it opened in 2011, Dre would park his car in Target's garage and walk three blocks to his shop instead of parking on Penn or Highland and paying the meter. When I asked if he was ever scared he'd get caught on camera and towed, he said that Target let him steal parking so niggas don't steal shit out the store. His logic was unorthodox but sound. When Target appeared, the Kingsley building—which would have sat across from Target on the opposite side of the Centre and Penn intersection—disappeared. As did the Shadow Lounge and Ava, the adjoined clubs where I partied with the PhDeez, posed at First Fridays with my best United Colors of Benetton suit when Brotha Ash had his flash ready, danced at every Thursday Reggae Night in the summer of 2008 to Sister Nancy's "Bam Bam" and Estelle's "American Boy," and first met my wife. And Royal Caribbean, which served convenient Jamaican food to Pittsburghers who hadn't known actual Jamaicans from Jamaica and couldn't tell a quality oxtail from a pork rind. And Dress Up, the spot on Penn Avenue where I copped my first faux-leather MCM hat and sweatshirt in 1989. And East Mall, the twenty-story high-rise that straddled Penn Avenue and dominated East Liberty's landscape. Before it was demolished, in order to get from Garfield to the East Liberty business district, you had to literally drive through the tunnels comprising East Mall's base. It was ugly as fuck, an eyesore haunting East Lib's topographical feng shui, but it was a fortress keeping interlopers and gentrifiers out. Even the neighborhood's name didn't stand a chance. By 2010, the area south of Penn Avenue became known as Eastside, an obnoxious portmanteau of East Liberty and the neighboring and predominantly white Shadyside.

East Liberty Kutz changed too. Some of this change was due to the natural transient state of the black barbershop, which exists as one of the few places where black men with papers and without degrees could find honest employment. There's no union to join, no good-ole-boys network steeped in bias and nepotism to navigate through, no apprenticeship requiring current driver's licenses not possessed because of active child support payments, and no real background checks other than "You know this nigga? Is he cool? Can he cut?" All you need are clippers, clients, and a barber's license. But sometimes barbers would disappear. For three weeks, for three months, for three years. And you'd learn perhaps that they got sent back to county. Or went back to college. Or that they bounced to a new shop in Lawrenceville that has more foot traffic and an owner who takes less of the chair each month. And then, after the chair was empty for a long enough time, they'd get replaced by someone else.

And like the rest of East Liberty, Dre got swept up in the

tide of progress and redevelopment and rapidly encroaching and colonizing whiteness. Because of some leasing issue I never was quite sure of, Dre was forced to move to a much nicer space two blocks away on Highland Avenue next to Sneaker Villa. When I asked if the new spot was more expensive, he gave me an exaggerated *nigga please* face. And then he actually said, "Nigga please." He never spoke much about money. But after the move, he started playing the lottery more. Sometimes he'd stop midcut to run across the street to Highland News and play a number or buy a dozen scratch-off tickets.

Back in 1995, while walking up Highland to David's Shoes on Penn, I happened to have on a red Nike sweatshirt. Tommy Ray, a nigga I knew from Mellon Street, was across the street with a couple of his Crip homies, but his perpetually squinty ass didn't know it was me. So he crossed the street all menacing and reaching in his pockets before stopping, smiling, and saying, "Damn, D. I ain't know that was you. You gotta be careful with that red shit, yo." "You need glasses, nigga," I replied, while emptying my bladder in my Karl Kani's. Seventeen years later, the experience of going to East Liberty Kutz became more and more surreal. I'd look out the window while sitting in Dre's chair and see white women in yoga pants walking bouviers and drinking kombucha on the same street I almost got shot on. I'd be tempted, sometimes, to ask these oblivious Beckys and the Saucony-rocking Brads jogging past and checking their Fitbits and nipple tape if they were lost and needed directions. Not to be helpful, but just to be an asshole. I'd never follow through, though, because East Liberty didn't belong to me anymore. It was theirs now. I was the outsider who returned each week to sit in a time machine.

There was a time, from approximately 2008 to 2013—when both Ava and the Shadow Lounge were always hot, and the annual East Liberty Street Fest was still active, and the Kelly Strayhorn Theater found its footing—when East Lib seemed to find that sweet space between the neighborhood crashers and the neighborhood. Many of the markers of the usurping whiteness were already there. You could already buy fifteen-dollar burgers at BRGR and appropriated BBQ at Union Pig and Chicken and whatever the fuck they served at Spoon, you could already eat entire meals off of the free Saturday-afternoon samples at Whole Foods and Trader Joe's, and white people had already begun to grow confident enough to walk down streets they wouldn't have driven down ten years earlier. But East Liberty's central zeitgeist still *felt* black. It was still fucking *East Lib*. If gentrification is a hurricane, this was when East Lib was in the eye. Whiteness, however, proved to be too relentless and inevitable and ingurgitating to be stopped. Whiteness wasn't a hurricane. It was Jason Voorhees, and that space of safeness was just us wrongly assuming we finally killed him.

By 2014, East Liberty Kutz was the only part of the old East Lib that I engaged with. But I spent more time in the new East Liberty—in goddamn *Eastside*—than I had before Hellmann's mayonnaise was spread all up and down Centre and Penn and Highland. I'd drive twenty minutes from my house in Manchester on the North Side to work in the Bakery Square Coffee Tree Roasters. I'd lift weights and hoop at the Bakery Square LA Fitness—where the windows in the lobby would allow you to see where Reizenstein used to be and Bakery Living would soon be—and I actually really fucking liked those fifteen-dollar BRGR burgers and Trader Joe's turkey bacon. If it were somehow possible for the people of the old East Lib—many of whom were displaced and pushed out to Homewood and Wilkinsburg and Penn Hills—to return and enjoy and own these bougie amenities too, I would have preferred that. But my macro distaste for East Lib's cultural decimation was outweighed by my willingness to engage with all this new and shiny and fancy and *safe* fucking shit. That this new and shiny and fancy shit was white too mattered. And I'd write about how much it mattered, how fucked up it was that we had to be erased from the neighborhood for the city to give a shit about it, how we'd been appropriated and gentrified and colonized and occupied, how absurd it was that Pittsburgh could find $100 million to invest in a vacant fucking Nabisco plant but couldn't keep Reizenstein Middle School open, and I'd write this while sitting in the Bakery Square Panera Bread, eating a hefty bread bowl full of their seasonal turkey chili, and using the next door Marriott's Wi-Fi because Panera only allowed an hour on their network during peak times.

I've leaned on the term *cognitive dissonance* before when attempting to capture my thoughts about East Liberty and my behavior, as it's an easy and sharp-sounding crutch for uncomfortable feelings still not baked enough yet to process. But that term suggests contradictory thoughts in conflict with each other, and I didn't actually feel much conflict. The angst I'd express about patronizing the new East Liberty while lamenting what had been lost was self-conscious. I knew I was supposed to feel a struggle, but how sincere was this wrangling of racial anxiety if it had minimal impact on where I'd choose to work and eat?

Still, Dre and East Liberty Kutz kept me anchored to that past, and as whiteness continued to creep up Highland and down Penn, I'd treat my weekly trips to the barber like I was visiting a friend in prison whose other ties to the outside world had long since either cut him off or died. And this need to somehow grip what I could of the old East Liberty obscured to me a reality that had been present since I first set foot in that shop: Dre was a terrible barber. I'd regularly leave his chair with an uneven beard and an asymmetrical shape-up, and what should have been a fifteen-minute-long act would often stretch to forty-five minutes, because Dre would stop cutting my hair to argue with me about the Steelers while finishing his steak sub from Vento's. Or perhaps he'd run across the street for a bottle of Cherikee Red and a Snickers Ice Cream Bar. Or maybe his bookie would come through, and they'd go over the lines for Sunday afternoon's NFL games. Or maybe he needed to run to the post office real quick to pick up a package of Muscle Milk and Omaha Steaks. Every errand he ran while cutting my hair was "real quick"—"I'll be back real quick"; "I need to make this call real quick"; "Lemme finish these fries real quick. Do you want some?"—which made me wonder if Dre had secretly appropriated the words *real* and *quick* and decided to give them their own meanings. His cuts weren't always bad. When he concentrated, he was actually quite good. The right cut can make a nigga feel like King T'Challa, and over the sixteen-year span of our relationship, which was probably (at least) seven hundred haircuts, he gave me that feeling hundreds of times. But his moments of focus were fleeting, and my hair was forced to answer for his sins.

Unconcerned with my history with Dre and how my relationship with him kept me connected to East Lib, Alecia would stare at my contorted, Frankenstein-at-an-eleventh-grade-semiformal shape-ups and ask why I'd allow Dre to turn my head into a Pez dispenser. I'd lie and say I hadn't noticed that I looked like I just slept nine consecutive hours on the left side of my face, and she'd walk away, perhaps to Google if *my fiancé won't tell his barber to do his fucking job* was sufficient grounds for ending our engagement. Alecia didn't care that much. But she knew how particular I was about my hair, and she just couldn't understand why I'd be okay with this. She even offered to learn how to cut hair herself so she could cut mine.

The last straw came a few months before our wedding. I returned home from East Liberty Kutz with a line that looked like two separate people's haircuts fused into one. Or perhaps two separate barbers cutting the same head. I'm leaning toward the latter, as Dre cut the right side of my head, left the shop for twenty minutes to pay his electric bill, and then returned in a much less anxious mood to cut the left side. During these breaks I'd play on my phone and watch TV. I'd get annoyed, sure, but I figured it was a surcharge for the privileges Dre provided me. Unlike most patrons, I never had to set appointments. If I walked in the shop, I was next in his chair. Also, while the rates of haircuts had slowly risen, my cuts with Dre stayed a flat ten dollars. This, plus our relationship, allowed me to look the other way when he was clearly looking the other way when cutting my hair. But this time, it was so bad that even I noticed it when I got home and looked in the bedroom mirror. For the rest of that night, I sat at awkward angles and in dimly lit corners of the rooms we were in so Alecia wouldn't notice my hair. This was enough for me to finally decide to see other people.

While standing in line at Panera two weeks earlier, I'd received a business card from a nigga who said he worked at a new barbershop that had opened on Baum Boulevard, five blocks away from Dre's shop. He looked at my beard and said, "We could do some work with that," and I'm still not quite sure whether that was a compliment or him sensing I was a nigga in need. After a day of hiding my Jekyll and Hyde hairdo from Alecia, I decided that, when it was time for my weekly shape-up, I'd try this new shop—which would be the first time as an adult that I sat in any Pittsburgh barbershop other than East Liberty Kutz.

The new shop was an upgrade. The main room was spacious, with two leather couches, a pool table, a table and chairs devoted to chess or checkers, and two large flat-screen TVs—one for watching Netflix and bootleg DVDs, and the other for Xbox. There was even a refrigerator stocked with juice, pop, beer, and liquor. The good shit too. Hennessy, Honey Jack, Crown Apple, Maker's Mark, Patrón, Cîroc—all the hood-rich-nigga staples. It felt like I was in the barbershop from the movie *Barbershop*. The nigga who'd passed me the card a month earlier wasn't there, though, so I sank down in one of those buttery couches and waited for one of the barbers there to ask if I needed help. Moments later, one did. The only white barber there.

White barbers in black barbershops exist under the same set of unspoken regulations as female barbers. If there is a white guy there, you better believe he's a great fucking barber—and can hold his own in a ripping session—because that's the only way he'd be allowed to be there. Ain't no country for mediocre white barbers in the hood. Half-assed white people in the White House? Sure. But not in the fucking barbershop. I didn't doubt that he'd do a fine job. It just didn't feel right to leave my black-ass barber and the janky shop I called home for an upgrade *and* a white nigga. For the first time, I felt like a true gentrifier. Or one of those dark-skinned male characters in Tyler Perry movies that get successful and leave their black wives for Becky McWhitey. And then the black wife gets depressed. And goes to church. And meets a God-fearing and hardworking redbone man at Bible study, whose strong jawline fulfills that wife in a way the ex never could. She even grows to accept and appreciate his blue-collar job—he's an exterminator—and eventually support his dream to own his own extermination company. She's alive again. She's smiling again. She's glowing again. She has seventeen thousand orgasms every time they fuck. And then they all see each other one day at Outback Steakhouse. And the bald-headed ex doesn't even recognize her anymore. Says, "Wow, Tameka, I didn't know that was you. You look . . . good." And Becky McWhitey looks at her all snooty, because that's the primary purpose of white women in movies about black women's spiritual and sexual awakenings. And then the bald-headed nigga and Becky get in the car and leave. And then Becky McWhitey asks him, "How do you spell 'dashiki'?" And he just stares out the driver's-side window. I DID NOT WANT TO BE THAT LAMENTFULLY BALD-HEADED NIGGA STARING OUT THE DRIVER'S-SIDE WINDOW!

Speaking of nigga, a white barber would make the barbershop another place I couldn't say *nigga*, and the thought of that upset me too. If a white person happens to be in the room while I'm with a bunch of my boys, he'll probably hear a *nigga* or two. Shit, he might *be* a *nigga* or two. The barber-client dynamic is more intimate, though, and I just wouldn't feel comfortable letting *nigga*s fly while this nigga caught them. I'd never be as free and familiar with him as I'd been with Dre. Plus, he'd be an inch from my face and holding a razor. Couldn't chance him hearing that word and then trying to lynch me after some overseer flashback embedded deep in his DNA burst out.

I eventually got over myself and sat in his chair. He put the cape on me and did the questionnaire thing all good barbers do with new clients.

"How much am I taking off?" "Do you want the back faded out?" "Should I use the razor or just the clippers?" "How high and dark do you want your beard?" "How sharp do you want the clippers to be?"

This was already a stark contrast to Dre, who would sometimes start cutting my hair *without even asking me what I wanted*. The cut itself was . . . perfect. Every line was symmetrical and sharp, my hairline was more Paul George than George Jefferson, and my beard was even and sexy. I officially had a new (white) barber and a new barbershop. Now I just had to find a way to tell Dre I was moving on. And by *find a way to tell Dre I was moving on* I mean *make sure Dre and I would never, ever, ever, ever cross paths again.*

I'm confident that, a millennium from now, someone will have invented a good way of breaking up with a barber. I'm even optimistic that this discovery might actually happen within the next five hundred years. Now, though, unless the breakup is due to you moving to a different city or balding a bit earlier than you'd like, there's no "*It's not you, it's me.*" You're not leaving to "*find yourself.*" Or because you're "*not ready for something so serious.*" You're not going to be "*pressed for time*" because you're "*starting a new job*" or "*going to grad school.*" You won't be "*better as friends*" and you won't introduce them to a friend that they'd be "*much more compatible with.*" You're not going to request an open relationship or the chance to "*see other people.*" And you will definitely never tell a barber that you're ending things because "*you don't deserve them*" and they "*need someone better.*" Someone who will "*appreciate them better than you ever could*" because you still need to "*mature*" and maybe one day "*catch up to them.*" There's just no way of euphemizing the fact that you're getting a new barber because you just believe the new barber is better, so instead of having that conversation with them, you ghost.

This would have been much easier if East Liberty Kutz had been Mount Lebanon Kutz or Stanton Heights Kutz or some other neighborhood I could avoid. But I had no plans on staying away from East Liberty, which meant I had to find a way to patronize the Eastside while avoiding the place and the person that kept me connected to East Lib. I agonized over this for weeks. I even created a script in my head for what I'd say if I ever bumped into Dre, and I plotted out secret ways to move and side streets to travel to get where I needed to get without seeing him.

But avoiding him wasn't that hard, really. Aside from parking in Target's lot, Dre mostly stayed on the side of Penn Avenue the redevelopment hadn't swallowed yet. And the only business on that side of Penn I still frequented was Sneaker Villa. I'd see him occasionally when I was driving past—the same baggy black T-shirt and blue jeans shuffling up the street, clutching a carton of Turner's Raspberry Iced Tea and stopping every seven seconds to joke with someone—but he didn't see me. At least I don't think he did.

And then, after a year of this, we bumped into each other on Highland in August of 2015. He was leaving the shop, and I had just parked and was walking to Pizza Sola on the corner of Centre and Highland. We both smiled, and then we gave each other a pound and a hug. He asked how the married life was and if I was still hooping. He also said something about "my boy LeBron" that I couldn't quite make out. I answered his questions ("Wife is great"; "I'm still hoopin' at Central every Thursday and Saturday"), and asked about the shop ("It's still the same . . . same ole niggas doing same ole shit, you know?") and his son ("He doing aiight"). He looked the same. Sounded the same. Moved the same. He was the same. I probably was too. (But with a better haircut.)

We were walking in opposite directions, so we did the pound and hug again, and both kept going our separate ways. Our conversation was so easy and natural that I got embarrassed that I'd dreaded a confrontation for so long. Maybe, I thought, I'd even stop past the shop every once in a while to say what's up. He'd like that. I'd like that.

The plan never materialized. The sentiment was there

whenever I was in East Liberty, but life interrupted the follow-through. And that grade of nostalgia just wasn't strong enough to pull me back into a place I had no use for anymore to talk to a man I still cared about but didn't need to see.

That conversation was the last time I saw or spoke to Dre. In November, while scrolling through Facebook, I saw his picture attached to an article. A eulogy. Dre had been battling a mysterious illness, and died three weeks before I saw the status. The article was from a small East Liberty periodical remembering him. I read this while sitting in Panera. After the shock wore off, I went to my car and cried.

Two weekends later, I spent the morning working at Everyday's A Sundae; a cafe on Centre Avenue in East Lib that I began to frequent because the owner is nice and it happens to sell two of my favorite things: breakfast sandwiches and ice cream. After my ten-thousand-calorie meal—consisting of bacon, egg, and cheese on a croissant, washed down with a Moose Tracks milkshake—I walked a half block up Centre to Target to buy a Diaper Genie for my ten-day-old daughter. And then, after leaving Target, I walked a block down Penn Avenue, made a right on Highland Avenue, and went into Sneaker Villa, which had recently undergone a name change and was now just called Villa. I'd been jonesin' for a new pair of butters for a long time, and a post–Black Friday sale was all the urging I needed to break down and go shopping. After leaving Villa, I finally did what I had been meaning to do, and dreading doing, that day. I went next door to East Liberty Kutz to find out what happened to Dre.

It was here, after talking to a couple of the barbers, that I learned how he died. He had cancer. Not sure which kind. His death was a shock to them too. None of them knew he was sick. They also shared that with Dre gone, the shop would be gone soon too. December would be their last month. There just wasn't enough revenue or will to keep it open without him.

Before I left the shop, I asked one of the barbers if he had anything from Dre's wake or funeral, and he gave me a program for the homegoing service that was pinned to one of the mirrors. I thanked him, read it, then put it into my pocket and left.

Three days later, I went to my no-longer-all-that-new-anymore barber, and told him about Dre. He actually already knew. Apparently the Pittsburgh barber world is small and tight. He didn't know Dre was my old barber, though, and he offered his condolences once I told him.

After the New Year passed, one of the barbers from the now vacant East Liberty Kutz starting manning a chair in my new shop. The first time we saw each other we both made the *fancy seeing you here* face before talking.

"How long you been on this chair here?"

"I just started Monday. I should have been here years ago, though. It's nice as fuck in here."

"I know, right? Floors is all crisp and shit. Shit's crazy."

"How long you been coming here?"

"Bout a year and a half now. Almost two."

"Yeah, I remember when you stopped coming to the shop. I thought you moved or something."

"Nah, I just . . . you know how Dre was."

"You ain't gotta explain shit, bro, I know. He was a great dude. But as a barber? Shit. Surprised you ain't bounce sooner. But yeah, I'm here now, though."

"Me too."

# 15

# THURSDAY-NIGHT HOOPS

My point guard is a conservative.

He's a lawyer too. I'm not quite sure what his specialty is, but I did once hear him say that he and several colleagues started their own practice a few years ago. He's a husband and a father, and up until last year, he was the owner of a burgundy Nissan Pathfinder. Now he drives a medium blue BMW X5 with a sunroof and black leather seats. It's a really nice car. It's the type of car you'd find displayed in an indoor shopping mall somewhere, parked outside Express and reeking of new-car-smell spray.

He's also actually more of a hybrid one (point guard) and four (power forward) today than a pure point. Think Boris Diaw, but if Diaw was five foot eleven, (approximately) 275 pounds, middle-aged, bald, and white. He played Division II ball at a small school in New Jersey back in the day. I didn't know him when he was younger (and thinner), but according to those who did, he was a "dog"—a hoop colloquialism for someone who's a tough motherfucker to guard. Still, despite his age and the vertical and horizontal limitations imposed by his weight, flashes of the dog persist. He's a sure ball handler with long arms and disproportionately large and strong hands—his palms are the size of the Williams Sonoma mixing bowls I bought my dad for his sixty-fifth birthday. You will not strip him and he will not lose the ball. His girth also assists him here. If you dare reach, he'll dip his shoulder and you'll be left with a chunky blade to your thorax and a sheet of Irish man sweat on your cheek. He doesn't have great range—you guard him "toes on the line" instead of "heels on the line" (you don't have to venture past the three-point line to contest his shot)—but he's a dependable and deceptively clutch shooter with his feet set. In the paint, he's tricky and crafty and ambidextrous, using his sizable ass and his unfathomably round and hard stomach—his stomach is a fucking medicine ball dipped in plutonium—as leverage to pin and seal people off. On D he *competes*, conjuring every inch of guile and grown-ass-man-with-a-retirement-plan-and-a-lawn-guy strength to attempt to contain people six inches taller or three decades younger than him. He possesses a generous amount of what Mr. Seneca, my sixth grade gym teacher, would call "spunk" and what my uncle Danny likes to call "sticktoitiveness."

The best part of his game, however, is his passing. He delivers the ball with accuracy, verve, and velocity: line-drive skip passes whizzing past eardrums and outstretched fingertips, pocket bounce passes off high ball screens and between limbs, vertical baseball hurls with arc and touch, underhanded post entry passes under intense ball pressure but in rhythm and away from too-anxious defenders, Unseldesque overhead outlet passes in perfect stride. Those who play frequently and seriously know that this is the rarest and most precious of commodities, valued by all ballplayers and even fetishized by some with indecent vigor. (This is no hyperbole, by the way. Some guys—and by *some guys* I mean *middle-aged middle school basketball coaches*—talk about pure point guards and "making the extra pass" the way Bengal tigers talk about fat and flirty gazelles. Shit, they talk about them the way *I* talked about my mom's smothered pork chops and gravy. It's disturbing.)

This feeling exists because a guy who makes the right pass, delivers it the right way, and does it for the right reasons has a way of permeating and eventually cultivating a team's collective spirit. It becomes a weaponized virus, infecting even the most reluctant teammate with the disease of magnanimity and trust. This is what Magic and Larry and Isiah did; what Oscar and Cousy and Frazier did before them; what Kidd and Stockton and Nash did after them; and what LeBron and Steph and CP3 do now. And this is why, out of the twenty or so regulars of the weekly Thursday-night pickup hoop games at Central Catholic High School—games that start at seven, end around nine, and have been held consistently for thirty years—"Law" is my favorite teammate.

But as my team checked the ball to start the game on the second November Thursday in 2016, my thoughts were possessed by the fact that my point guard is a conservative. Who stumped for, gave money to, cheered for, declared allegiance to, and even once took a selfie with Donald Trump. And who definitely, absolutely voted for him two days earlier.

*This motherfucker voted for that motherfucker,* I thought while spitting into my hands before rubbing them together and wiping them on the soles of my gray-and-black Kyrie 1s to gain some sort of traction on the bit-too-slick gym floor in need of a scrub. And again while tightening the DonJoy Legend SE-4 brace stretching from my upper left thigh to the shin below it, swallowing and protecting my knee. The thoughts dissipated when the action began; can't exactly be mindful of blind back ball screens or finish in traffic while obsessing over your point guard's bitch-ass political leanings. But they returned during each extended break in action. When games ended or subs were made, I became anxious again. And not necessarily because of what I thought I might do, but what I knew I wouldn't.

Trump's win provided no grand epiphanies for me. Perhaps I underestimated the appeal of the preservation of white privilege and white supremacy, but the idea that racism is an essential and inextricable part of America's identity is not particularly novel. I've never been a postracial Pollyanna, even in the years directly following Obama's election, when postracial Pollyannaism was in vogue and marketed as a soothing, restorative, and pumpkin spice–scented balm for America's unseemly cold sores. The only "New Black" I've ever been interested in is the color of the discontinued 522 Levi's I've considered ordering on eBay. Believing America had somehow grinded and hoped and wished its way out of its racially antagonistic history wasn't just myopic and foolish; it was time consuming. I had much better things to do, like watching *Shark Tank* marathons or removing the lint from my beard. But still, even with all of this awareness and consciousness and performative sobriety, Tuesday, November 8, was an earthquake. That shit fucking *hurt*, man. And the following morning was the postquake tsunami. America's tectonic plates had shifted, and I wasn't as sure of my footing.

In the following days, I incorporated my usual coping mechanisms when faced with intense stress in order to deal, including (but not limited to) writing, consuming various foods covered by or infused with bacon, and frequent masturbation. My acid reflux also flared up, and I attempted to alleviate it with Advil and Seagram's Raspberry Ginger Ale. But mainly I limited my interactions with white people. Not just suspected or actual Trump voters, but *all* white people. They all were equally culpable. By supporting a man who campaigned on a platform of bias and proud ignorance so unambiguous it bordered on parody. Or supporting him specifically because of this platform. Or, if they didn't happen to support Trump—if they fashioned themselves liberals or progressives or allies or just sane—not doing enough at their Thanksgiving tables and country clubs and home and garden tours and company potlucks and family barbecues and each other crucible of whiteness I'm not privy to in order to sway those who do. Perhaps this blanket characterization was unfair, but, all things considered, being fair to white people felt (and still feels) irrational.

Fortunately, I had an occupation where literally zero white people worked in my office (the street-facing bedroom on the third floor of the house my wife and I were renting), so no chance of running into one in the break room (my kitchen), the restroom (the third-floor bathroom), the exercise room (the space in the hallway leading to the stairs where I occasionally do pushups), or the water cooler (the two bottles of Deer Park and the half-empty bottle of Jack Daniel's Tennessee Honey sitting on that bedroom's dresser). And, since I'm one of the only Thursday-night regulars who happens to be black, I considered skipping the games that week as well.

This would have been the first time I ever intentionally skipped Thursday-Night Hoops. For the decade or so that I've been a regular, it's existed as an essential part of my weekly routine. So essential that I've rescheduled family commitments, passed on work-related opportunities, and postponed first dates just to ensure I was available. For the stretch in 2012 when my car was repossessed for two weeks, I just made the mile-and-a-half walk down Fifth Avenue from my place in Point Breeze.

In 2013, when a tweak of the same knee I had ACL reconstruction on in college sidelined me for three months, I signed up for Obamacare after not having insurance for four years just to be able to see an orthopedist and buy a discounted brace so I could play again. When my car was the only car my wife and I owned and she needed it that evening for errands, I'd either Uber or convince her to restructure her itinerary to allow her to drop me off and pick me up. And when my daughter was a newborn and my wife happened to be in Chicago or Denver for work—rendering me the sole available parent—I'd *take her to the gym with me*, propping her up on the bleachers in her car seat, checking on her, feeding her, and changing her diapers between games. (Whether I washed my hands afterward depended on the intensity that night. If it was a particularly heated and competitive day, whoever was guarding me would have to just deal with me and my skunky, baby-shit-scented hands.)

The value I attached to Thursday night is mined from its scarcity. It's rare in a football town like Pittsburgh to find a consistently good pickup basketball game as an adult; even rarer to find one with guys who can actually play; even rarer to find one with guys you actually *enjoy* playing with; and finding one with each of these characteristics *and* a game that isn't bogged down with heedless foul and travel calls *and* half-hour-long arguments over those foul and travel calls is like finding a fucking unicorn.

To gain entry, you need to be either a graduate of Central or somehow connected to a regular. Even then, you're subtly vetted on the court. If you shoot a bit too much or call a few too many fouls or talk a bit too much shit or play a bit too little D, a couple of well-placed eye rolls, exhales, and smirks will communicate to your host that he probably shouldn't invite this wack motherfucker back. I gained entry via Alex, the oldest son of Paul—Central's sixtysomething head basketball coach and Thursday night's alpha dog. I'd known Alex and his brother Kenny since we were grade-school Pittsburgh Diocese rivals in football and basketball, me at St. Barts and them at St. Sebastian. (In eighth grade, I hit a half-court buzzer beater against them to win a game. This is a sore spot for Kenny, who, twenty-five years later, still insists I traveled before letting it go. He's probably right.) We played with and against each other as teens in the summer at Expos Camp at the Shadyside Boys & Girls Club and the Ozanam League in the Hill, became rivals again in high school (they knocked us out of the playoffs my senior year), and played against each other again in the Connie Hawkins Summer Basketball League at Pennley Park in East Lib while in college. We've never been close friends, but we've always been cool. So when I happened to bump into Alex outside the Macy's at Ross Park Mall in 2006, and he invited me to come through that Thursday, I obliged.

I've been a part of the runs long enough now to chart the ebbs and flows. From 2007 to 2010 they'd often be packed with as many as thirty people, some of whom were twenty-two-to-twenty-five-year-olds who'd played ball in college, recently graduated, and still desired opportunities to prove that they should have been recruited by bigger schools out of high school. They'd carry petty eight-year-old grudges no one gave a shit about around their necks like tennis sweaters, and each game was played like an assistant coach from Pitt or Duquesne was in the stands, ready to offer a scholarship to whoever had the prettiest step-back J. It was an awkward mix. These whippersnappers— some black, some white, all thirsty as fuck—shared the same court every Thursday with thirty- and forty- and fifty- and sixty-year-old (mostly white) men who still possessed some competitive fumes in their tanks but mostly just wanted to play and sweat and drink beers in Paul's office afterward. And then, of course, there was me. Sometimes the only guy in the gym who'd played Division I basketball. But although I was more than a decade removed from those days, my ego wouldn't allow me to allow them to forget who I was. So I spent many Thursdays—maybe three out of every five Thursdays—rocking my twelve-year-old Canisius College practice jersey while playing; its tattered and tired sleeves clutching my shoulders for dear life, its once vivid and vibrant blue base and yellow stitching faded so definitively that it became the tint of mashed bananas mixed with baby oatmeal, its threads reeking of caked, decade-old sweat and fresh Bounce fabric softener. It looked like plantain peel marinated in almond milk. It looked like I was hooping in a fucking dish rag.

By 2011 the herd began to cull, eventually settling into a group of regulars so regular I have extensive scouting reports and abridged Wikipedia pages on each of them. Both Alex and Kenny work at Central, Alex as an assistant principal and Kenny as a math teacher. They're also assistant coaches for the basketball team. Tall (six foot four) and lean, Alex looks a little like Neil Patrick Harris and carries himself like someone doing an impression of a Mormon. Preternaturally earnest, honest, and forthright, he shakes hands with enthusiasm and integrity, never not making eye contact, never not expressing a genuine interest in you. He's one of the few people who, when they ask "What's up?" or "What's going on?", always gives a damn about your answer. His game fits his personality. He's so fundamentally sound—the perfect jump stop here; the textbook chest pass there—that it sometimes veers into mechanical and predictable. He also gets hot, both with his J (he'll have stretches where he'll make three-pointers five or six times down court in a row) and with his temper when antagonized by Kenny, Alex's opposite in build (also six foot four, but probably 260 or 270), looks (he's regularly mistaken for Ben Roethlisberger), temperament (sarcastic, fun, and a little dickish), and skills. While Alex is an objectively better basketball player, his game comprising a concrete sequential distillation of tens of thousands of Mikan drills and lane shuffles, Kenny is a better and freer natural athlete. Faster and springier than his size would suggest, he played football in college, and hoops unconstrained by the pressure of always making the perfect play.

Paul, the oldest of the regulars, is the living personification of old-man balls in YMCA locker rooms. Old-man balls, of course, are the languid and smirking testicles possessed by the type of middle-aged and elderly men who, decades ago, auctioned away their last fuck about being bare-assed in the locker room. While most men attempt to spend the least amount of time possible naked there, these guys will hold entire conversations while their still-dripping-'cause-they-haven't-dried-from-the-shower-yet nuts sway fuckless and free beneath them. Utterly and completely devoid of fucks, Paul regularly takes shots off the dribble from thirty-five feet, but has enough gravitas—and, admittedly, makes enough of them—that no one bats an eye if he misses five or six of those heaves in a row and doesn't even feign to bother to get back on D.

There's Kenny, the genial accountant whose release is so deliberate and slow it's like a disconnected Wi-Fi signal rebooting. His jump shot is a process. A gotdamn *parable*. But if no one's within seven feet of him, he'll knock it down. His nephew Jackson is in his midtwenties, played lacrosse in college, and hoops like the world's most athletic nine-year-old. Frank is a twenty-eight-year-old engineer and annoyingly relentless back-door cutter. Sometimes he cuts oblivious to the ball; his only purpose is to amuse himself by possibly tricking or fatiguing the guy checking him. He's also a much better shooter and ball handler (and player) than he thinks he is. Sixty-year-old Lonnie runs an accounting firm, is impressively athletic—think Santa after eight months of CrossFit—probably smokes an ounce of weed per week, and is by far the worst player of the regulars. Carson is the best. He's thirty, but one of those rare thirty-year-old ex-college ballplayers who's stronger and in better shape than he was at twenty-five. He plays with a pulsing and frenetic rage; I've called him White Russell Westbrook but a more apt determination is that he hoops like he'll only be allowed to eat dinner if his team wins.

There are also several semiregulars—guys who show up once or twice a month. Most notably Rakeem, who's forty-nine years old, black, has a practically unguardable right-shoulder turnaround J, and comports himself like a sitcom dad perpetually annoyed that his wife orders so much junk from QVC, and Tucker, who walked on at Pitt, is in *phenomenal* shape—his abs and pelvis actually do the V thing that Olympic swimmers and H&M mannequins possess—and recently did a bid in prison for drug trafficking. Occasionally Tucker will bring his boy Chevon, a former University of Pittsburgh star and recently retired pro who, against us, is essentially a hybrid of Wilt Chamberlain, Draymond Green, Jesus, and the alpha velociraptor from the first *Jurassic Park*.

Games are played to twenty-two. And instead of twos counting as one and threes counting as two—as is the case at most pickup games—twos are two and threes are three. There are six people on each team (five players and one sub) and subs are made after each team has combined to score eight points. (For instance, if one team scores five points and the other team hits a three, it's time for a sub.) Fouls are not called, they're *given*. If you foul someone you're expected to acknowledge it, stop play, and give them the ball, which is also a stark contrast from most other pickup games, where arguments over foul calls often comprise the bulk of the time on the court. This honor system extends to other violations, where instead of a travel or a double dribble forcing the guilty party to relinquish possession, the team is just forced to preempt their possession and check the ball up. Basically, they receive a do-over.

At first, these rules seemed impractical and even foolish. But as a veteran of roughly two thousand different pickup games at maybe a hundred different parks and gyms—with dozens of different rules and park-specific variations of those rules—this is easily the best and most efficient set of rules I've ever encountered. It is, truly, a gentleman's game. A *fair* game. With rules that make sense and are followed by everyone, with no exceptions. Imagine that.

After the runs conclude, most of the regulars stay behind another hour or two to shower, drink beer, and talk shit in Paul's office. The beer-buying and -bringing duties rotate; you're expected to bring a case at least twice a year. And, if you happen to go an extended stretch without coming, you're expected to bring a case when you return. The acronym FUBAC (Fuck U Bring a Case) is often attached to the texts informing the regulars of cancellations or changes in date or start times.

These runs have cultivated new friendships and strengthened old ones. Many of these men have been invited to each other's homes, bachelor parties, and weddings. I am not as close to them. I've been invited to Alex's house a few times, and even attended a couple of Memorial Day barbecues there, but I've never invited anyone from Thursday-Night Hoops to spend time with me and my people. I've attempted to convince myself that this lack of reciprocation is for their own good, assuming none of the Thursday-night regulars would be very interested in bringing a case of Woodchuck to an all-black game night where the jokes and conversations occasionally veer into some variant of "funny and/or fucked up shit white people do." But I don't invite them to my house because I just don't want them in my house. I haven't been possessed with the inclination to grant them that privilege, and I wouldn't want my friends or my family or my wife to feel the need to redact themselves in one of the few spaces we're able to freely regard white people with callousness and mundane and hilarious cruelty. These are not bad guys. But they are white, and whiteness already takes up too much space for me to volunteer my own.

This dynamic lives in paradoxical concert with these men existing as the *only* men I do "man" shit with on a regular basis. I've downed more drinks with them than I have with each of my closest friends—most of whom have long moved away from Pittsburgh. Brian, for instance, moved to Europe in 2010 to coach basketball, and comes back home each year for a week during Christmas. I've seen and spoken to and played with Kenny's son twenty times more than I've seen and played with either of Panama's. When Zoe was born, I honored the Thursday-night tradition of new dads bringing a bottle of whiskey instead of beer, and the shots we shared that night remain the first and only group toasts ever made to my daughter. I've even leveraged those relationships to my family's benefit, asking Alex and Kenny to assist me in getting my nephew Maurice into their prestigious and exclusive school. They happily obliged, with Alex even meeting personally with Central's head of admissions to express how much it would mean to him if Reese was granted entry.

Still, despite my decade-plus membership to Thursday-Night Hoops, I've never quite felt completely comfortable there, particularly during the post-hoop beer sessions in Paul's office. I've never felt *unwelcome*, but while clutching and pretending to enjoy Labatt Blues, sitting on those beat and cracked-to-the-bare-cushion couches, makeshift stools, and ice-filled beer coolers repurposed as benches, it's as if they're all in on a joke. It's a joke I *get*—I understand why it's funny and appreciate its humor—but don't *get* get it because I wasn't there for its inception. This sense of abstract discomfort doesn't exist in a vacuum. Conversations about politics are infrequent. Most revolve around sports (the Steelers, Pitt football, college basketball, the Pens, and WPIAL sports, mainly), the games just played, and shit presently happening in each other's lives. (Socks are also discussed far too frequently.) But they happen enough for me to know just how much of an outsider I am there—how different my world is from theirs, and how my world *exists within* theirs—and how this outsider status extends through the door to Paul's office; past the visitor lockers, urinals, and showers in the hallway leading to the gym's main entry; into the just-recemented parking lot; onto both the Fifth Avenue exit wrapped around the school's entrance and the Neville Street exit parked behind the gym; and wherever either of those paths take me. There is nowhere in America I can drive, walk, shit, write, scream, sleep, fuck, eat, sweat, lie, spit, die, conjure, see, touch, sit, dream, drink, run, jump, dunk, dribble, shoot, pass, steal, guard, catch, screen, block, lob, assist, or win without a similar sense of estrangement. Nowhere that I can have a moment of respite—a house party, a family reunion, a conversation with a friend at a bar or in my car or in a house I *own*—without knowing that relatively safe and superficially black space is enveloped by whiteness.

And, whether it's a driver's license or my eyeglasses or a navy blue Yale University tote bag Yale gave me after I spoke there in February 2016 or a threadbare practice jersey stuck like a Post-it to my sweaty skin, there's nowhere I can be without always being possessed to carry some form of ID. Something to let *them* know that *I'm* safe. Something to assure *them* that, despite my being surrounded and outmanned and outresourced and outflanked and outgunned by *them*, *I* am not a threat.

But, for two hours a week every week, I'm able to forget about that. The white men surrounding me, bumping me, chasing me, fouling me, calling my name, flanking me, defending me, blocking me, and stopping me are either my teammates or the team my teammates and I are trying to beat. And it's difficult to resist the temptation of romanticizing Thursday-Night Hoops; of shoehorning some sort of allegorical commentary about race and racism between Central's baselines. Particularly because we're playing basketball, a sport where the inherent culture—a difficult but voluntary coagulation of distinct and encouraged individuality to achieve a collective goal—closely mirrors what America wants us to believe it's aspiring to.

*Perhaps*, I've been *this close* to thinking a few more times than I care to admit, *this is what America needs. Just a group of black and white men joking and laughing and sweating and swearing and having fun together. This will solve racism.* I get so desperately close to *Remember the Titans*–ing it all that I can hear the zippy Motown montage music and taste the spittle exploding from Denzel's mouth.

And then I get smacked back to reality, like the Thursday I overheard Law talking to Jeremy (another regular) and sharing his experience at a Trump rally earlier in the week. He was even close enough to the stage to take a selfie, apparently, which he excitedly showed Jeremy, pressing his stupid fucking phone in Jeremy's palm for him to get a clearer look. (Jeremy, to his credit, didn't seem very impressed. Even said, "He's fatter than he looks on TV.")

There are several more instances like this I can cite, none particularly egregious or obscene, but all notable for my reaction to them: *nothing*. I'd do nothing. I pretended not to hear Law fawning over Trump, and whenever I'd maybe overhear another one of the regulars say something that revealed his politics, his *whiteness*, I'd take that opportunity to become fiercely interested in the debate about beer nut brands the rest of the room was having.

When that would happen—and it didn't happen often, but enough for me to be affected by it happening—I'd leave questioning my blackness. My manhood. My *balls*. I'd ask myself why it was so easy to write about race and racism behind the safety and the space to marinate in outrage and the access to Thesaurus.com that a laptop provides but so difficult to challenge it when in this room. Even if it wasn't blatant, it was there. It was an opportunity for me to do all the things I challenge white people to do. I'd been granted access to this portal of whiteness, the coach's office at Central Catholic High School, sharing beers and shots and sweat and stories with these very Pittsburgh and unambiguously white men, and I'd always decide to pass. And then convince myself I'd engage the next opportunity I had to. But when the opportunity came five weeks or four months or two years later, the same thing would happen again.

These decisions weren't fear-based. I knew there'd be no physical confrontation, no collective decision to jump the black guy who dared ask Paul how he really felt about Black Lives Matter. I also knew they were mostly aware of what I did for a living. A few are my Facebook friends; they undoubtedly saw the hundreds of pieces about "White Tears" and "Darth Becky" I share on my page. And among the dozens of newspaper clippings adorning the office walls is a 2015 *Post-Gazette* profile of me and my work. So there was no trepidation of being outed as some sort of closet Erik Killmonger biding my time, waiting for the opportunity to shame and stab Whitey. Instead, I chose not to acknowledge these moments because *I just didn't want to*. I preferred keeping these relationships superficial, so that I didn't have to feel anything about these men other than whether I enjoyed playing with them. If I took them out of that box I kept them in, maybe someone would say or do something that would make his whiteness too hard to ignore, and I didn't want to have to process and access that and have it dictate my attendance. Knowing how rare and treasured something like Thursday-Night Hoops is, I just didn't want to strangle the unicorn.

For those two hours every Thursday, I wanted to be able to not be so fucking aware. So hypersensitive to language, enunciations, inflections, connotations, and mannerisms; so cognizant of our prolonged state of houselessness. Of being othered. Of the hysteria, the psychosis, and the claustrophobia. I just wanted to be a *guy* who happened to be black hooping with other guys who happened to be white. I just wanted to finish post moves and make nice passes and make it through another week without tweaking my knee and then drink beers afterward and maybe get a slice of vegetable pizza from Maximum Flavor on Craig Street on the way home. That's it. It's just too fucking much to always have to be angry and alert. To always have to be ready and willing to challenge whiteness. To always have a perfectly pithy tweet or a thousand-word screed ready in response to the next Trayvon Martin, the newest Sandra Bland, and the latest

Eric Garner, and to feel all the same feelings again. And again. And again. I just wanted a fucking break.

Before the games started on that second Thursday in November of 2016, two days after my country decided that Donald Trump would be the best person to lead it, I saw Law and Lonnie embrace in an exaggerated and performative manner. The hug was an inside joke that only the regulars would be privy to. Lonnie was a staunch progressive, and throughout the election season the two had ribbed each other about their "teams." Them wrapping their big beige arms around each other represented them calling a truce to everyone's amusement and delight, effectively serving as some sort of postelection, postgame handshake line. It must be nice, I thought while stretching my hamstrings underneath the east wall backboard. To be able to exist here without ever questioning your existence here. To be able to treat something I'm treating like Hurricane Katrina like a highly contested but cleanly fought game to twenty-two.

Teams were chosen shortly afterward. It's a process where the first twelve to get to the gym are divided in a way to make the first game as evenly matched and competitive as possible. The younger guys would guard each other, as would the older guys. I was matched up with Carson. Law was on my team, matched up with Jimmy. I barely acknowledged him before the games started, spending extra time tightening my brace and tying my shoes instead of giving him and the rest of my teammates a pregame pound.

And then the game started. And a couple of well-placed post entry and outlet passes reminded me why Law was my favorite teammate. And I forgot about it all: the election; Donald Trump; the country; my country; my perpetual otherness in my country; my anxiety about my safety and the safety of my wife and daughter; my shame at bringing an infant girl into this fucking world the year before; the pain of seeing those results that Wednesday morning and seeing those motherfuckers beaming, gleeful, and cocky; my urge to punch each and every person on Fox News in their goddamn white fucking faces.

We won that first game easily. And as I sat on the bleachers, taking a breather, gulping the sour apple Gatorade I brought with me, and basking in postvictory glow—another Thursday-Night Hoops session off to a great start—I thought of the irony of my needing to be *there*, in *that gym* and surrounded by *those people*, *that week* to exhale. And of all the negotiating and navigating it requires to exist while black and relatively sane. And how, for the rest of them, for my teammates and the guys we just played against and the guys waiting to play next game, this was just another game. Just another week. Just another day. Just another election. Just another president. Just another Thursday. Whiteness in America exists and thrives in that *just another* space, where things will always be fine. Things will always be all right. Things will always work out. And then I wondered (again) if I should even be there. And if, by being there, I was choosing sanity over integrity. Sanity or integrity? That's such a fucked-up question to ask someone and to require someone to answer. Such a fucked-up circumstance to even allow such a fucked-up question to exist.

And then it was time to get back on the court for the next game. We won the next two, lost one, sat for one, and then won the last two. I left the gym that Thursday night feeling better than I had before I entered. *Sanity or integrity?* I thought again as I walked to my car. I guess I found my answer.

Carson was parked next to me, and was sitting in his car with his window down when I walked past him. He looked frustrated.

"My fucking phone won't link up with my Bluetooth, and I don't know if it's the car or my phone," he said when he noticed me noticing him.

"Shit, I hate when that happens," I replied before getting into my car and driving back home. I hope he found his answer too.

# 16

# ZOE

When I was seven years old, a miscommunication between my parents and my aunt Toni about who was picking me up after school one day led to me just catching the school bus to my Nana and Papa's house in Belmar Gardens, which is what I did most days. Unfortunately, they weren't home yet and I did not have a key—which is why I was supposed to get picked up from school—so the space between their screen door and their front door was my only shelter from a storm so severe that, decades later, I still remember the crack of the hail as it shot off the pavement into their garage door. By the time they got home an hour later, I was soaked in equal parts rain, tears, sweat, snot, and urine and also in possession of a new and paralyzing fear of lightning. It was such a traumatic experience that my immediate reaction to it was to dive into meteorology. I begged my parents to buy me every book they could about clouds, lightning, hurricanes, cyclones, tornadoes, and all other weather-related phenomena. I studied the almanac and the *Guinness Book of World Records* and eventually was able to recite weather stats like how my friends recalled Garbage Pail Kids. I began reading *USA Today* just for the color-coded national weather map on the back page of the A section. I'd spend hours watching the Weather Channel, and I'd even tell people I wanted to be a meteorologist when I grew up until I realized that was the quickest way to get disinvited to birthday parties.

I needed to know as much about the weather as I could in order to predict when there might be a storm and take the necessary measures to protect myself. And while I knew I had a better chance of dying by toaster than getting struck by lightning, that didn't stop me from believing it would happen to me. Fortunately, I have mostly grown out of this fear. Although the thuds and claps of thunder sometimes induce tension in me, I no longer duck under tables and dive into coat closets when I hear a storm approaching. I have matured. I am brave. I am a functional fraidy cat.

I am also a dad now—which is exactly what I attempted to convince myself when first carrying my newborn daughter into our home. *You are a dad now, Damon. A fucking* dad. By that point, I'd already been a dad since the moment, five days earlier, when I stood behind a wall of glass and watched a room full of doctors pull my daughter out of Alecia's stomach. It reminded me of when Simba was presented to the kingdom by Rafiki in *The Lion King*. But Zoe didn't yet feel like she was my child. Between having to be taught how to hold her, wrap her, wash her, clothe her, change her, watch her, burp her, and feed her— and also how often they'd whisk her away those first few days to take some measurement or perform some test—I felt like she belonged to the hospital. Almost as if Alecia and I were wide-eyed tourists attempting to convince the nurses to loan her out for a few hours, like a city bike-share program for babies.

But mainly she just looked too tiny, too pale, too delicate, too soft, and too *alien* to be something that we were somehow supposed to take care of until she was mature enough to take care of herself.

*How is this uncut loaf of ciabatta bread with eyes Velcroed to it . . . human? Wasn't it just inside of Alecia? Are we sure it's not just Alecia's spleen? I've never seen a spleen in person before, so how would I even know? How is it not cold? Wait—is it cold? How is it going to grow? What type of food can this tiny little ciabatta thing possibly eat? A drop of Gatorade? A single Frosted Flake? How are we supposed to keep it alive?*

When we finally brought her home, her presence in our apartment felt like a clerical error. Like Citizens Bank had placed ten thousand mystery dollars in my checking account and I didn't know whether to spend it quickly or report it. We were living in a two-story loft space above a coffee shop on the corner of North and Federal on the North Side. It was a nice place for a young-ish married couple—it had two spacious bedrooms, hardwood floors, and exposed brick throughout—but it didn't feel like a place that this tiny little human who now lived with us should live. She belonged back in Magee-Womens Hospital, where it was bright and secure and safe and where professionals would be able to watch over and water her until she blossomed into a fully formed adult.

I didn't dare share my thoughts with Alecia, who was in a postepidural haze and dealing with residual pain from her C-section. She was immediately smitten with Zoe and might have bitten my nose off if I suggested that her baby was a baked good. Compared to me, she seemed so damn *natural* with the parent thing—as if being a mom for her was like catching a samba beat—so I just took her lead and went along with the flow.

As I hoped, these feelings faded over time. When Zoe was

born, she was a full shade lighter than both Alecia and I, which was a bit of a surprise because we're both quite brown and were anticipating a Hershey's Kiss of a baby. She wasn't *lightskint*. This wasn't a real-life example of what sometimes happens on sitcoms where you'll have two dark-skinned people as the biological parents of a shade-away-from-passing little girl who could never ever be the product of that union. Of course, black people have enough DNA in us that a medley of skin tones and hair textures are always possible when we have children. But sometimes, on those shows, the differences between the parents and the kids are so unbelievably stark that you can picture the casting director thinking, *Yeah, we need a light and wavy little mulatto-looking girl to contrast these black-ass nigger parents. Our mean grade of darkness needs to get down to a six. Anything above an eight won't test well in the Rust Belt.*

Yet, while Zoe's complexion was not what we expected, a quick glance through my baby pictures shows she was the same color I was then. I got progressively more brown as I grew older, and the same thing is happening to her now. At two, she's still too young for her personality to be much more than a sketch of what it'll eventually be, but I can already see pieces of mine in hers. Most notably, she's an introvert who laughs at her own jokes and enjoys routine and familiarity and treats all new things with skepticism. If, for instance, we introduce a new food to her, she'll grab it with her hand, inspect it to ensure it meets her standards of quality, raise it up to her mouth, and then touch it ever so slightly with her tongue. If she doesn't hate it, she'll touch it twice. If she likes it, it's going *in* her mouth on the third touch. And if something happens while it's in her mouth that she doesn't agree with—maybe it's a bit spicier or mushier than she expected—she'll spit it out. But politely, as if to say, "*I appreciate your efforts to expose me to Indian cuisine. Perhaps, if I were so inclined, I'd complete the eating experience. But alas, my palate is discerning and you will instead find the remaining contents of the samosa on the floor beside your right foot. Namaste."*

In the summer of 2017, more than a year and a half after Zoe was born, I finally shared with Alecia my thoughts from that first week. We were driving back from Home Depot. Zoe was asleep in her car seat. When we made it home, we sat in the car in front of our house for an hour so Zoe could keep napping. We also relished those increasingly rare moments when we'd be able to sit in the car watching the street and talking, like we did for hours when we were still just homies.

"You know, that first week when we brought Zoe home, I was scared shitless. I felt . . . I felt like . . . like she didn't belong to us. Like 'What the fuck are we supposed to do with her?' I just didn't feel like my life was worthy of taking care of hers. I felt . . . unqualified."

I stared straight ahead instead of looking at Alecia during this admission. When we were both single, this lack of eye contact during car confessionals would turn the front seat of my Charger into a therapist's office. Not looking into someone's face when talking to (and sometimes about) them allowed us the freedom to expound and purge without pressure. That day, however, I was just glad I couldn't see any disappointment in her eyes.

While I waited for her to acknowledge what I'd said, it started raining. I was immediately reminded of how, in *High Fidelity*, Rob Gordon was caught in the rain so often that it began to defy reason. Did this nigga just chase torrential downpours for opportunities to emote?

*And this is why,* I thought, *things like marriage and parenthood will always be uphill battles for me. Here we are, in the middle of this intimate moment, something that has been weighing on my mind for eighteen months, and I'm daydreaming about the moisture-retentive properties of John Cusack's hair. Why can't I just exist in the now? Shit, even now*—literally right now—*I'm stressing over existing in the now instead of just existing in the motherfucking now.*

Before I had the chance to answer, Alecia replied.

"Me too."

"What?"

"I felt the same way. I didn't know what to do with her. I remember thinking, 'I guess we'll figure this out somehow,' but I didn't have shit figured out. I didn't feel like we were ready to bring her home and start her life. I was terrified. I think most new parents are, though."

Throughout my life, nigga neurosis would form alliances with the dozens of other anxieties and hang-ups I carried to conspire against my common sense. And it usually worked. They'd convince me that I was the only one who experienced the doubt and angst I lugged around, tricking me into believing that my self-consciousness and the familiar diffidence it culti-vated were singular. I remember, in 2009 or 2010, appearing on a panel where I shared the stage with another blogger I'd ad-mired for years. I was in awe at how articulate she seemed—so natural, so unbothered by the audience. There were hundreds of people there, but she carried herself with the supinity of someone holding court on their couch during game night. I was intimidated by how, well, *unintimidated* she was, and the bigger she seemed, the smaller I made myself. I said maybe five words the entire night. I just couldn't compete. A year later, we ran into each other at another event, I shared how impressed I was with her on that panel, and I asked if she had any tips for being more comfortable onstage. She smiled: "Jack."

"Huh?"

"A shot of Jack Daniel's does the trick. Anything brown, re-ally. White doesn't agree with me."

"You drink before you get up there?"

"Need something to take the edge off. I ain't up there drunk, of course. I just always need a little Jack to calm my nerves down."

Sometimes that lie would reveal itself while I was on dates and perhaps even in bed with women who, I learned much later, were as anxious to impress and as terrified with disappointing me as I was with them. And then, occasionally, an especially sneaky mutation of nigga neurosis would worm itself into my brain, where instead of questioning whether a thing that happened to me happened because I'm black, I'd fear I'd been colonized by shit my blackness was supposed to shield me from. Because I'm black and male I'm not supposed to feel anxiety. I'm not supposed to feel doubt. I'm supposed to be *cool*, and that cool should be as effortless as Tracy McGrady jaunting back on D after hitting a hesi and laying a nigga with a lefty jelly. I should be as sure of myself as my man Rus Johnson was in eleventh grade, when I watched him get a smile and a number from that dime at Foot Locker in Monroeville Mall by just swagging up to her and saying, "So, we doing this or not?" I'd allow myself to feel—not believe, but *feel*—that I wasn't who I was supposed to be.

I've grown less susceptible to that lie and progressively more confident that I am exactly who I'm supposed to be, but the belief that I'm somehow defective unmasks itself at inopportune times. And while sitting in my car that day with my wife and my sleeping daughter, I wondered how much better that first year and a half of being a parent and adjusting to the myriad changes parenthood imposes on a marriage would have been if I'd just allowed myself to remember that other people—including Alecia; *especially* Alecia—feel anxiety too. Other people doubt themselves too. Other people—other parents—are scared shitless too. Although it would be wonderful if all the world's angst and nervousness and restlessness and situationally inappropriate daydreams just existed in one person—an eggheaded East Lib Jesus who lied for all of our sins—I am just not that special.

I am, however, terrified for Zoe.

I presume that as she grows older, the parts of me that are in her may grow more noticeable. I am also hopeful that her journey to accept and appreciate herself doesn't last as long as mine did, and I am committed to doing whatever it takes to prevent myself or others from sabotaging it. But I don't know how to pass on the good things without also passing on the bad things, and I want those bad things to end with me. I want her to be observant and thoughtful, but not so thoughtful that she gives herself, as I have, acid reflux from the stress and anxiety that come from overthinking. I do not want her to be on Nexium and/or Prilosec, and I do not want her to be compelled to get multiple endoscopies just to ensure her esophageal lining is still intact. I want her to continue to regard new things with a healthy and safe skepticism that allows her to stay true to her convictions and not be as susceptible to peer pressure as many of her friends and classmates might be. It's an attribute that has served me well. I am writing this in 2018, which means I will be forty at the end of this year, and I've never had a homie or a girlfriend who played me or was revealed to be a fraud. But sometimes this reluctance to ignore my reservations and worries paralyzed (and still sometimes paralyzes) me, where my reticence and doubt congealed (and still sometimes congeals) into a lack of assertiveness and I ended (and still sometimes end) up not doing things I wanted (and still sometimes want) to do because I just couldn't (and still sometimes can't) find the will to

be fearless. I want her to be too empathic to bully and humili-
ate people she's bigger than or smarter than or cooler than, but
if she ever has to compete—in sports, in school, wherever—I
want her to possess the killer instinct that her dad just never
had. I want her to continue to be able to entertain herself and
make herself laugh. But I don't want her to be so lost in her
thoughts and herself that she forgets to experience the now.
How can I calm her during a violent thunderstorm if lightning
still shakes me?

And this is only what she might inherit from me, her dad.
She's also a little black girl and will eventually be a black woman
in a world that is more dangerous for her than it has been for
me. Alecia and I have already begun to think about how we're
going to teach her about race and racism and whiteness and
white supremacy and racial profiling and police brutality and
implicit bias. She will know what *redlining* and *gerrymandering*
mean. She will be aware of gentrification and displacement and
will know about what happened in East Liberty between 2000
and 2015 to provide an applicable and intimate context. She will
be taught, as Mom and Dad taught me, about how the lynching
of black Americans was once such a mundane function of her
country's ecosystem that not only were postcards made depict-
ing lynchings but they were sold during other lynchings. She
will know that 1839 is both the date of the *Amistad* slave revolt
and the home address (1839 Wylie Avenue) of Aunt Ester, the
iconic matriarch in August Wilson's *Gem of the Ocean*. She will
know who Ruby Bridges was, and she will be taught before she
is a teen that four little black girls not much older than her
were killed in 1963 when their church was bombed by a racist.
And if she ever attempts to discount that sort of racial violence
as something from the distant past, she will be reminded that

five months before she was born a terrifying twenty-one-year-old white man sauntered into a South Carolina church and executed nine of its members moments after sitting and praying with them.

She will also be exposed to Toni Morrison and Beyoncé. To bell hooks and *Black Panther.* To Octavia Butler and Ava DuVernay and *Moonlight* and Alex Haley and Chinua Achebe and *Love Jones* and Wu-Tang and Ruth Carter and Kara Walker and LaToya Ruby Frazier and both Smokey's and D'Angelo's "Cruisin'." Just as our house is and will continue to be a living and breathing paean to black culture, black art, black language, black history, black food, black joy, black love, and black people, her bedrooms will be museums of carefully curated blackness, brimming with black dolls and black figurines and books by black authors about black people, with little black girls like her on the covers. Her hair is kinky and thick and nappy, and she will know that, if someone ever says those things about her hair to her, the proper response will be "Thank you!"

She will know why there's a small broom on the wall underneath a picture of our wedding day, and she will know what "jumping the broom" means and where that act originated from. If she is interested in college, she will know that, despite neither of her parents attending a historically black college or university, black colleges are legitimate options. She will be able to code switch, but she will never be pressured by her parents to do so. She will be taught the third verse of "Lift Every Voice and Sing," which I didn't even know existed until a year before she was born. She will eat (healthy-ish) soul food. I haven't quite decided yet when an appropriate age for her to use *nigga* would be. But I want her to know and be comfortable with that word. I want her to eventually be a veteran *nigga* user like her mom and dad. I desired meeting and marrying a woman I could *nigga* banter with. Now that I've found that, I look forward to providing *nigga*-use mentorship for our daughter. Perhaps she'll never be interested enough in Spades to learn how to play it, but she'll see Alecia and I challenge (and beat) our friends enough—and have so much fun doing it—that it'll be hard for Zoe to resist that temptation. And she will also know that her grade of blackness cannot be determined by how quickly she takes to Spades, how easily she learns to Wobble, or how interested she is in rap music. She will know that there's no such thing as grades of blackness. She will know that she was born black, and there's nothing she can do to not be black, and that if she chooses to do or be a thing—anything—that thing is officially "black enough" by virtue of her deciding to do or be it.

She will be taught that while black people have been victims of oppression, subjugation, bias, and hate—and while we've faced these things, in various forms and in various measures of intensity for the duration of the hundreds of years we've been in America—blackness itself is not the problem. Her blackness is not a problem. It's not her skin. It's not her hair. It's not the way she looks. It's not the way she talks. It's not the blood coursing through her veins. It's none of the trillions of particles and elements that decided, through divine providence, to comprise her. She will be taught that whiteness needs blackness—the nigger, specifically—in order to possess and retain its value. She will learn that whiteness requires something it can point to and claim itself to be better than. She will know that it needs that whipping boy and that bedtime story and that cautionary tale in order to sleep and to find a reason for waking. She will be told that the man who was elected president in 2016 was anointed because of whiteness's urgent desire to preserve its supremacy and be elevated above the nigger, even if that elevation is self-destructive.

Since whiteness was invented, blackness has been positioned as unseemly and uncivilized and demented and dirty. Blackness is to whiteness the puddle you attempt to avoid when crossing the street. And, if whiteness is feeling particularly ambitious that day, blackness is the puddle you place a jacket over so that other whites can step across it without being muddied. Perhaps, after learning this, she will be compelled to believe that blackness is the antithesis of whiteness. After nearly a half millennium of the nimble propaganda of white supremacy, it is natural and freeing and vindicating and deliciously petty to believe that whiteness is the source of all evil and blackness is the light. However tempting this is, I will remind her that this belief would merely mimic the humanity of whiteness, which is a lesser and incomplete way of encapsulating our existence. She will be taught that while humanity can be sublime, if you are human, you are capable of evil. You are capable of oppressing. You are capable of everything the invention of whiteness has done to the people who have not been deemed white, and everything that inventing whiteness has done to the people deemed white.

But, she will also be taught that, because of this ceaseless racial antagonism, blackness allows her humanity to be stretched and extended and amplified and evolved in a way both those who oppress and those who have benefited from oppression aren't able to experience. Blackness forces you to love harder. It forces you to entertain the concept of forgiveness and choose whether or not it's a thing you're interested in possessing. It forces your hugs and your kisses and your daps to be tighter and longer, like a book you read ever so slowly because you're just not quite ready yet for it to end. It forces improvisation to be an immutable function of life. It forces you to seek solace and respite and community wherever they can be found, which makes you more cognizant of the world's crevices and margins and ellipses and any other space where those twinkles of colony might be stashed.

She will be taught, above all else, that she can be whoever and whatever she wants to be.

And this is where I have to stop, because this is where I'm stuck.

This is where, if she retains the things I will teach her, and if she continues to be as curious and as thoughtful and as intuitive and as quick and as skeptical as she currently is, she might eventually ask, "How?" How can she be whoever and whatever she wants to be if there's a hulking and devious five-hundred-year-old force constructed specifically to prevent her from doing that? How can she have a limitless future in the same America that killed the grandmother who died two years before she was born? She might not yet know what the word *paradox* means, but she will know that what I have taught her is paradoxical. How can all of those great things about her potential be possible—be *true*—if they exist at the same time this other thing, *the* other thing, does?

If my daughter asks me those questions, I will have no choice but to be honest with her. "I don't know."

I will tell her that despite the knowledge and experience her dad possesses, I do not know *how* such a thing is possible. I don't know how my little black girl can be all she can be when she can bounce in the lap of her grandfather, my dad, a man who is so much wittier and kinder and worldlier than so many of the white men who have been my teachers and lawyers and doctors and accountants and college basketball coaches but has never and will never experience the success and the status and the privilege that has come to them. Dad is sixty-eight years older than Zoe is, and the America he was born into is different from the one she was. This is true. The ceiling that lurked above him and everyone else born black back then has been punctured.

There are holes in it now wide enough to inch through. But the ceiling is still there.

She is still in danger. She is still thought to be a threat. She will still have people see her and assume she's older and stronger and tougher than she actually is. She will still encounter nurses and doctors who'll assume she doesn't experience pain the same way little white girls do. She will still have her intelligence doubted, as if it's not possible to be that black and also be that sharp. She will still have to watch racism and sexism join forces and attempt to pathologize her. She will still contend with the Chinese water torture of racial microaggressions. She will still exist in the same country, in the same region, in the same state, in the same county, in the same zip code, in the same city, in the same voting district, in the same neighborhood, in the same block, in the same school, and in the same classroom as people who will look at her sweet and brown and perfect little round face and see nothing but a nigger.

"I don't know," I will tell my daughter if she asks me how it's possible to be all of the things I've told her she can be if America is all the things I've told her it can be. "I don't know *how* it happens. I don't know *how* it's possible. I don't possess the level of intelligence necessary to understand how both those things can exist at the same time. But I know it happens, Zoe. I know it's possible. I know you can and will be those things I said you can be."

If the conversation goes anything like the conversations we have now, she will ponder what I said, she will nod her head, and she will leave to go find another adventure to lose herself in. I will watch her scurry away, this miracle, and I will see Alecia. I will see Dad. I will see Mom. I will see me. And I will smile.

And then I will hope, and I will wish, and I will dream, and I will pray to God that she believed me.

# ACKNOWLEDGMENTS

To Alecia Dawn, for too many things to mention, but specifically right now for (1) allowing me to convince you to have brunch food at our wedding and (2) your spontaneous freestyle variations of the *Golden Girls* theme song, including that time in 2015 when you made me laugh so hard that I had hiccups for thirty-seven minutes.

To my dad, the man, for being generous, gracious, good, and my nigga.

To the Youngs, the Freemans, the Coles, the Crunkletons, the Hunts, and the Hambricks.

To Brian Carroll, for never once, in twenty-five years, asking me for gas money.

To sarah huny young, for creating the places that have housed and covered my work—platforms and web designs and book covers so spectacular that my writing feels anticlimactic when existing next to it.

To Panama Jackson, for being my lightskint brother from another mother.

To my niggas who were somehow involved with the events that occur in this book, including Marguerite and Raymar and Alicia and Taaliba and Andre Fleming (RIP) and Heath and Paul and Warren and Tracey and Jessica and Camille and the rest of the PhDeez crew. I love y'all, and the next wing night is on me.

To Natalie Degraffinried, for reading and critiquing my work (and me) at aggressively random hours while also indulging my bad jokes about volleyball.

To everyone else whom I've asked, in the process of writing this, to read a paragraph or a page or a chapter because I either didn't feel quite right about it and needed their opinion or I felt right as fuck about it and needed their opinion; a list that includes Shanae Brown, Anne Branigin, Zaynab Aden, Terryn Hall, Sai Grundy, Porscha Burke, Susette Brooks, Rae Gomes, and Clare Polke.

To the writing-ass niggas I know whose work and whose way of stitching words together has had any sort of conscious influence on mine. I'm going to name Samantha Irby and Kiese Laymon and Angela Nissel and Tony Norman and Kara Brown here, and I know that there are more I just can't think of right now and I promise that if you are one of these people I will tweet your name out or send you coins through Cash App as soon as I remember it.

To the extended VSB crew, which starts with Liz Burr and continues with Shamira Ibrahim and Alex Hardy and Jozen Cummings and Tonja Stidhum and Lawrence Ware and Mylon Medley and Aliya King and Brandon Harrison and Corey Richardson and Dustin Seibert and Malaika Jabali and Danielle Butler and Agatha Guilluame and ends with everyone who's been with us since March 31, 2008—writing, commenting, emailing, tweeting, and promoting—and just fucking stayed because the couch was comfy and the chips were still crispy. Thank you.

To all the black-ass editors and publishers at the black-ass publications that first paid me for my work, starting with Deanna at Clutch, Demetria and Veronica at Moguldom, Kierna and Jamilah at *Ebony*, and then Donna and Lynn and Danielle and Genetta at the Root.

To Tanya McKinnon, for pushing me, for scolding me, for believing in me, and for occasionally interrupting your full-time job of being a force of nature to find enough space to be my agent.

To Denise Oswald, for finding paragraphs and pages that I didn't realize I had in me and convincing me to allow you to pull them out of me.

And, last, to Nexium.